CW00343140

Basic Research Methods

Basic Research Methods

An Entry to Social Science Research

Gerard Guthrie

www.sagepublications.com

Los Angeles • London • New Delhi • Singapore • Washington DC

Copyright © Gerard Guthrie, 2010

All rights reserved. No part of this book may be reproduced or utilised in any form or by any means, electronic or mechanical, including photocopying, recording or by any information storage or retrieval system, without permission in writing from the publisher.

First published in 2010 by

 SAGE Publications India Pvt Ltd
B1/I-1 Mohan Cooperative Industrial Area
Mathura Road, New Delhi 110 044, India
www.sagepub.in

SAGE Publications Inc
2455 Teller Road
Thousand Oaks, California 91320, USA

SAGE Publications Ltd
1 Oliver's Yard, 55 City Road
London EC1Y 1SP, United Kingdom

SAGE Publications Asia-Pacific Pte Ltd
33 Pekin Street
#02-01 Far East Square
Singapore 048763

Published by Vivek Mehra for SAGE Publications India Pvt Ltd, typeset in 11/13pt Charter BT by Star Compugraphics Private Limited, Delhi and printed at Chaman Enterprises, New Delhi.

Third Printing 2012

Library of Congress Cataloging-in-Publication Data

Guthrie, Gerard.
    Basic research methods: an entry to social science research/Gerard Guthrie.
        p. cm.
    Includes bibliographical references and index.
    1. Social sciences—Research. 2. Social sciences—Research—Methodology. I. Title.

H62.G847   300.72—dc22   2010   2010011342

ISBN: 978-81-321-0457-5 (PB)

The SAGE Team: Elina Majumdar, Sushmita Banerjee, Vijay Sah and Trinankur Banerjee

For Karina

Contents

SECTION 1   THE PROBLEM

1   Approaches to Research

2   Research Ethics

3   Research Proposal and Literature Review

List of Tables and Figures

Tables

Figures

List of Boxes

Preface

This book is intended for students undertaking a first social science research project in anthropology, education, geography, psychology, sociology or other subjects. You probably have taken undergraduate or postgraduate subject courses and now you are getting into research methods. Here your task is to complete a research paper, dissertation or thesis containing primary data collection and analysis. The report will have to be tight, logical and detailed, presenting the evidence before you and only that evidence.

The deadline seems quite some time away, but it will arrive impossibly fast. Suddenly your prior study does not seem to help very much. That study was probably about academic issues and theory derived from research findings. Now, the methods behind the findings have to be learned. You understand some of the Why, but the issues you face are practical: What? Where? How? This manual gives practical guidance on some of the basic principles and practices of research.

Textbooks dealing with research methodology have two approaches. One is a deductive approach of studying research principles before practice is developed. By helping students learn the theory and principles, the assumption is that you will better deduce their application to research projects. The approach in this book is a second, inductive one that points you in the direction of practical experience. From an experiential base, you should be able to build a more advanced conceptual and theoretical understanding of research.

Three learning objectives are implicit. You should:

1. understand social science research design and methods, including conventional data collection and analysis techniques;
2. apply practical skills in a first research project; and
3. value a systematic approach to problem solving.

I have aimed for very clear and direct English to make a difficult subject easier to understand. The start of each chapter outlines its contents, and the conclusion is a brief summary supplemented by annotated references for further reading. In between are examples of the practices discussed. Learning exercises are not included within each chapter because the assumption is that you will practicse the skills, first, on a research proposal and, then, on your project itself.

Throughout are practical illustrations of research techniques from research in the Asia-Pacific region. Many of these come from research projects in which I have been involved because they allow me to add more flavour to research techniques by explaining some of the background reasons for taking certain paths. The examples are a starting point for thinking about similar parts of your own work.

The ideas in here are distilled from experience gained over 40 years of carrying out research in many forms. Most of the research methods in this book are 'common knowledge' and in wide use. It is impossible to reference this common knowledge to the many books, experiences and people from which it derives in my case, except for citations about specific borrowings. Books particularly useful when I was learning to research included *Zen and the Art of Motorcycle Maintenance* by Robert Persig (1974), which is a novel that makes some of the metaphysics underlying thinking about research very accessible. Karl Popper's *Objective Knowledge* (1979) is a formal but understandable work on the philosophy of science that resolves some metaphysical conundrums for researchers. Fred Kerlinger's *Foundations of Behavioral Research* (1986) is the best advanced methodology text that I have used. Sidney Siegel's seminal *Nonparametric Statistics for the Behavioral Sciences* (originally published in 1956) is a classic text that very clearly relates tests to particular types of data. Graham Vulliamy, Keith Lewin and David Stephens' book, *Doing Educational Research in Developing Countries* (1990), on qualitative research in developing countries, is grounded in practical experience. William Strunk Jr and E.B. White's *The Elements of Style* (2000) remains a model of brevity and clarity for written English.

So, this is a 'how to' book that provides a map of where it all fits. The book aims to demystify research and to provide clear and direct instruction on carrying out research projects. It takes you through the stages of a project by giving practical guidance on conducting some of the more common types of social science research. The techniques are basic ones, but many masters and doctoral research studies use them. Unlike many introductory texts that focus on abstract methodology, this one is mainly about research in practice, and it therefore contains more than usual information about data analysis and presentation, which is where many projects become stuck. However, advanced research does require an understanding of the methodological principles from which basic techniques derive. You will need to add deeper conceptual understandings as you undertake more research.

There are good reasons to learn about research and its methods. Not only can you learn more about the world around you, your own thinking can become clearer and more disciplined. Whether or not you become a professional researcher, you will find that understanding research methods helps you better understand scientific information. Your ability to think should also improve, helping give clarity in both your private and professional lives. Whatever you take out of this book, I hope research is as satisfying and interesting for you as it has been for me.

Gerard Guthrie
<gerardguthrie@hotmail.com>

Acknowledgements

Some portions of Chapters 1, 3 and 9 of *Basic Research Techniques*, DER Report No. 55, published by the National Research Institute, Papua New Guinea, have been used with the kind permission of the Institute.

SECTION 1

THE PROBLEM

Research projects have four stages: *(a)* definition and analysis of the problem and methodology; *(b)* data collection; *(c)* data analysis; and *(d)* action, including but not necessarily limited to write-up.

In a project, each of these stages should take roughly the same time. The amount you can spend on each is simple mathematics: the length of time before your project is due divided by four. If you have about one semester, say 16 weeks, each stage can have about four weeks.

Planning your time carefully is very important. A common mistake is to spend too long on the theory and methodology, then to find time compressed towards the end of the assignment. This especially affects data analysis and write-up, which often overlap, ending up in long nights of work to finish. The result is that many research papers do not do justice to the work that has gone into them simply because the final product is rushed and full of minor errors.

This first section of the book deals with the first of the four stages: the problem, the literature review, research methodology and the ethical issues that might arise. This stage should be the easiest for most students because the review most closely resembles the essays that you have been writing. However, there are three traps. One is to put too much time into the research proposal because the theory and methodology can be very interesting. A second is to have difficulty synthesising all that literature. The third difficulty is narrowing down the review to provide a practical research problem on which data can be collected.

This leads to one more important point. Although the book presents research from a formal point of view, as a logical sequence of events from Stage 1 through to Stage 4, research does not actually happen like that. Unanticipated fieldwork issues appear, and, in fact, the whole project might be an exploratory one or looking to find out what people think and do rather than prejudging their thoughts and actions. The literature review and the methods do not have to be perfected upfront because many things will change along the way. Some draft material will not remain relevant as the project develops.

This is normal. To shape your project, you should read over the following sections and then study more thoroughly the chapters that are most relevant to your research problem, but you do not have to close off the write-up on one stage before moving to the next.

Approaches to Research

1

R esearch is concerned with collecting and analysing data systematically to help solve problems that concern us. In common usage, research has wider meanings. Often, people refer to reading books or searching the internet as research. For research purposes, these activities are only part of the job at hand. *Basic Research Methods* looks at research in the sense of collecting your own original data and analysing the information collected thoroughly and methodically. Data does not necessarily mean numbers. Words are data too.

This book is for beginners in research in the social sciences, perhaps in anthropology, education, geography, political science, psychology, sociology or other subjects such as management. Social scientists have a wide variety of perspectives, and attempts to develop theories that integrate all these subject areas have not been successful. There is a lot of disagreement about methodology, too. What the subjects do have in common is an interest in real-world problems involving people, directly or indirectly. As scientists, we usually use some form of data to study these problems. We also expose our thinking to careful intellectual analysis because social science research is not an excuse to argue for preconceived social, political or religious beliefs. In social science, we scrutinise our viewpoints in a disciplined way before reaching conclusions.

The approach taken in this book is predominantly one of philosophical pragmatism. Pragmatism views knowledge as useful in terms of its practical effect. It puts prime emphasis on objectives and what is useful in achieving them. From this perspective, the value of research methodologies lies in their usefulness in engaging with the real world. The book synthesises various methods from the perceptive of their usefulness in addressing research problems. Ideas fit where they belong according to their role in research projects: not 'have theory (or methodology), will travel'; rather 'have problem, will attempt to solve'.

The study of research will require defining many terms. As the same term can have different meanings in different fields of research (and, equally, different terms can have similar meanings), definition is a chronic problem in research. The solution is always to define clearly the particular sense in which key technical terms are used.

At this point, four terms need clarifying so that their usage is clear in the organisation of the book. One term is *research methodology*, which refers to the broader principles of research underscored by philosophical rationales. The book will only introduce the main schools of methodology. The key concepts presented aim to give an understanding of why we do certain things in research, but you will need to do further reading on advanced methodology. The second term is *research methods*, which are the focus of the book, by which I mean the key principles of research design brought together in material on measurement principles, sampling and the case study, survey and experimental methods. The third term is *research techniques*, which are particular approaches to collecting and analysing data, found in the chapters on available data, observation, interviews, questionnaires, tests and data analysis. The fourth term is *research tools*, which are resources used in conducting research, such as computers, the internet and libraries. Your intellectual skills are a research tool as well. Studying research should help you improve them.

Rather than begin with a theoretical overview of research, we are going to plunge straight into research projects and how they are conducted. This chapter will:

1. look at four types of research: Pure, Applied, Policy and Action (PAPA Model);
2. consider the four stages in the research cycle: the problem, data collection, data analysis and action;
3. introduce examples of research projects that will reoccur throughout the book; and
4. consider four issues to do with accuracy: relevance, validity, reliability and generalisability.

1.1   The PAPA model of research

To help understand the emphasis in these guidelines on practical research, it is useful to consider the full range of research. The PAPA Model is my way of conceptualising four main types: Pure, Applied, Policy and Action. Each has a different purpose, as Figure 1.1 illustrates.

Pure research is concerned solely with scientific outcomes. The purpose is to expand knowledge and to discover new things because they are of interest to the scientist and to science. Scientists of all types are continually reading about their field, which generates many ideas about the nature of its theory and methodology. Pure research is essentially driven by curiosity. Early anthropological research on tribal societies in Africa and the Pacific is an example. The research was often motivated by the researchers' interest in what were, to them, new and strange societies. Through their studies, they hoped to

Figure 1.1   Types of research

Pure	Applied	Policy	Action
Concerned solely with scientific outcomes of interest to scientists.	Concerned with topics that have potential for practical application, but without a particular way of implementing the results in mind.	Based on practical issues of interest to those who make decisions about them.	Concerned with working on particular practices in order to improve them.
Increased emphasis on practical action			
→			

Source: Author.

learn how different people lived in other parts of the world, but practical action based on the findings was not usually a priority.

Applied research is concerned with topics that have potential for practical application. The research often begins with scientific curiosity, but is not designed keeping in mind a particular way of implementing the results. The researcher wants to find out how things work and wants the findings to be used, but does not intend to become involved in implementation. Sometimes, for inventors, the interest is purely technical; other researchers have a social orientation. For example, a project might investigate how the community views banks to find how banking could more effectively meet community needs. However, the researcher might not know in advance whether the findings could best be implemented by particular banks or through government regulation. The researcher then has the problem of 'selling' the results to the implementer.

Policy research is based on practical issues of interest to those who make decisions about them. Governmental authorities, for example, might have a policy of reducing crime and want to know whether the policy is having an effect. They might want to know if crime victimisation levels are changing and, if so, whether property crime, for instance, is changing more than violent crime. Often, policy research is commissioned from consultants, who are given the terms of reference. Usually, this type of work is strictly time bound and, often, requires research teams with specialist skills and considerable experience.

Action research is concerned with working on particular activities to make direct improvements. For example, teachers in a school might decide to compare test results from different classes to see if differences follow from using a new textbook so that the school can decide whether all the teachers should use the book. An organisation might review some of its systems and procedures to make them more efficient, or review its staffing arrangements. Action research is quite common, especially to evaluate the success or failure of new projects.

All four types of research have their place in science. The underlying dimension is to do with practical action. Pure research aims to develop theory while action research does not, but properly carried out, all four use scientific theory to improve their quality. The difference is that pure research is mainly concerned with developing theory as an end in itself, but action research is only concerned with theories that will help improve practical action.

The research methods and techniques presented in this book can be used with all four types of research.

1.2   Stages of research

There are four main stages in doing research (Figure 1.2).

1. *Problem*: The first stage is to decide which topic to research. Here, we can distinguish between theoretical questions of relevance to the development of science and practical problems to do with real-world issues. There are five steps in deciding fully on the problem:

   (*a*) Topic selection: First, decide on a general area of study.
   (*b*) Problem definition: Next, narrow the topic down to a smaller aspect that can be studied properly in the available time.

Figure 1.2   Simple research model

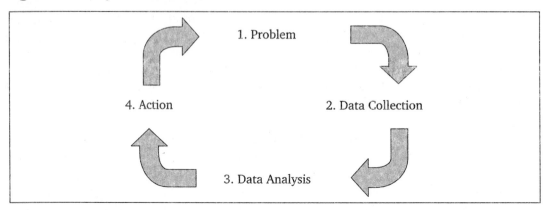

Source: Guthrie (1985: 6).

(c) Literature review: Many things have been researched before, so now use the library and the internet to see if the problem has already been studied and to find ideas on how to approach your own aspect. This will probably result in several revisions of the problem statement to make it more focused.

(d) Hypothesis formation: Then it is often helpful to define research hypotheses, which are informed guesses about what is the answer to the problem. They can guide the methods and data collection by clarifying the type of data needed.

(e) Methodology: Now comes consideration of the methodology and the data collection issues that arise from your approach to the problem.

2. *Data Collection*: The second stage is to apply the research methods and techniques to collect the necessary information. Sometimes the data can be found in the library or in files, but for most primary social research, it is collected in the field. There are three steps:

(a) Definition of the universe: The *universe* is the total number of people or things to be studied, so first it is necessary to define exactly what or who is to be studied to answer our problem.

(b) Sampling: To study everything in the universe would take a great deal of time and effort, so usually only a small part is studied by taking a sample.

(c) Data collection: Then collect the information that is actually needed.

3. *Data Analysis*: The next stage is to analyse the data in order to find out if it answers the problem.

(a) Organisation of information: First, organise all the information that has been obtained so that it can be analysed.

(b) Analysis of results: Next, examine the data to see if it is reliable and valid, and to describe, classify and interpret it. Sometimes, but often not, statistics are used.

4. *Action*: The final stage is to do something with the information and findings.

(a) Report writing: Results are written up in research reports, for administrators and for publication in places where interested people can read them.

(b) Distributing information: Ensure that interested parties receive findings from the research.

(c) Putting results into action: The final step (which often does not include the researcher at all and which is often the hardest) is attempting to make any changes that the research might have shown to be desirable.

We now come back to the starting point, hopefully with a solution to the problem, but invariably with more problems to research and more hypotheses to explore.

One reason why the model in Figure 1.2 is a simple one is that it makes research seem linear: a step-by-step procedure from start to finish. The way research reports are written up follows the formal linear logic, which reinforces this impression. Actually, it is far more complex than that. The research process is iterative. You will find that you move backwards and forward through all the stages in a constant interaction. You will revisit earlier stages (perhaps modifying the methods) and also, revise your plans about future ones (perhaps adjusting the data analysis techniques). Sometimes, brilliant ideas seem to pop into your head in the middle of the night (actually, this is the result of the subconscious quietly processing the information that you have been absorbing) and you then work backwards from these 'conclusions' to possible reasons.

Sometimes, indeed, you will not use all the sub-stages (for example, formal hypotheses). If you do not, this should be a conscious decision, not one based on ignorance of the standard procedures. If you omit steps, justify the omission.

1.3   Some actual research projects

To illustrate the four types of research and the four stages in each, Box 1.1 summarises four research projects in which I have been involved. The projects ranged from a pure library study into economic systems, through an applied teacher education evaluation, to

---

BOX 1.1 FOUR RESEARCH PROJECTS

1. Pure Research into Economic Systems

(*a*) **Problem:** Could Harvey Franklin's classification of economic systems of production be refined by developing his parallel concept of systems of appropriation? (Guthrie 1977).

(*b*) **Data Collection:** The analysis was a theoretical one illustrated by a case study that used library research into key anthropological texts about traditional Australian Aboriginal economic organisation.

(*c*) **Data Analysis:** The analysis developed and extended Franklin's work to clarify the conceptual basis of appropriation and to include the tribal system. The conceptual framework was illustrated with the case study of the tribal system of appropriation in pre-European Aboriginal Australia.

(*d*) **Action:** Publication in an academic journal specialising in development issues.

2. Applied Evaluation of Teacher Training

(*a*) **Problem:** Were the graduates of formalistic pre-service diploma training programmes in Papua New Guinea more professionally effective as secondary school teachers than those with more progressive bachelor degrees in education? (Guthrie 1983a).

(Box 1.1 Continued)

(Box 1.1 Continued)

(b) **Data Collection:** Five teacher training programmes were evaluated, primarily using 870 formal reports by school inspectors based on observations of 578 graduates in classrooms from 1977 to 1980. A graduate tracer study and documentary analysis of the training programmes supplemented the reports.

(c) **Data Analysis:** Parametric statistical analysis led to a rejection of both research hypotheses. There were no statistically significant differences in programme-based graduate performance. Of the two main programmes, the longer, more expensive degree based on a general education foundation was not more professionally effective than the shorter and cheaper diploma based on professional training.

(d) **Action:** The research was an influence on the subsequent amalgamation of secondary teacher education in Papua New Guinea some 10 years later.

3. Policy Research into Crime Victimisation

(a) **Problem:** What were the levels, extent and types of crime in Bougainville's two main towns in the period following a civil war? (Guthrie et al. 2007).

(b) **Data Collection:** Surveys of the adult populations of Arawa and Buka were undertaken in 2004, 2005 and 2006. Random area samples identified clusters of houses where quotas were selected based on age and gender. Statistically representative samples of the adult populations were gained from 290–307 interviews in each of the six surveys.

(c) **Data Analysis:** The 2006 report allowed analysis of trends in crime victimisation from 2004 to 2006. Large, statistically significant reductions occurred in both property crime and violence.

(d) **Action:** Independent evidence in reports to senior administrators provided reassurance that, following the civil war, the policies and programmes of the recently elected autonomous Bougainville government were contributing to reductions in crime victimisation and should continue.

4. Action Research into Teaching Styles

(a) **Problem:** How could my university teaching become more appropriate when returning to teach in Papua New Guinea in 2002 and 2003? Would students prefer a formalistic lecturing style or self-directed learning?

(b) **Data Collection:** Pedagogic lecturing was used in one undergraduate and one postgraduate course. A student-centred andragogic approach was used in a second undergraduate course and a participatory tutorial approach was used in another postgraduate course. Student feedback was sought at the end of each course using a standard course evaluation sheet.

(c) **Data Analysis:** Academically stronger undergraduate students preferred the flexible andragogic approach, while others preferred the more structured lectures. The postgraduates preferred the greater opportunity for student discussion in the informal tutorial style.

(d) **Action:** The feedback informed my own teaching. It was discussed informally with colleagues who were interested in trying different teaching methods and was used by one of them as data in an article discussing the issues (Boorer 2004).

a policy study into crime victimisation, and a small action study of teaching techniques. Even though the projects were very different, the underlying formal logic was the same, with each one structured around the four stages of research. The teacher training and crime victimisation projects will return as practical examples in later chapters along with research by others.

One feature of these studies is that they involved different academic subjects, including political economy and economic anthropology, education and the sociology of crime. With the exception of the pure research into economic systems, where the aim was to analyse the theory itself, the studies drew on whatever theory was appropriate to the research problems rather than being driven by theory. Indeed, the policy research into crime victimisation went further than this: the reports were virtually without theory in their presentation. Their role was to provide data for decision makers. They had their own conceptual frameworks and were interested in practical action rather than the development of academic theory.

1.4   Research accuracy

As the research studies illustrate, one of the underlying themes of this book is encouragement of research that is *disciplined* (systematic and accurate), but not *disciplinary* (defined by academic boundaries). The methodical approach used throughout the four stages of research should provide accurate results, but accurate in what ways? All research involves trade-offs between relevance, validity, reliability and generalisability. The crime victimisation surveys in Bougainville illustrate some of these competing aspects.

The *relevance* of collecting data is established by the usefulness of research to consumers of the results. High-level law and justice sector decision makers commissioned the crime surveys. They wanted independent, objective, factual data about crime victimisation levels and public perceptions of crime. The credibility of the surveys for these clients was dependent on providing such information. This meant that the surveys had to be representative population samples, not case studies or focus groups. The trade-off was between relevance to the decision makers and validity for other users, such as social workers. The decision makers who commissioned the research wanted it for planning purposes. The data collected was relevant to planning, but did not have enough detail for social workers.

Validity refers to the correctness of the data collected. Is it really measuring what we think it is measuring? For example, we might want information about particular types of violence affecting women, but will we get the truth? A survey using a questionnaire will probably not get past the barriers that victims have about discussing very personal events. They might not tell the truth because they are too embarrassed to talk about sexual assault, for example, especially if men interview women. The crime surveys used same-gender interviews, but in-depth interviews over extended periods would have been needed to gain more detailed understanding of victims' experiences. We did not have the time, nor did the interviewers have the necessary background in counselling. Thus, the need for planning data about overall patterns meant that the surveys could not get valid data about some types of crime. Figures on domestic violence and sexual assault were likely to be the minimum levels that occurred.

Another validity issue in policy or action projects is the independence of the data collectors from the sponsoring organisations. If researchers are closely associated with the agencies, they might not be objective. Just as important, interviewees might not perceive them as objective, especially if interviewers ask questions about their own agency. Interviewees might even think that they could get into trouble for telling the truth (in another crime survey, a pilot test of questions about corruption had very high non-response rates because the questions implicitly asked respondents to incriminate themselves). To get around such problems in the crime research, agency staff were not involved. Nor, despite safety concerns, did we maintain contact with the police, who were often perceived negatively.

Reliability is defined as the ability to replicate the same results using the same techniques, that is, to provide results that other researchers could repeat. In the crime surveys, reliability was obtained through random sampling methods backed up by consistent management, training, quality assurance and reporting of the survey methods. If changes in methods and techniques had occurred, each report would have to be qualified by explanations that changes in results could be due to the changes in methods (that is, stem from lack of reliability) rather than be genuine changes in crime victimisation (that is, be valid measurement of real changes).

Generalisability is the ability to predict accurately from a sample to the whole population from which it is drawn. This is addressed usually through random samples that are as accurate as the field conditions and the available background data permit. The Bougainville studies were part of 16 crime surveys conducted from 2004 to 2008 in eight of Papua New Guinea's 25 cities and towns with populations over 1,500 according to the 2000 Census. A total of 6,781 interviews with adults in 2,683 household visits were statistically representative of towns with 72 per cent of the country's urban population of 601,000. This meant that reliable nationwide generalisations could be made about urban crime victimisation (Guthrie 2008).

A first research project will be much less ambitious than these large-scale surveys, but relevance, validity, reliability and generalisability issues will all arise. For example, if you conduct a survey among fellow students, a relevant issue of great interest to them (for example, grading systems) would probably increase cooperation. On the other hand, an issue such as sexual harassment might be relevant but not get cooperation because it threatens people's own gender identity. If you take the hard path and research date rape, for example, you will strike gender validity issues. Could you reliably get a sample of men's or women's views, and how? Generalisability will also be an issue, depending on what you study and whom you sample. Similarly, if you take the easier route, but only interview students in notoriously hard courses about grading, this will not reflect on all students' experience.

All research projects involve trade-offs that generate strengths and weaknesses. This is normal. The point is that you must recognise the limitations and discuss them in your report. The implication is that research projects must be transparent. They must give honestly and accurately the background on the methods and provide the operational details on the techniques and their strengths and weaknesses so that readers can judge the quality of the research.

We will return to all these issues as we proceed through this book.

1.5   Summary

Whether or not you become a professional researcher, understanding research methods will help you better understand scientific information and to think more clearly.

Types of research

1. Research is concerned with systematically collecting and analysing data so that it will help solve problems of interest.
2. Social science systematically exposes viewpoints to disciplined analysis before reaching conclusions.
3. The four main types of research are Pure, Applied, Policy and Action. All four use theory to improve their quality.

Stages of research

1. The four main stages in research projects are: *(a)* problem, *(b)* data collection, *(c)* data analysis, and *(d)* action.
2. The result should be an answer to the problem, but invariably with more problems to research and more hypotheses to test.
3. Research reports follow the formal linear logic, but the actual research process involves a constant interaction among all the stages.

Quality issues

All research involves trade-offs between relevance, validity, reliability and generalisability.

This textbook is concerned with all stages in basic social science research projects. The intention is to help you gain practical experience on which to base further study and more advanced research. It helps to remember that your first research project is a learning exercise. You do not need to be ambitious about selecting a topic that will change the world. Think of this as driving lessons, not a championship race.

1.6   Annotated references

There are dozens of good advanced textbooks on research methods. Use whichever ones are available in your library or bookshop. The following long-standing examples all cover research design and a wide range of methods, but with different emphases according to their subject areas (respectively, education, sociology, psychology and geography):

Best, J. and J. Kahn. (2005). *Research in Education*, 10th edition. Needham Heights: Allyn & Bacon.
Babbie, E. (2007). *The Practice of Social Research*, 11th edition. Belmont: Wadsworth.
Cozby, P. (2009). *Methods in Behavioral Research*, 10th edition. Boston: McGraw Hill.
Scheyvens, R. and D. Storey (eds). (2003). *Development Fieldwork: A Practical Guide*. London: Sage.

A search of the internet or a bookstore might find you earlier, yet good editions re-printed cheaply. You should also use the internet to search the key words italicised in the text or the headings in the summaries, but keep in mind the need to check the quality of internet material.

Additionally, you should become familiar with journals in your field that are available in your library. The following list indicates some current journals across a range of subjects and types of research that focus on the Asia-Pacific, South and Southeast Asia regions:

Asian Journal of Social Psychology
Asian Journal of Social Science
Asian-Pacific Economic Literature
Asia Pacific Journal of Anthropology
Asia Pacific Journal of Education

Asia-Pacific Journal of Public Health
Contributions to Indian Sociology
Hong Kong Journal of Social Work
Indian Geographical Journal
Indian Journal of Social Work
Indian Journal of Gender Studies
Journal of Indian History
Journal of South Asian Development
Journal of Southeast Asian History
Malaysian Journal of Economic Studies
Pakistan Journal of Psychological Research
Papua New Guinea Journal of Education
Philippine Journal of Public Administration
Singapore Economic Review
Singapore Journal of Tropical Geography
South Asia Economic Journal
Sri Lanka Journal of Social Sciences

Research Ethics 2

Being social science researchers does not give us any special powers or entitlements. We are merely citizens conducting professional work with fellow citizens who have the same rights as ourselves. We have no authority to direct the subjects of our research, and we must ensure that their engagement in our work is done freely. We do gain, however, some extra responsibilities.

Before commencing research, it is worthwhile giving some attention to the ethics required in conducting this exercise. This chapter is placed near the beginning of the book to emphasise the importance of ethics, especially because research involves new professional roles and behaviour. The chapter will look at:

1. a code of ethics;
2. the range of permissions needed to research;
3. researcher responsibilities;
4. confidentiality of information given to you;
5. feedback to participants; and
6. participatory research.

2.1 Codes of ethics

Ethics are standards of professional behaviour. They guide us so that we act with integrity, especially towards participants in the research. They also view technical competence as an ethical obligation, which also helps ensure that we are regarded as credible when we provide research results and that our work is held in high repute.

A code of ethics sets out principles of behaviour that professionals should apply to their work. A good example comes from the American Sociological Association (1999). It lists five general ethical principles to which social scientists should adhere:

1. Professional competence.
2. Integrity.
3. Professional and scientific responsibility.
4. Respect for people's rights, dignity and diversity.
5. Social responsibility.

Associated with these principles are certain professional standards. The ones most relevant to students learning to research are:

1. Adherence to the highest possible technical standards.
2. Ensuring that you are competent in your research.
3. Correct representation of your own expertise.
4. No discrimination, exploitation or harassment.
5. Avoidance of conflicts of interest or their appearance.
6. Protection of confidentiality.
7. Seeking informed consent.
8. Avoidance of plagiarism.

In practice, you need to be particularly aware of these ethical standards at certain points in your project. One point is seeking permission to research. A second relates to responsibilities as a researcher in the community. A third relates to the need for confidentiality about private information to which you might gain access. A fourth relates to feedback to the people among whom you research.

2.2 Permissions to research

Permissions in research apply in two main areas. One is where approval is needed from authorities to carry out the project. The other is obtaining informed consent from participants.

Approval of research project is usually required first by your academic institution. Each institution will have different rules for approving your research. Find out what they are and discuss them with your superviser or course lecturer.

If your project is approved, you might need subsequent agreement from particular authorities to carry out your work in places for which they are responsible. These authorities might be senior managers of organisations in which you want to collect data, community leaders or heads of households where you want to interview.

Sometimes organisations lay out formal rules and procedures if they often receive requests to permit research. Usually, these rules are designed to prevent parts of the organisation being overloaded with research. For example, a Department of Education might often have educational researchers wanting to research in its schools. School principals complain that too much research is interrupting classes, so the department sets up procedures to vet requests. The procedures aim to ensure that the research is legitimate, the researcher has appropriate credentials, the research is consistent with departmental policy and potentially useful to the education system, it will not be disruptive and that it is ethical. The department will usually want to see the research proposal, the researcher's qualifications and supporting material from supervisers or referees. All this is legitimate. The primary responsibility of the department is to ensure that children's education is not interrupted unnecessarily.

The approval process can involve bureaucratic delays. Procedures are often slow and this can be frustrating. So, think ahead and apply as soon as possible. Sometimes too, organisations procrastinate because they do not want their activities exposed to outsiders whom they might perceive as hostile or they do not like the interruptions that research generates.

Otherwise, to be very practical, choose a research project that does not require outside approvals, for example, by researching among fellow students.

Once you are able to proceed with data collection, the main ethical issue is informed consent from participants. Before you start interviewing or testing, you should briefly:

1. Tell participants the purpose of the research.
2. Tell them what you will do with the results.
3. Answer their questions about the research.
4. Ask their permission to continue.
5. Respect their right to refuse to participate.
6. Respect their right to withdraw at any stage.

Box 2.1 is an example of a questionnaire introduction used in an international study of attitudes to the environment held by students in 12 different countries across the Asia-Pacific region. The introduction clearly explains the purpose of the survey, seeks the students' cooperation and explains the anonymous nature of the data so that there is informed consent.

Sometimes respondents are paid to participate in research. Indeed, I argued for this approach in the crime victimisation surveys. Here were we, well-paid researchers, asking for free information from people, some of whom lived in poverty. Practically as well, this would have increased cooperation and decreased our obligations to provide feedback, because we would now own the data. Some of the arguments against were self-serving but one argument persuaded. The likelihood was that if word went out in poor communities that families were being paid to answer questions, these families would suddenly become bigger. We would not be able to tell who really was a member. Thus, payment would have involved unacceptable trade-offs with validity.

There was not much point in adding an ethical payment if it invalidated the research, which did have widespread potential benefits for the community.

BOX 2.1   INFORMED CONSENT

Introduction to Questionnaire

'Dear student,

'This questionnaire forms part of a study of the environmental attitudes of young people we are carrying out in two cities in Australia and in a number of countries in the Asia-Pacific region. The aim of the study is to compare environmental attitudes, knowledge and behaviour in these different cities and countries. We hope that the study will help to develop greater international understanding so that people across the region can work together more effectively. Your contribution is greatly valued.

'Before you answer the questionnaire, please read these instructions carefully.

'Please note that this is not a test and we do not ask for your name. Your answers will not be graded or seen by your teacher and will remain anonymous. Please, however, take the survey seriously because we are trying to find out some important information about environmental attitudes.

'Please be as honest as you can and answer every question to the best of your ability. It is important that everyone answers all the questions, so that we can get a proper picture of student attitudes.

'Thank you.'

Source: Fien et al. (2002: 173).

2.3   Responsibilities

In research, you play roles that are different from your usual roles in daily life. As a researcher, you have professional responsibilities, the first one of which is *competence*. If you do not have confidence in your skills for particular research, ask for advice, undertake further study, modify the project or even reconsider whether to proceed. Ask your superviser for advice if necessary—supervisers are more likely to be impressed by a willingness to seek advice than by avoidance of such issues.

Another responsibility is *respect* for people's culture, especially their moral and legal standards. If you are working in a culture that is different from your own, consider whether your research might be detrimental to the community. Try to become aware of and stand outside your own cultural biases. Try to see things from the point of participants, whether or not you agree personally with those viewpoints.

It is not uncommon to find people who are shy or embarrassed about talking with you. Occasionally, you will find people who are uncooperative or even angry. If this happens frequently, you should stop your research and try to work out what is wrong. If your work appears to be creating the problem, you should discuss the situation with sympathetic informants, local leaders and your superviser if you cannot resolve the situation in the field.

Other responsibilities require that you:

1. Do not get emotionally or sexually involved with participants.
2. Do not break the law.
3. Never invent information (for example, filling out questionnaires without interviewing people).
4. Do not misrepresent yourself or your role.

Your responsibilities include anybody who works with you on your project. You must give them proper training in technical skills and ethics, and actively supervise their work. Box 2.2 has a training example from a large and well-funded series of surveys, but the same issues apply to you too.

Box 2.2   TRAINING ABOUT ETHICS IN FIELDWORK

Survey Training

In all, some 170 people were involved in 16 urban crime victimisation surveys in Papua New Guinea, many on more than one occasion, and some in multiple roles. The fieldwork was staffed by the Survey Director, Survey Managers, Field Supervisers, from 8 to 20 interviewers for each survey, and casual Field Assistants.

To ensure consistency (and therefore reliability of results), a five day training programme for supervisers and interviewers included three days of induction and interview practice, plus two pilot days in the field. The training programme particularly covered ethical issues such as interviewer competence and confidentiality. Interviewers had to become informed about the surveys so that they could answer questions from interviewees to ensure that informed consent occurred. They were also instructed about right of refusal to participate and privacy of interviewees.

The induction covered the survey background, the parties involved, the objectives of the surveys, key aspects of the methods, and fieldwork protocols. An introduction to the questionnaire was followed by extended interview practice using versions in two languages. Finally, administrative and contractual arrangements, field management and security requirements were discussed.

Two days in the field under close supervision ensured that fieldwork protocols were closely followed. All completed questionnaires were checked by the Survey Director and individual and group feedback provided.

Subsequently all completed interview schedules were checked by each interviewer's partner and by the Field Supervisors, who held daily debriefings with the interviewers.

Source: Adapted from Guthrie (2007a).

2.4   Confidentiality

Remember that interviewees have the right to refuse interviews or to answer particular questions. Privacy entitles people to decide how much of their lives they will expose to you. As a researcher, you are obliged not to reveal information about participants in any way that might allow them to be identified.

1. Interview notes and completed questionnaires should not have the name of the interviewee written on them.
2. Only a code number should identify interviewees (in the crime surveys, we did not even identify individual respondents, but used only household IDs).
3. Notes and questionnaires should be kept locked up and not left lying around.

Never gossip about answers or respondents' personal information with fellow researchers or friends of family. Do not tell funny stories about the people you interviewed.

When you write up the report, you might well want to illustrate information about groups of people with some of their individual stories. These stories should be anonymous and written in such a way that readers could not identify the person. Box 11.5 later shows an example.

2.5   Feedback

Community feedback is very important, both from ethical and practical perspectives. People are curious to know about findings from research involving them. They have assisted you and you have a responsibility to inform them about the results. Feedback is also important if you want cooperation on follow-up visits.

In small-scale studies, feedback is not particularly difficult to set up, perhaps by holding information sessions with families or having small community meetings. That does not necessarily mean the meetings will be easy. Not everyone will be as excited by the results as you will be. Some people will deny the findings and blame you and your methods for misrepresenting what they think is the real situation (this occurred in two of the communities in the crime victimisation surveys where some residents disagreed with findings about high crime rates in their communities). Others will be offended because they think (perhaps wrongly) that they can identify themselves in your report and they do not like what your say. Sometimes, people might recognise privately that your findings are accurate but have vested interests in opposing them or action arising from them. The best that you can do in these situations is to accept, calmly and objectively, any valid criticisms, and explain why other criticisms might not be valid. Usually, discussion will lead to a balanced reaction to your report, with some community members starting to speak up in agreement with your findings.

Where you have undertaken a large survey, feedback is more difficult to arrange. A variety of approaches can be taken:

1. Put summaries of findings on community or work notice boards and give them to leaders for discussion in their own meetings.
2. Arrange public meetings through community leaders to talk about the findings, answer questions and participate in discussion.
3. Deliver summaries to houses at sample sites.
4. Arrange interviews on local radio.
5. Write articles for newspaper columns.
6. Call meetings with interest groups and agencies to present the reports.
7. Hold workshops with key agency staff.

All these approaches were used in the community crime surveys with uneven success. In communities where literacy was low, public meetings were more effective than written reports. Articles in papers were more likely to be read by suburbanites than by squatters in settlements. Agency staff sometimes found difficulty understanding the relevance of findings to their own work. The lesson is to be flexible and adapt approaches to the particular situation.

2.6   Participatory research

The various ethical standards outlined apply to all projects. For some researchers, however, they are not separate issues, but are manifestations of a scientific methodology that is itself the problem. In the positivist tradition, the researcher is an independent expert who studies a topic scientifically, analyses the results and perhaps makes recommendations to implementers. Some find major ethical problems with this. The key difficulty is that research 'subjects' often see no benefits from their contribution. Perhaps the researcher communicates only with the scientific community or high-level decision makers, or communicates poorly with the subjects, or the subjects do not understand the role of research or some combination of these difficulties.

In many minority communities and in many developing countries, this concern has resonance. Some people feel exploited by research, which they can think is a tool of their oppression, and they will cooperate only if they see a direct benefit. This is a valid position for many individuals and communities to take.

One consequence is the proposition that researchers should stop thinking about subjects and should start thinking about participants. In this view, research should be a process of reciprocal social action in which researchers and participants are on an equal footing in participatory research. Participatory research openly recognises that research is a political process, the researcher's own constructs or ways of thinking affect their behaviour, and that this behaviour is not an entitlement from independent scientific rules that override other considerations.

Participatory research requires full and active involvement by the participants in an educational process to empower the community. The intention is that participants gain benefits from the learning process in defining the research, collecting information, contributing their interpretations to the data analysis and knowing the results, and are therefore in a better position to carry outcomes forward. As the researcher, you are less of a leader and more of a fellow participant and technical resource. You might find the research going, quite legitimately, in different directions than anticipated. The effect is that participatory research becomes an approach to action research that has a particular ethical viewpoint. The most appropriate method is usually community case studies.

Flexibility and plenty of time are important for effective participatory research. Because too much time is required to do it properly in a short introductory research project, we will not deal with participatory research further here. If you go down this path, many books contain a wide range of special techniques.

2.7   Summary

Being social science researchers does not give us any special powers or entitlements. However, we do gain ethical responsibilities to act with integrity, especially towards participants in the research. Technical competence, too, is an ethical obligation.

Codes of ethics

Ethics include professional competence, integrity and responsibility.

Permissions to research

1. Find out your institution's rules for approving research.
2. Subsequent approvals might be needed from the research site.
3. The main ethical issue in data collection is informed consent from participants.

Responsibilities

1. Researchers' professional responsibilities include competence and respect for people's culture, especially their moral and legal standards.
2. Do not get emotionally or sexually involved with participants, break the law, invent information or misrepresent yourself or your role.

Confidentiality

1. Privacy entitles people to decide how much of their lives they will expose to you.
2. Do not reveal information in any way that might identify participants.

Feedback

1. Community feedback is very important ethically and to ensure ongoing cooperation.
2. In small studies, feedback is not very difficult but it is more difficult in large surveys.

Participatory research

For some researchers, the ethical problem is positivist research methodology, from which research 'subjects' often see little benefit. Their position is that research requires active involvement by the participants.

Ethics are not only a consideration when formulating your research project. The research project cycle is iterative. As you proceed, you will have to anticipate many issues and revisit previous ones. Ethics are no different. You need to consider upfront your role as a researcher and consider its ethical implications for you personally and for any others participating in the research. You also need to remain alert to ethical issues as you progress through the project and reflect continually on daily events. When in doubt, talk the issues through with others and seek advice, but often you will not find easy answers.

2.8   Annotated references

American Psychological Association. (2002). *The Ethical Principles of Psychologists and Code of Conduct*. Washington: APA.
An example of a Code of Ethics, available at <www.apa.org>.

American Sociological Association. (1999). *Code of Ethics*. New York: ASA.
  Another example of a Code of Ethics, available at <www.asa.org>.

McNamee, M. and D. Bridges. (2002). *The Ethics of Educational Research*. Oxford:
  Blackwell.
  A comprehensive collection of articles on research ethics, relevant to many subject
areas and types of research.

Scheyvens, R. and D. Storey (eds). (2003). *Development Fieldwork: A Practical Guide*.
  London: Sage.
  Another comprehensive collection of material on doing fieldwork in developing
countries. The book discusses participatory research and fieldwork ethics, including
many examples from across Asia.

Research Proposal and Literature Review 3

Writing up a research proposal is the required first step for many academic studies. This is the formal way of clarifying your own ideas and convincing a superviser that you know what you are doing. When you start the proposal, you will probably have only a general idea of what your research topic will be. The research proposal helps define the problem statement so that it provides a manageable topic on which to collect data in the available time.

The research proposal has two main elements. The first is a literature review, which this chapter considers. By the time you have finished the literature review, you should have a clearly defined research problem and, perhaps, a research hypothesis. The second element is the methodology (which the next chapter considers) so that you know how to collect data.

This chapter provides guidance on:

1. the content of the research proposal;
2. literature reviews and the issues in developing them, including use of the library and internet;
3. abstracting, which is a useful technique for synthesising review material;
4. some word processing techniques, which may save time at a later stage; and
5. plagiarism.

3.1 Research proposal

Often, each university department has its own particular set of requirements for the structure and style of the research proposal, which you should follow. Many specialised texts discuss in detail the writing of a thesis and research proposal. The following guidelines give an indication of what is usually expected and provide a format if nothing is laid down for you.

The research proposal requirement for a short introductory study might be only one or two printed pages. For a longer study, it is normally between 4–10 pages, depending on the size of the study. The proposal is written in the present or future tense, whereas the final study normally uses past tense because it describes completed research.

The left-hand column of Table 3.1 lists sections that can be included in a proposal. A short proposal can omit Sections 2, 6 and 7 and use the others only for summaries—but seek advice from your lecturer or superviser about what is acceptable for your own project. The right-hand column indicates accessible resources that can be used to find material for the literature review.

By the time you have worked through the list for the first time, you will probably be confused and will need to revise it repeatedly to get the proposal down to the key elements. The superviser for my first major research study made me go away the first time I tried (badly) to tell him what my project would be. 'Come back when you can say it in 30 seconds,' he said, which was really good advice that got me very focused.

Table 3.1   Contents of research proposal

Structure	Types of source
1. Title	
2. Introduction	
3. Problem Statement	
(a) Establish the purpose of the study.	(a) Framed by theory in key subject textbooks and articles, also previous research and social concerns.
(b) Overview the variables or issues to be examined and the research questions to be asked.	
4. Context	
(a) Identify the context and background of the study.	(a) Textbooks, research articles, literature reviews, research reports.
(b) Review important literature relevant to the problem and cite key references dealing with each of the variables/issues in the problem.	(b) Identify from previous course notes, book and article reference lists, library indexes, subject bibliographies.
(c) Show how results in the research literature are related to the study and identify differences in findings.	(c) Use key word and author searches with online search engines such as Google Scholar.
(d) Indicate how the proposed study relates to other research and the contribution it might make to gaps in existing knowledge.	

(Table 3.1 Continued)

(Table 3.1 Continued)

Structure	Types of source
5. Research Problem and Hypotheses	
(*a*) Statements of research problems are appropriate to both quantitative and qualitative studies. They help to focus a study and give it direction. They should be stated clearly and concisely.	(*a*) Find guidance on narrowing the problem in this and other research methods texts as necessary.
(*b*) Care should be taken here to judge whether the questions are manageable and worthwhile.	
(*c*) Formal research hypotheses are especially appropriate for quantitative research methods.	
6. Assumptions and Limitations	
(*a*) Identify any assumptions made in the study.	(*a*) Guidance from research methods texts.
(*b*) Indicate awareness of its limitations and delimitations.	
7. Significance of the Problem	
(*a*) Indicate relevance or potential significance of findings.	(*a*) Framed by theory, previous research and social concerns.
8. Research Methods	
(*a*) Methods and techniques to collect and analyse data.	(*a*) Research methods textbooks and handbooks.
(*b*) Participants involved.	(*b*) Research reports (especially appendices detailing techniques).
(*c*) Tasks (if any) to be assigned to participants.	(*c*) Research articles.
(*d*) The order in which various procedures will be used.	(*d*) Standard instruments may have protocols to follow.
(*e*) The timing of different procedures.	(*e*) Statistics textbooks.
(*f*) Data gathering instruments.	
(*g*) Statistical design (if any).	
(*h*) Statistical analysis (if any).	
(*i*) Conducting a pilot study.	
(*j*) Ensuring high degree of validity and reliability.	

Source: Column 1 adapted from Maxwell (1992: 16).

If you can, choose your superviser carefully. The legitimate role of research proposals and literature reviews is to be a quality control device for supervisers. However, some supervisers can be quite demanding in exercising their power by orientating your research towards their own academic position and refusing permission to proceed unless they are satisfied. If you have more than one superviser and they have differing viewpoints, you can be caught in a crossfire of contradictory revisions. A consequence is that, often, far too much time goes into this part of the research project, leaving you short of time for data collection and, especially, data analysis.

3.2   Literature review

The literature review is a major component of the research proposal. It is an analysis of relevant publications (usually from the previous ten years or so) that help set the context for and define the research topic. The review is always oriented towards narrowing the field to provide a research problem that can guide operational research.

The review should be the easiest part of the study for many students because it is quite close in format and style to an essay. However, there are two traps. One is to put too much time into the theory because it is very interesting: do not forget that the review of theory is only one part of the research proposal. You also have to consider the next chapter on methodology and the following section on data collection.

The other trap is to have difficulty narrowing down the review to lead to an operational research problem on which data can be collected in the available time. A precise definition of the research problem is critical. The examples in Box 1.1 demonstrate that research problems should be stated simply, clearly and analytically. Without focus, research will be vague and lack rigour. With it, there will be a good start to an analytically tight project, a strong indication of the data to be collected and a solid start on methods.

An almost invariable rule is, *the narrower the focus, the more likely the research project is a practical one*. The correct approach is to break down big problems into small ones, into their component parts. Next, focus on one of the parts and keep breaking it down further until there is a problem that you can realistically research in the available time. For example, you might have an interest in why university students choose some subjects rather than others. However, the university could be very large, so you might narrow the focus to internal day students (rather than distance education students). The university probably has a diversity of subjects, so for an introductory project, you might further narrow the focus to arts students, or to education students or finally, settle on engineering students. You could then choose between studying why they took up engineering in the first place, or why they later specialised in different branches of engineering, such as civil or mechanical. Furthermore, you might focus on first years or postgraduates. Your research problem now becomes manageable. Instead of a broad research problem that asks why university students in general choose their subjects, you have a focused one that asks why postgraduate engineering students specialise in different branches. Instead of a three-year project requiring a survey of the whole student population of many thousands with questionnaires covering all the subjects, you have a three-month project than can survey a few dozen engineering postgraduates using a more focused questionnaire.

One role of the review is to exclude those parts of the literature that are not relevant to the approach you will follow, to give logic to the exclusion of other approaches. Published literature reviews that classify theory and methods can be very useful. Reference to these reviews gives legitimacy to your decision to follow one approach and not others.

A legitimate option is to identify an existing study to replicate, and use its methods to retest its findings. If you do this, you have to demonstrate in your own words your understanding of the methods. However, gaining access to the full details might be difficult. Commercialisation of research in recent decades has resulted in lower standards of public transparency, in part because data and the techniques of gathering it can be commercially valuable. Do not try to repeat studies that report inadequately about research techniques (for example, sampling and questionnaires) because this means that the research is suspect.

The literature review is a funnel that narrows down your topic to a research problem that you can study in the available time and within your available resources. Sometimes, abstract theory can provide concepts that are difficult to research in practice. In this situation, find another theoretical approach that is practicable for research and use that approach.

3.3   Levels of analysis

One of the hard parts of a literature review is showing that you have a critical understanding of the literature. This requires a demonstration of higher order intellectual skills. You have to do more than just quote or paraphrase material from articles, textbooks or your professors. Describing others' ideas only demonstrates lower level intellectual skills of remembering and understanding. This is not enough. Your own research project means that you are now contributing to knowledge yourself and you have to demonstrate the necessary higher order skills.

In essence, a literature review has to operate at the three higher levels given at the top of Table 3.2, which shows the cognitive domain of Bloom's Revised Taxonomy of Educational Objectives. The taxonomy has six levels from lower to higher order thinking. The levels are remembering, understanding, applying, analysing, evaluating and creating. The typical actions (which you will recognise from many essays and exams) indicate what is expected at each level. A literature review should work at the three higher levels to:

Table 3.2   Cognitive levels

Cognitive levels	*Typical actions*	
Creating: generating new ideas and patterns.	Construct Design Devise	Formulate Propose Synthesise
Evaluating: making judgements.	Assess Critique Interpret	Judge Justify Rate
Analysing: breaking material into parts to explore understandings and relationships.	Classify Compare Contrast	Distinguish Illustrate Investigate
Applying: using information in another situation.	Calculate Construct Illustrate	Practice Show Use
Understanding: explaining ideas or concepts.	Compare Describe Explain	Outline Paraphrase Summarise
Remembering: recalling relevant knowledge.	Define List Present	Quote State Tell

Source: Adapted from Anderson and Krathwohl (2001).

1. Analyse the literature actively.
2. Evaluate its relevance to the project, including only selected material directly relevant to the review.
3. Create a conceptual framework for the project, including an operational research problem.

Additionally, the review needs to:

1. Show extensive reading. These days a literature review might have to cite dozens of articles (your superviser or lecturer should make clear the extent to which you are expected to go into a topic for your particular assignment).
2. Have a scholarly style, including proper acknowledgements and references.

3.4   Using the library and internet

The material for the review usually comes from the internet and libraries. My suggestion is to use both, if available. Key word searches on the internet are a very good starting place, but be very selective.

The internet is fast, efficient and offers a huge range of access to material. Some universities offer a seamless transition between internal and external course materials and provide online access to course materials. If your library provides computer access to publishers' websites, you have a very good starting place. Target academic, university, think tank, official and non-governmental websites that have open access publications. Use all these sites' search engines—they often bring up material that is not found by following the site map. With official sites, you need to assess the quality of material and the political policies that it promotes. They often contain both legitimate research and public relations material. Ask yourself whether each publication is genuine research or is heavily massaged for public relations purposes. Public relations material can be an object of study, but it is usually highly selective of the information presented and is not a reliable data source.

Google is a very good tool for searching topics and authors, in particular Google Scholar searches academic sources. For example, search any topic from this book (which you should do as part of your study) and you will find a huge range of material. I searched for 'literature review' on Google and found some 70,900,000 results! The first search result screen displayed information only from universities providing guidance for students on literature reviews, which provide good reading for this topic. There were also unpublished papers and student essays, which like much informal material on the internet can help introduce topics and contribute to your own understanding, but are not for serious citation. Open source materials such as Wikipedia can be very helpful, but they, too, are not refereed and are often devoid of citations (although Wikipedia's entry on literature reviews was quite good in this regard). Still other material was actual literature reviews. There were also results for commericial books and for journals, but with restricted access to their contents. What all this means is that you must assess critically the results of internet searches.

Libraries have one major advantage over the internet: they filter material. They rarely have huge budgets and have to be selective about purchases. They usually use academic advice about purchases and generally accession materials that are refereed formally and published, which means that their content has been vetted for quality. The reference sections also contain many bibliographies and indexes which provide short cuts. In contrast, any clown can put rubbish on the internet, and many do. So,

1. Do not cite ephemeral material in a formal literature review. Use only formally published material as references.
2. Make use of professional search engines, such as Google Scholar.
3. Target websites with open access publications.
4. If you have it, use online access to publishers' lists, especially academic journals.

Whichever the search tools used, the result should be a small number of key books or articles that you judge to be the most appropriate to your level of knowledge and to the research topic. At first, these will probably be introductory overviews that help map the field, later they will have a more technical focus.

3.5   Abstracting

As you grind through readings for the literature review, you will often think, what is its relevance? What principle does it demonstrate? One very useful skill for answering such questions is abstracting, which is a technique for analysing that requires active and critical thinking about the written word. Abstracting is a higher order intellectual skill that much improves the clarity of academic reading and writing. Spend some time and practice it on some material that you are reading. If you do not already have this skill, gaining it will lift your analysis to a higher level.

Abstracting in the way used here derives from a legal principle that applies when a court case is heard. The legal question is: what legal principle applies? Take the following story:

> One day Ravi was riding his Honda motorbike. Without looking very carefully, he started to ride across an intersection. To his surprise, he was knocked off his bike by a big green Tata truck. Fortunately, he was not hurt. Unfortunately, a police officer saw the accident and gave Ravi a ticket, which made him angry. Subsequently a court fined him for failing to give way at an intersection.

What is the legal principle here that applies to other cases? Most of the details in the story do not matter. It does not matter that Ravi rode a Honda, was hit by a truck, was angry or even that it was Ravi. The legal principle is independent of all these facts: *Drivers who fail to give way at an intersection are in breach of the law.* When Ravi tells the story to his friends, the facts will be part of the colour to show what happened and how he felt. However, for the court, the legal principle is what matters.

Similarly, academic work often requires identification of the basic principles from one piece of research that might be relevant to another. An *abstract* presents key concepts, bringing in details only in outlines to show the type of evidence used to support the main ideas. This is not the same as a summary. A *summary* shows understanding by representing evenly all parts of an article and includes more detail. The following summary compresses Chapter 17 on 'Social Science English' by following closely its structure and content.

> More than anything else, the quality of your research will be judged by your final written report. A poor report will reduce the credibility of research no matter how good the research design, the data collection techniques, and the data analysis. The scientific task is to write clear, direct, correct English.

1. Words used in your sentences should be: 1. short, 2. accurate, 3. unambiguous, 4. necessary.
2. Sentences put words into meaningful order. Sentences should: 1. use the active voice, 2. be direct, 3. keep related words together, 4. use the past tense.
3. Paragraphs place sentences into meaningful order. They should not normally be very long: 1. the most important sentence in a paragraph is the 1st one, 2. the 2nd most important sentence in the paragraph is usually the last one, 3. the sentences in the middle should expand on the main idea.

Three general rules apply on spelling, punctuation, citation, and layout: 1. be consistent, 2. do not make up your own rules, 3. avoid footnotes.

These guidelines are a good foundation for clear English writing. You can break all of them on occasion to improve interest and you should adapt them to whatever discipline, publication, purpose or university department you are writing for.

That summary is 208 words long. The following abstract is only 60 words. It includes some of the material in the summary, but omits the step-by-step details to focus on the main ideas.

A good report must be based on good research. A poor report will reduce the credibility of research. Quality in scientific writing is assessed by accuracy and lack of ambiguity. Short sentences, concise wording and clear meanings are signs of good report writing. The task is to write clear, direct and correct English. Guidelines give a foundation for clear English writing.

Both summaries and abstracts are useful when reading for your research project. A summary is useful when you want to know details (of a research procedure, for example). For higher order analysis and synthesis in your literature review, you need to abstract.

3.6   Word processing

The research proposal and literature review provide material to build upon as the study develops through cutting and pasting into different parts of the report with your word processor. Writing the literature review can speed up if reformatting is not needed when cutting and pasting material from other documents. Set up your word processing package in a common format to use for all assignments. You might not need the basic guidance in Table 3.3, but check it anyway.

I have learned some of these techniques only in the last few years despite having used word processors for 25 years. These techniques have saved me days of minor layout editing. The guidance applies to Word 2003, which is used (like Excel 2003 in Section 3) simply because it is by far the most common word processor worldwide, but the same principles apply to other packages too.

Table 3.3   Word processing guidance

Task	Operations
Set standard language	Windows > 'Control Panel' > 'Regional and Language Options'. Also in Word > 'Tools' > 'Set Language'.
Set standard document features	In Word, open a 'New Document', then 'Format' > 'Reveal Formatting'. Set defaults: A serif font such as Times New Roman 12 is most appropriate for the main text. A sans serif font like Arial 10 is clearest for tables. Check the default language. Set page margins consistently. Keep paragraph spacing simple, e.g., 0 spacing before and after, single line spacing. Set tabs consistently, e.g., tab and default positions at 1 cm.
Set bullets and numbering	'Format' > 'Bullets and Numbering' > 'Customize'. Set consistent indent and tab spaces, e.g., 1cm intervals.
Cut and paste, copy	After pasting, set 'Paste Options' drop-down box to 'Match Destination Formatting'.
Set up cross references	'Insert' > 'Reference' > 'Caption' to set up table references, then 'Insert' > 'Reference' > 'Cross-reference' for cross-references within text to tables. To update, place cursor at the beginning of the document > 'Control/Shift/End' > 'F9'.
Lay out tables evenly	'Table' > 'AutoFit' > 'Distribute Columns Evenly'. 'Table' > 'Table Properties' > 'Row' (for heights) and 'Cell' (for text placement).
Align columns in tables	'View' > 'Ruler' > highlight all columns to be aligned > 'Align Right' > adjust tab.
Set up contents and tables lists	In the contents page of your document, 'Insert' > 'Reference' > 'Index and Tables' > 'Table of Contents'. Identify 'Levels' in text and for table headers using 'Style' drop-down box in Formatting toolbar. Repeat for tables. The results might require manual formatting.
Spell check	'Tools' > 'Spelling and Grammar'. Before electronic submission, reset using 'Options' > 'Hide Spelling Errors in this Document' and 'Hide Grammatical Errors in this Document'. In Reviewing toolbar hide editing with 'Display for Review' drop-down box > 'Final'.
Update contents page	Highlight Table of Contents, place cursor to left > 'F9'.
Accept editing changes before electronic submission if 'Track Changes' has been used	'Tools' > 'Track Changes' > drop-down box 'Accept All Changes in Document'.

Source: Author.

This advice goes further than formatting and writing up. It is best to do all note taking straight onto the computer if you can. This avoids double entry and makes drafting much easier. Also, keep all your files backed up. Do not learn this lesson the hard way. The editing for an earlier edition of this book was lost when my computer was stolen and it took months to redo the work. Now I copy files onto a flash drive every time I finish using one. The flash drive is kept separate from the computer and my hard drive is backed up weekly.

3.7   Plagiarism

Academics take intellectual honesty very seriously indeed. Partly, this requires openness and objectivity in writing about the strengths and weaknesses of our own research. Another aspect is giving credit to fellow researchers for their contributions to our work, either through their direct involvement or through use of their publications. If we quote their material, we must quote it exactly without mistakes. The ethical requirement is to respect their intellectual property rights.

Plagiarism is failure to give due acknowledgement by copying material from other people's work without citation, or by copying the work of other students. This is cheating, as is copying ephemeral material or buying research papers from the internet. Get caught and you will lose all academic credibility. Any of these practices could find you excluded from your university. Do not do them.

You can save a lot of time and effort and reduce the risk of plagiarism if, when taking notes, you double check the citation and pagination of the source material before moving to the next piece of note taking. Likewise, when drafting the report, complete and double check quotes and citations, and insert references before returning books to the library—it can save days of frustrating follow-up later.

3.8   Summary

Writing a research proposal is a required first step for many academic studies. Even if a proposal is not a formal requirement, an informal one will be useful.

Research proposal

1. Follow each university department's requirements for structure and style.
2. Proposals can range from two to 10 printed pages. They are written in the present or future tense. A typical proposal includes: Title, Introduction, Problem

Statement, Context, Research Problem and Hypotheses, Assumptions and Limitations, Significance of the Problem and Research Methods.

Literature review

1. The literature review should narrow the field to provide a research problem stated simply, clearly and analytically.
2. The narrower the focus, the more likely that the research project will be a practical one.

Levels of analysis

Reviews require a critical understanding of the literature that demonstrates the higher order intellectual skills of analysing, evaluating and creating.

Using the library and internet

Use both the internet and library if possible. Be selective about information on the internet by using only formally published material.

Abstracting

Abstracting is a key intellectual skill for analysis and synthesis of key concepts.

Word processing

Set up the word processor in a common format for all assignments.

Plagiarism

Plagiarism is cheating, as is copying research papers from the internet. Do not cheat.

At first, the theory guiding the research may seem the most difficult part of your study. As you proceed, you will find that this is not necessarily the case. Though the theory and methodology in the literature review might be high level and abstract, a whole new set of mental disciplines comes from examining research techniques, collecting data and analysing it. You will need to become obsessive about detail. This will, in turn, help you upgrade the quality of your theoretical work by making you more conscious of unsupported leaps in logic and by helping ground your work in real-world data. Say goodbye to waffle—there is no role for it in research.

3.9   Annotated references

Anderson, L. and D. Krathwohl (eds). (2001). *A Taxonomy for Learning, Teaching, and Assessing: A Revision of Bloom's Taxonomy of Educational Objectives*. New York: Longman.
   This is a fundamental book used in this text at several points to provide a structure for abstracting and, later, for analysing data. The book revised Bloom's earlier taxonomy using slightly different terms and labels, which should be used in preference to the earlier ones.

Cozby, P. (2009). *Methods in Behavioral Research*, 10th edition. Boston: McGraw Hill.
   Orientated towards psychology, Chapter 2 of this book has solid material on getting ideas to start research projects.

Punch, K. (2006). *Developing Effective Research Proposals*, 2nd edition. London: Sage.
   A short and clear guide to developing proposals, including the role of theory and methods.

Strunk, W., Jr and E.B. White (2000). *The Elements of Style*, 4th edition. Needham Heights: Allyn & Bacon.
   Writing up research requires much more precision in your use of language than do essays. This short book gives excellent advice on clear English.

Research Methodology 4

A good draft of the research proposal should contain both a literature review and a considered approach to research methodology. Both can be very complicated, especially because there are many competing theories and methodologies. If only a very short proposal is needed, you may only have space to state the data collection techniques. However, you do need to understand the principles on which they are based and what they imply for data collection and analysis.

To help you through the maze, this chapter will cover some fundamental and difficult methodological ground. This is not a time to practice speed reading. Read each sentence slowly and think about it carefully—there is no hurry. Do not worry if it all seems too complicated. You can proceed with your research without fully understanding all the issues (actually, I doubt that anybody really does). If you continue in research, you will find that these issues keep reoccurring. They can become a lifelong study in themselves, but if your interest is problem solving, you need to be familiar with them but not too obsessed or you will never complete the project.

This chapter will:

1. consider the use of research hypotheses;
2. discuss the meaning of objective and subjective data;
3. outline positivism, post-positivism and their competing claims;
4. provide a solution to the claims rooted in commonsense and pragmatism (which for our purposes have philosophical meanings); and
5. outline mixed methods and triangulation of data.

4.1   Research hypotheses

A useful but not compulsory test of a successful literature review is a research hypothesis that clearly identifies the type of data you need to collect to investigate the research problem. A research hypothesis is the researcher's prediction about the answer to the research problem, presented in such a way that it can be tested and either accepted or rejected.

One reason for having research hypotheses—and the reason we are considering them here—is that they can act as a bridge between the literature review and the methodology. They help define the type of data that you need, which in turn helps decide your choice of methodology and the framework within which to interpret the findings.

This type of formal research hypotheses is a *deductive hypothesis*, in other words, derived beforehand from existing theory. If you use a formal hypothesis, it should:

1. Provide a possible explanation for the findings.
2. State a relationship between variables.
3. Be testable.
4. Be consistent with existing knowledge.
5. Be simply and concisely stated (Ary et al. 1996: 107–12).

Formal hypotheses are not an essential part of research, especially exploratory and qualitative research. You might be unable to formulate a hypothesis because so little is known about your problem that a hypothesis would not be very meaningful. Alternatively, you might want to do *grounded research* based on participants' experience and not biased by academic preconceptions. The role is not to review theory, deduce hypotheses and use data to test the hypotheses. Rather, the role is to review the data and see what patterns might emerge. In this case, you will probably generate *informal inductive hypotheses* later, that is, derive them from the data that you collect.

Even if you do not use a formal research hypothesis, you will probably have several informal ones buzzing around your brain. Understanding the logic of hypotheses is important. The logic applies to all research, with or without formal hypotheses. It helps us to be more systematic in testing our ideas, including in grounded research.

A theory only has to be disproved once to show that it does not have universal application. If research shows that a hypothesis is not supported, it is *rejected, refuted* or *falsified*. The hypothesis and possibly the theory from which it was derived are not true or they need to be modified (or perhaps the research was not reliable). If a formal or informal research hypothesis is rejected, it is not a sign of a failure by the researcher; it is a positive sign of clear thinking.

While research can disprove research hypotheses derived from a theory, the reverse does not apply. Research can never prove the theory beyond all doubt, and this is the difficult part about scientific logic. Theories are generalisations that apply to all possible situations, but it is not possible to actually test all future instances. The possibility of disproof always remains open. Just because research supports a hypothesis does not mean that the hypothesis is correct. Evidence *supports* it now but does not prove beyond all future doubt that it is *correct*. The more support a theory gets from a range of research studies, the more confidence we have in it; but a future study might still disprove it.

This principle was demonstrated over two centuries ago, when some philosophers in Europe framed an argument that all swans are white because all swans then observed were this colour. In exploring Australia, black swans were discovered. The theory that all swans are white was refuted, but this did not prove correct the proposition that all swans are only black or white. This proposition is now supported, but perhaps someone will discover pink ones in the future (pink iguanas were recently discovered in the Galapagos Islands, so the idea is not as silly as it seems).

One effect is that all research findings are *probabilities*. Nothing is proved correct, although there might be extremely low levels of probability that it will be refuted. For practical purposes, it is commonsense to accept such findings as correct, but researchers cannot have closed minds about this.

Box 4.1 expands on my own research into teacher education systems in Papua New Guinea to illustrate the logic of hypotheses. The research problems specified how the effectiveness of teacher training programmes would be measured, that is, by assessing graduates' professional performance in schools according to school inspectors' ratings (Guthrie 1980, 1983a, 1984). This determined the type of research methods because the written comments had to be converted into numerical ratings and tested statistically. The result, commonly enough, was that 'objective' statistical tests measured 'subjective' inspectorial ratings.

Other ways of rating were open. I could have measured classroom interaction (however, the techniques were culturally biased); or tested student performance (which would have turned the research into an exercise in testing techniques because there were no reliable tests available); or measured graduates' attitudes to their training courses (which was too indirect). Each of these approaches required different techniques for data collection and analysis. In turn, they had implications for the research methodology because some possibilities were more subjective than others were.

The two formal, deductive research hypotheses added predictions of results derived from the theoretical framework. The hypotheses guided the research but did not pre-empt the findings. In fact, both were rejected, which led to suggestions for further research based on inductive hypotheses grounded in the research data about formalistic teaching. The formal rejection of the research hypotheses was actually what I expected, but the research process had to test formally and very carefully whether my assumption was sound.

BOX 4.1   ROLE OF RESEARCH HYPOTHESES

Evaluation of Teacher Training Programme

1. **Problem:** Were the graduates of formalistic pre-service diploma training programmes in Papua New Guinea more professionally effective as secondary school teachers than those with more progressive bachelor degrees in education? The two major research problems, derived from the work of C.E. Beeby (1966), were formally stated as:

P_1 Do graduates of the secondary teacher training programmes differ in their professional acceptability in schools as evaluated by secondary school inspectors?

P_2 If so, do higher inspectorial ratings correlate with greater amounts of professional training and general education in the programmes?

These problems lead to two research hypotheses:

H_1 Increased amounts of professional training will result in graduates being rated as more professionally acceptable by inspectors.

H_2 Increased amounts of general education will systematically add to the professional acceptability of graduates.

2. **Data Collection:** Five teacher training programmes were evaluated, primarily using 870 formal reports by school inspectors based on observations of 578 graduates in classrooms from 1977 to 1980. Manpower data and documentary analysis of the training programmes supplemented the reports.

3. **Data Analysis:** Parametric statistical analysis led to a rejection of both research hypotheses. There were no statistically significant differences in programme graduate performance. The results for each hypothesis showed:

H_1 Increased amounts of professional training did not result in graduates being rated as more professionally acceptable.

H_2 Higher inspectorial ratings did not correlate with greater amounts of professional training and general education.

Of the two main programmes, the longer, more expensive degree based on a general education foundation was not more professionally effective than the shorter and cheaper diploma based on professional training.

4. **Action:** The research had little immediate effect on the structure of the teacher education programmes, but was an influence on the subsequent amalgamation of secondary teacher education in Papua New Guinea some 10 years later.

Source: Adapted from Guthrie (1983a, 1984).

4.2   Objective and subjective

A research hypothesis shapes the type of data that we need to collect. In social science, we research both the objective and the subjective. *Objective research* treats the physical and social worlds as objects that we can sense in some direct form, for example, by seeing them. The objective social world consists of people, for example, as counted in censuses. *Subjective research* considers what people think about objective things. It deals with mental constructs that we cannot directly see but which we infer from what people say about them or from various forms of measurement such as attitude scales. For example, the physical environment is an objective thing, but people have subjective views about it (witness the debate on climate change, for example) that we can research. Subjective in this sense does not mean our own personal opinions, but concerns research into others' subjective views.

In considering the objective and the subjective, we face a diversity of complicated and difficult issues in the research methodology literature, which are not helped by confusing labels. Frequently, the methodological issues are typified as objectivist versus subjectivist, sometimes as quantitative versus qualitative, or as positivist versus postpositivist. I am also going to refer to philosophical pragmatism.

All this brings us to some really complicated stuff. Whether the objective or the subjective is more important is an issue that reflects long-standing philosophical arguments in western science about *metaphysics* (the study of the nature of reality). The metaphysical issue for science is this. Does the world and the things in it really exist outside our perception of them? Are they subjective and exist only in our minds (the *idealist* position), or are they objective and exist outside our minds (the *materialist* position), and can we actually prove any of this (the doubting *sceptic* view being that we cannot)?

Some people say that the argument is nonsense, and that the world obviously exists, but this is not actually easy to prove logically. Others with the opposite view (including Buddhist philosophers) say that the world is an illusion that exists only in their own minds, but if so, how can they prove it to somebody else? Still others agree that the world does exist objectively, but that any meaning is what we believe it to be. This position is reflected in the saying that 'perception is reality'.

These arguments are fun intellectually, but they can go round and round in circles. In the social sciences, both the objective and the subjective are frequently studied. As commonsense, we accept that the world does exist, but we know the logical implications of not being able to prove it beyond all doubt, as represented operationally in hypothesis testing. We also know that people can have very different interpretations of the same events (for example, one person's terrorist is another person's martyr).

Additionally, we do not treat knowledge only as subjective. We treat formal written knowledge as objective once it is written down and is available in print independent of the minds that originated it, for example, doing this in literature reviews. In practice, social science looks at both the objective and the subjective, although individual researchers might specialise in either or both.

You will have to make up your own mind about where you stand on all this, and you will probably find that your mind changes anyway. To me, the most interesting research tries to see how the objective and the subjective match up. What do people think subjectively about objective events? Do their perceptions match reality? What importance do they place on different events? What do those events mean to them?

4.3   Positivism and post-positivism

Different schools of research take different positions on objectivity and subjectivity, sometimes with an almost religious fervour. We can understand the methodological issues a little better by considering two opposing *paradigms* (systems of intellectual thought) about research methodology to establish some contrasting principles.

In the pursuit of scientific research, some social scientists have pursued 'scientific', 'objective' research methods. Positivist, quantitative methodology is found, among other places, in experimental psychology and quantitative survey research, but has its roots in natural and physical sciences. The essence of *positivism* is that it:

1. studies the world and people in it as objective things;
2. views data as being independent of the observer;
3. accepts data as scientific evidence only if it is collected by direct observation according to strict rules;
4. breaks down data to isolate elements that demonstrate cause-and-effect and, ultimately, scientific laws; and
5. considers that the scientific method is itself objective.

In this paradigm, research is about the scientific rules that researchers follow.

In contrast is the post-positivist view that knowledge is cultural and has many forms. Post-positivist, qualitative methodology largely derives from sociology and anthropology. The essence of *post-positivism* is that it:

1. regards knowledge as subjective and value laden;
2. views data as dependent on the relationship between the knower and the known;
3. favours naturalistic, non-experimental research where the researcher does not manipulate the research setting or subjects or put data in pre-defined categories;
4. views knowledge as subjective, holistic and not based on cause-and-effect; and
5. considers that scientific methods are social constructs.

In this paradigm, research is what researchers do rather than a set of scientific rules.

While offering high levels of reliability, the positivist approach is commonly criticised as suffering from low levels of validity because experiments, in particular, might not realistically reflect social settings. In contrast, the qualitative case studies typically used in post-positivist research, interesting as they may be, offer little beyond the immediate experience of the actors. Ecological validity can be high, but little is possible in the way of generalisation to different ecological niches. So,

1. Narrow positivistic use of formal scientific theory and methods can raise the reliability and generalisability of research, but lower the validity and relevance.
2. Narrow post-positivism can improve validity and relevance, but at the expense of reliability and generalisability.

There is no absolute right or wrong in this. Adopting one methodology or another only offers trade-offs.

4.4   Commonsense and pragmatism

A problem with both positivism and post-positivism is the tendency to treat them as mutually exclusive. Is it really so? Does the use of subjective methodologies and qualitative techniques necessarily exclude the use of objective methodologies and quantitative techniques, and vice versa? Fortunately, social science methodology has become more inclusive over recent decades and there is no need to feel obliged to follow the methodological extremes.

One view, put by the philosopher of science Karl Popper, is that science does not require a secure metaphysical base at all.[1] Popper considered that a commonsense scientific starting point is *realism*—acceptance that the real world exists, even though this can be neither demonstrated nor refuted. Rather than pondering upon the metaphysics, we can progress from this starting point through problem-centred research. The implication is that there is no reason to assume that the use of a particular research technique necessarily locks the researcher into its conventional assumptions because there is no need to be locked into such assumptions at all.

The term *commonsense* also helps us unlock whether or not positivism and post-positivism are incompatible. Essentially the meaning of commonsense is 'shared understanding' (common as 'in common' or 'shared', sense as 'understanding'), which is synonymous with *social construct*. Both positivism and post-positivism can be understood as social constructs. This is a position held also by a subjectivist school of methodology called *phenomenology*, which holds that all researchers are actors whose belief systems are integral to their research.

The viewpoint can be illustrated by statistics, which seems very objective and positivist. Nonetheless, statistics is a subset of mathematics, which is now well recognised

---

[1] This chapter follows Popper (1979: 33ff., 153–68) on commonsense realism, objective knowledge and falsification, although not on commonsense as inter-subjectivity.

as a social construct invented by people, even in such fundamentals as the true zero and base 10. The true zero was introduced into European mathematics from Arabia predated by India. Some preliterate Papua New Guinean cultures had traditional counting systems with bases from 12 to 47 rather than the base 10 system now prevalent internationally. These irregular systems used body parts as a reference for counting, with the base depending on the number of body parts used and how they were combined.

In effect, positivism and post-positivism are both social constructs developed by people and with procedures debated and often agreed among them. This being the case, there appear fewer in-principle objections to combining objective and subjective methodologies because they both can be taken as negotiable products of thought rather than incompatible alternatives.

How can we do this in practice? Philosophical pragmatism provides a point of reference for judging the application of methodologies. *Pragmatism* views knowledge as useful in terms of its practical effect. It lays prime emphasis on research objectives and what is useful in achieving them. From this perspective, the value of research methodologies lies in their usefulness in engaging with the real world. In effect, the pragmatic starting point is the research problem. The research problem implies the data that we need to collect, which leads the research proposal to specify the data collection techniques, research methods and methodology. Otherwise, predetermining the methodology restricts our choice of methods and techniques and their appropriateness for problem solving. Indeed, I actually work backwards from the data to the methodology, but not many take the pragmatic view this far, and in any case, my formal presentations still follow the conventional logic.

You should be aware that these methodological viewpoints exist (indeed, many courses in social science research methods revolve around them), that there is much disagreement about them and that many social scientists dislike Popper because he is often identified as a hardcore positivist. Many other books do have the same viewpoint as this one about data driving methodology, but there are many ways of reaching this conclusion.

4.5   Mixed methods

An increasingly important part of social science research is the use of mixed methods. In general, mixed methods combine both qualitative and quantitative techniques to cancel out their weaknesses.

The pragmatic approach means that we can combine methodologies even within the same project as it enables us to use those research techniques which suit the research problem at hand. The social constructs that are positivism and post-positivism provide the researcher with options, separately or together, depending on the nature of the problem under investigation and the data to be collected. We can measure the subjective and also analyse subjectively the objective world. Sometimes, we need to study the objective, in which case quantitative methods may be the most relevant. Other times, we need to study the subjective, where qualitative methods may be more appropriate. To know the details of a particular situation, the qualitative case studies that are a common feature of post-positivism are appropriate. For generalisations about the attitudes of a population, collection of qualitative opinions using quantitative surveys is appropriate. Positivist experiments can give more rigorous assessment of cause-and-effect.

We can also mix data collection techniques together. As an example, a case study of a small town can use quantitative census statistics about the local area (which would give facts about population numbers but not people's opinions), qualitative open-ended interviews with residents (which would find out what they think) and qualitative observation of community life (which might show whether their behaviour reflects their professed views). A community survey can supplement quantitative individual questionnaires with qualitative discussions in focus groups. An experiment can combine objective tests with controlled observation. In each case, different types of data are collected and analysed using different techniques.

4.6   Triangulation

If similar findings come from different sources, the findings have greater credibility. Triangulation is a particular application of mixed methods. The term comes from mapping, where it refers to taking multiple bearings on a geographic feature to cross check its exact location. In research, triangulation is a process of bringing multiple types of data to bear on the one problem, using the different techniques to study the issue from different angles.

Box 4.2 shows several techniques that were combined in a study of malaria in part of Vietnam. The researchers wanted to investigate social, cultural, economic, environmental and health system influences on the persistence of malaria. This required multiple and mixed methods, both qualitative and quantitative.

Sometimes, triangulation is in the research design from the beginning, especially if you are interested in both the subjective and the objective. However, triangulation can also come from an open eye for apparent contradictions in research data. If you find an unexplained difference, be flexible and add a new research technique to try to find an explanation.

A further application is meta-analysis, that is, an analysis of large numbers of similar studies to see if an overall pattern emerges. Box 4.3 summarises one such analysis, covering teacher education in Asia, Africa and Latin America that was conducted as part of the international background to the teacher education study.

BOX 4.2   MIXED TECHNIQUES IN A HEALTH STUDY

Study of the Persistence of Malaria

The formative stage of the research comprised:

1. Community meetings.
2. Observation of bed-net use.
3. Focus group discussions and semi-structured interviews with health managers, providers and the community.

Formative results were used to guide development of tools for the assessment stage, which included:

1. A provider quiz.
2. Structured surveys with 160 community members and 16 village health workers.
3. Quality checks of microscopy facilities and health records at district and commune levels.

Source: Adapted from Morrow et al. (2009: 85).

BOX 4.3   META-ANALYSIS OF EDUCATIONAL FINDINGS

Teacher Education Effects

1. **Question:** Why did three literature reviews of teacher effectiveness in developing countries have apparently inconsistent findings related to the research hypothesis (that there is a positive relationship between teachers' general and professional education as independent variables and teacher performance as dependent variable)?

2. **Data Collection:** The latest published forms of the reviews had collected research studies covering large parts of Asia, Africa and South America. The task was to review the interpretations placed upon the collected studies.

3. **Data Analysis:** Meta-analysis of the reviews found they had differing disciplinary approaches, different search strategies for the studies included and different limitations placed on the methods in the studies accepted for review. The most detailed of the three reviews included studies covering 19 developing countries in three continents. It found varying results on the three variables most relevant to the research hypothesis. Depending on the groups of variables studied (which ranged from 11 to 194 tested effects), 55–57% of findings supported the hypothesis, 27–35% were null and 10–19% were negative. The positive skews in the sampling distributions were consistent with the research hypothesis.

4. **Action:** The conclusion was that there was considerable support for the general relationship hypothesised, but the exact nature was complex and varied between different educational and cultural contexts. This conclusion guided the main body of the research into the particular characteristics of secondary teacher education in Papua New Guinea.

Source: Adapted from Guthrie (1982).

4.7   Summary

Research hypotheses

1. Usable research hypotheses provide possible explanations of findings, state relationships between variables, are testable, are consistent with existing knowledge and are stated simply and concisely.
2. Some research hypotheses are deductive; others are inductive. Formal hypotheses are not essential, especially in exploratory or grounded research.
3. The more support a theory gets from a range of research studies, the more confidence we can have in it; but a future study might still disprove it. All scientific findings are probabilities.

Objective and subjective

Social science can measure both the objective and the subjective.

Positivism and post-positivism

1. In the positivist paradigm, research is the scientific rules that researchers follow.
2. In the post-positivist paradigm, research is what researchers do.
3. Narrow positivist use of formal scientific theory and methods can raise the reliability and generalisability of research, but lower its validity and relevance.
4. Narrow post-positivism can improve validity and relevance, but at the expense of reliability and generalisability.

Commonsense and pragmatism

1. Schools of methodology can all be considered as social constructs. There is no necessary reason for a particular research technique to lock the researcher into its conventional assumptions.
2. Philosophical pragmatism views the value of research methodologies as being in their usefulness in engaging with the real world.

Mixed methods

Mixed methods include both qualitative and quantitative techniques to cancel out their respective weaknesses.

Triangulation

Triangulation uses different techniques to study the same issue from varied angles. This methodology can be used to investigate apparent contradictions in findings.

In sum, the approach in this book holds:

1. With the philosophical sceptics—that there is no absolute proof that the world exists independent of the mind.
2. With Popper—that assuming it does exist is a matter of commonsense.
3. With the positivists—that rigorous method has many quantitative applications in the social, biological and physical sciences.
4. With qualitative researchers—that understanding of human actors needs other methods too.
5. With the phenomenologists—that all researchers are actors whose belief systems are integral to their research.
6. With the pragmatists—that we can combine methodologies even within the same project and use whatever research techniques suit the research problem at hand.

All research methodologies, including positivism, are shared understandings, the usages of which should be governed by the research objective and the data that needs to be collected.

4.8   Annotated references

Desai, V. and R. Potter (eds). (2006). *Doing Development Research*. Delhi: Vistaar.
    This book has a good range of material on development research, including research planning and design.

Henn, M., M. Weinstein and M. Foard (2006). *A Short Introduction to Social Research*. Delhi: Vistaar.
    A well-written introduction to research taking a different, critical methodology approach from this one. Chapter 1 has background on positivism and Popper.

Persig, R. (1974). *Zen and the Art of Motorcycle Maintenance*. London: Bodley Head.
    This is a cult novel from the 1970s that was often used in postgraduate courses because it presents the case for idealist metaphysics in a very interesting and accessible fashion.

Popper, K. (1979). *Objective Knowledge: An Evolutionary Approach* (Revised edition). Oxford: Oxford University Press.

Popper is a very controversial figure heavily identified with positivism. This work provides a reasonably accessible discussion of philosophy and methodology.

There are also many handbooks, encyclopaedias and dictionaries on research. Try searching the library for some.

SECTION 2

DATA COLLECTION

The second section of this book is about research methods and data collection techniques, which are critical parts of research design. At this point in your project, you should have a good draft of the literature review and methodology in your research proposal and you should now move into this section to select methods and techniques.

This is the longest section in the book because it is convenient to consider both methods and the variety of techniques together. You need to gain an understanding of your options before deciding which will best provide the data you need. You can then use other textbooks that give more details on particular methods or which provide specialist techniques not covered here.

Whatever the method, the chances are that you will use more than one research technique. For example, in a case study of a village, you might use documentary analysis and statistics about the local area, hold open-ended interviews with residents, and observe village life. In a community survey, you might supplement individual questionnaires with discussion in focus groups. In an experiment, you might combine tests with systematic observation. The following table (Table 5.0) illustrates the most common combinations (XX) and those used less often (X).

Where there is a tight deadline, the best advice is to design your first research project so that data collection can occur within your own institution. If you are a university student, collect data about or from fellow students. If you are a professional undertaking in-service training, consider collecting data where you work, for example, if you are a teacher, you could collect data about your school community. Similarly, you could research a sports team, religious group or club to which you belong. You will probably find it much easier to get permission to research from fellow students in particular, especially if you reciprocate and help them with their own projects.

Table 5.0   Combinations of research methods and techniques

Research method	Research techniques				
	Available data	*Observation*	*Interviews*	*Questionnaires*	*Tests*
Case Study	XX	XX	XX	X	X
Survey	X	X	XX	XX	X
Experimental		XX			XX

Source: Author.

Sampling 5

Research design involves a great deal of careful planning. First, as part of the research proposal, a decision must be made on exactly what group of people or objects need to be studied to get the information that is required. Then, the study usually focuses on a sample taken from the entire group. Sampling is one of the foundations of research methods and design because research design nearly always involves recognition of samples.

This chapter provides fundamental understandings about three types of research method. The case study method uses very small samples that give data about individual situations, the survey method samples groups to generalise about them, while experimental designs use samples to identify cause-and-effect. Sampling has implications for dealing with the findings and the extent to which they can apply beyond the sample.

In this chapter, we will look at:

1. why sampling is done and how large samples should be; and
2. three main types of sampling (haphazard, random and systematic).

5.1   Justification

The total group to be researched, and generalised about, is the *population* or *universe*. The small group is the *sample,* and selecting the sample group is called *sampling.*

The main reason for sampling is very simple: it is both efficient and effective. Researchers' resources are usually very limited. Much time and money would be required to study all the primary schools in a province or state, for example. Instead, it is possible to sample a smaller number of schools. Because this approach is time efficient, each school can be studied in more detail, so sampling can also be more effective. Provided the sample is chosen carefully and data is analysed carefully, it is possible to generalise reliably from the smaller sample to the universe of schools.

5.2   Sample size

One of the problems in sampling is determining the size of the sample. Sometimes thousands of people are sampled to get the data that is required. Political telephone surveys are an example. On other occasions, a sample might be as small as one. This type of sample could be a case study of a family or a sports team. Usually, a sample lies between these two extremes, with between 30 and 400 people being part of the study.

Sample size depends on many factors, including the purpose of the study, the size of the universe and the research techniques used. Advanced statistical rules about sample size and selection are complicated and beyond the scope of this book, however some basics will help.

A sample of 30 will usually give results similar to a normal distribution. This will be sufficient for a small study, but your title should state that it is 'exploratory research' or a 'pilot study'. Small, first research projects do not need to go beyond this size.

For larger projects, a social survey sample is between 30 and 400 for populations ranging from about 30 to 1 million, although samples are often bigger. Table 5.1 shows sample sizes that are necessary for any given population from 10 to 1 million, where there is no information available other than the population size. This table is based on the conventional 95 per cent level of probability used in social sciences that the sample will accurately represent the population.

The table shows that for small populations virtually every member should be sampled (for example, for a population of 10, all 10 members should be sampled, while for a population of 30, 28 need to be sampled). For more substantial work with populations up to 400, half or more should be sampled. However, once larger population numbers are reached, sample sizes do not increase proportionally (for example, a population of 1,000 needs a sample of 278, but a population of 1 million adds only an extra 106 cases).

Table 5.1 also shows why it is not possible to generalise from a single case study to an entire population. A case study of one student cannot be representative of an enrolment of 5,000. To represent that number adequately would require a sample of 357. The purpose of a case study of one or two students would be to give detailed information about them and the research issue. The purpose of sampling 357 would be to give a general overview of the total enrolment.

The difficulty with Table 5.1 is that it gives very high *sample fractions* for small to medium-sized populations (that is, the samples as percentages of the population), sampling 80 per cent of a population of 100 and 49 per cent of a population of 400, for example. An alternative approach gives smaller sample fractions, but requires knowledge of the population standard deviation and some mathematics. Box 5.1 contains an example based on data for Port Moresby, the capital of Papua New Guinea. The calculation shows that a sample of 141 has a 95 per cent chance of getting a sample age

Table 5.1   Sample sizes

N	S	N	S	N	S	N	S	N	S
10	10	100	80	280	162	800	260	2,800	338
15	14	110	86	290	165	850	265	3,000	341
20	19	120	92	300	169	900	269	3,500	346
25	24	130	97	320	175	950	274	4,000	351
30	28	140	103	340	181	1,000	278	4,500	354
35	32	150	108	360	186	1,100	285	5,000	357
40	36	160	113	380	191	1,200	291	6,000	361
45	40	170	118	400	196	1,300	297	7,000	364
50	44	180	123	420	201	1,400	302	8,000	367
55	48	190	127	440	205	1,500	306	9,000	368
60	52	200	132	460	210	1,600	310	10,000	370
65	56	210	136	480	214	1,700	313	15,000	375
70	59	220	140	500	217	1,800	317	20,000	377
75	63	230	144	550	226	1,900	320	30,000	379
80	66	240	148	600	234	2,000	322	40,000	380
85	70	250	152	650	242	2,200	327	50,000	381
90	73	260	155	700	248	2,400	331	75,000	382
95	76	270	159	750	254	2,600	335	1,000,000	384

Source: Krejcie and Morgan (1970).

Note: N = population size; S = sample size.

mean within two years of the population mean for an adult population of 190,000. The sample size of 141 is well under the 383 in Table 5.1. This demonstrates that a higher level of knowledge about the population allows a smaller sample.

The bigger the sample, the better it will usually represent the population. Sample size estimates are based upon assumptions that might not always be met in practice, but the abovementioned estimates should be adequate for most purposes. However, they do not guarantee the result. The numbers collected need to be tested statistically once the sample is completed by comparing sample variables (for example, age means and standard deviations, gender proportions, educational levels and marital status) against the population parameters (the characteristics of the population) when they are known.

Once the sample size has been determined, there are three main types of sampling:

1. Haphazard sampling, which should be used sparingly.
2. Simple random sampling, which is the preferred option.
3. Systematic sampling, which is necessary in complex situations.

BOX 5.1 SAMPLE SIZE CALCULATION

Sampling a City

Suppose a sample is wanted for an estimated population of 190,000 adults aged 15 and over in a city with a total population of some 300,000. Fortunately, the population mean and standard deviation can be calculated from census data.

The sample size formula is:

$$S = \left(\frac{sd\ z}{E}\right)^2$$

where S = required sample size,

sd = the population standard deviation,

z = the number of standard error units equal to the desired probability level,

E = the error or range of variation in the sample mean from the population mean that the researcher judges is acceptable in the sample.

The mean age and standard deviation of the 15+ population is 31.0+/−12.1 years, so sd = 12.1. The standard 95% level of probability in social science research has a z score of 1.96, taken from a table of normal curve areas (for a higher 99% level of probability, z = 2.57).

E = 2.0 years. In other words, a sample with an age mean from 29.0 to 33.0 (i.e., within two years of the population mean of 31.0) is acceptable.

So:

$$S = \left(\frac{12.1 \times 1.96}{2.0}\right)^2 = \left(\frac{23.72}{2.0}\right)^2 = 11.86 \times 11.86 = 141$$

Source: Author.

Note: The original source for the formula in this box is Parten (1950: 316–17).

5.3 Haphazard sampling

We often use *haphazard* non-random sampling in everyday life. If we want to try a new brand of biscuits, we try one or two to decide whether we like the brand. We know from experience that one biscuit in a packet will taste like all the others and that all packets of the same brand will likely taste the same. Usually, factories have good quality control, but sampling people is not so easy.

A common form of haphazard sampling is interviews carried out for newspapers, radio or television. Sometimes, reporters walk down a street and interview people they meet. This is not scientific. The reporters will tend to interview people of the same age group, sex and race as themselves because it is easier to talk to people who are similar. Also, people on the street might represent only certain parts of the population, for example, shoppers or street sellers, but not people at work. Similarly, letters to the editor are not proper samples of public opinion. Only certain types of people (the literate and the vocal) write to newspapers.

Another haphazard sample is crude quota sampling. With *crude quota sampling*, you interview people until you have reached the required number. Suppose you have to interview 15 first-year and 15 second-year university students, you walk around the university asking for interviews until you have the correct number in each group. Since the choice of interviewees inside each strata is free, this is a form of haphazard sampling and results in a reliability problem because even if you consciously attempt to make fair selections, there will be an unconscious bias. Every interviewer would select a different set of 30 persons.

The situation can be improved considerably through *structured quota sampling*. This divides the population into groups or stratas and uses quotas from all of them. For example, in interviewing students from the science and arts departments, there should be the correct number of males and females, in proportion to their numbers in the total student population. The first-year group of 15 might have to include six female and four male arts students, and two female and three male science students. This essentially means that the population needs to be redefined to represent the sample more accurately. Probably, the sample never was all university students anyway. The group interviewed was really full-time on-campus arts and science students. In this case, any generalisations made must be specifc to the group and not to the whole student body.

The risk with haphazard samples is that our choices might be *biased*, that is, they might not accurately represent the population because the strict rules of random sampling are not used. Haphazard samples should be treated very carefully, especially while generalising from them. However, they can be very useful early in a survey when trying to get some new ideas for the study, when testing out some interview questions, when practising interviewing and survey techniques or in combination with systematic sampling. Sometimes, there is little choice but to conduct non-random surveys because it is not possible to construct a *sample frame*. In such cases, it is important to recognise the limitations, which the author of the study in Box 5.2 did.

5.4   Pure random sampling

Proper sampling in its most basic form is called simple random sampling. Random sampling occurs when every member of the universe has an equal chance of being included in the sample. To give every member an equal chance, certain rules must be followed very carefully.

Pure, one-stage random sampling is usually possible only with smaller populations whose members can be identified individually. First, prepare a sample frame, which is a list of all the members in the population. A sample frame should:

BOX 5.2   LIMITATIONS IN A HAPHAZARD SURVEY

Thai Migrant Workers in Hong Kong

1. **Problem:** Little information was available about Thai migrant workers in Hong Kong compared to domestic workers of other nationalities. The study aimed to establish basic data about them.

2. **Data Collection:** A non-random sample of 50 female domestic workers was interviewed with a 50-item Thai language questionnaire supplemented by focus groups. No sample frame could be constructed, so the sample was obtained haphazardly at locations in Hong Kong where Thai workers met on their day off from work. Importantly, the author pointed out that the sample was not statistically representative.

3. **Data Analysis:** The questionnaire gave basic socio-economic data such as age, marital status, family situation and place of origin and previous employment in Thailand. Previous employment questions indicated a pattern of step migration from village to Thai city to overseas. Income comparisons in Thailand and Hong Kong showed that higher wages and lack of social pressure on income made Hong Kong an attractive destination. The interviews also gave information about previous training, getting to Hong Kong, and living and working in Hong Kong, and remittances back to Thailand, which was the primary motivation for these workers.

4. **Action:** The research provided basic data that could be of use to government and non-governmental organisations in the absence of more reliable information.

Source: Adapted from Hewison (2004).

---

1. cover the whole universe to be studied;
2. be as complete as possible; and
3. not include the same member more than once.

A correct sample frame is surprisingly difficult to establish, but it should always be attempted. For example, for a sample to test the ability levels in mathematics of pupils in a primary school, the sample frame would be a list of names of all pupils on the school roll. Second, once there is a sample frame, select the sample randomly so that there are no biases in selection.

An easy to use tool is a calculator with a random number generator (you can also use Excel—use the Help function to search 'random numbers'). The set of 150 random numbers in Table 5.2 was generated on a Casio scientific calculator with a random number generator ('SHIFT'/'Ran#' > '=' > '=') that produces three-digit figures from 001 to 999, made up statistically so that every number has an equal chance of being chosen.

Suppose, following Table 5.2, a simple random sample of 108 students in a university class of 150 is required:

Table 5.2 Set of random numbers

072	600	686	694	093	450	165	400	424	949
440	496	720	875	370	278	128	863	031	433
484	415	218	234	168	698	807	581	639	597
451	254	605	569	964	245	305	363	035	765
179	014	898	239	017	669	065	140	978	454
329	658	124	398	023	976	551	889	703	229
414	729	736	081	929	246	994	324	819	667
219	435	796	181	479	437	237	058	169	820
643	979	144	870	844	139	347	580	399	025
552	249	359	462	584	355	914	057	391	731
403	877	131	304	385	568	241	419	959	167
442	714	908	526	251	932	052	654	533	063
118	341	280	220	775	344	668	396	812	758
375	090	847	589	485	480	524	273	109	066
519	543	925	741	421	565	376	342	725	772

Source: Author.

1. First, give all members of the sample frame (the student roll) a three-digit number starting at 001 and finishing at 150.
2. Then, choose 108 numbers up to 150. If using a random number table like Table 5.2, the starting point does not matter as long as you are consistent and systematic (although Table 5.2 has insufficient numbers to complete the exercise). The sample consists of those students with the first 108 numbers below 150. For example, you can start at the top left corner and read down the first column (getting 072, 118) then the second column (014, 090) etc. Alternatively, you can read in rows across the table (072, 093, 128, etc.). Ignore numbers above the total population size (151 and above). Check that you do not have the same number more than once.

The idea is the same as drawing a lottery. The aim is to avoid any personal bias in choosing sample members so that the data is more reliable by being representative of all types of people in the population under study. To maintain randomness, do not take substitutes if you cannot identify sample units in practice. Commonly, maps might be slightly inaccurate or houses demolished or replaced by apartment blocks, or people might not to be at home. In such cases, do not take a nearby replacement because this will introduce a non-random element into the sampling. Any replacements for non-existent sample units must be identified during the sampling process strictly in the order in which the random numbers are drawn.

5.5   Systematic sampling

Systematic sampling can be an alternative to pure random sampling, especially when a full sample frame does not exist. Each approach should, first, incorporate random sampling to the maximum extent that field conditions permit. If a sample or a particular sample stage is non-random, the research report must point this out.

1. *List sampling* saves time by choosing people at regular intervals in a sample frame list. Suppose there is a list of 750 names out of which 250 are to be sampled. This means sampling one person in every three. First, choose randomly a number between 01 and 03 (using the first two digits in the numbers in Table 5.2 and going down the column would give 01). Then, take that number and every third one thereafter, that is, 01, 04, 07, etc. This will give 250 numbers. The people with these numbers would be interviewed.

2. *Proportionate stratified sampling* is used to ensure that the sample includes people from different subgroups or strata in the population. These subgroups might be very important in making sure that the sample is *representative*, that is, it includes key groups. For example, you might have a primary school of 300 pupils and test a random sample of 30 pupils across the six grades. Here, each grade would be called a *strata* and the sample fraction is 10 per cent (that is, a sample of 30 pupils out of 300). Instead of taking a simple random sample of the school, you would take 10 per cent of the pupils randomly within each grade. If there are 50 pupils in Grade 1, you randomly select five from the grade sample frame. If there are 10 pupils in Grade 6, you randomly select one. The total sample would still be 30, but it would equally represent all grades.

3. *Disproportionate stratified sampling* can be used when you do not want the same sample fraction from all strata. For instance, if Grade 6 has 10 pupils, then a 10 per cent sample only gives a sample of one. You cannot generalise from such a small number, so you might decide to sample 60 pupils, 10 from each grade. This would give a sample fraction of 20 per cent in Grade 1 and 100 per cent in Grade 6. In other grades, sample fractions might be 25 per cent, 33 per cent or 50 per cent, depending on the numbers in each grade. Account of the disproportionate sample can be taken while analysing the data.

The first three systematic sample types just identified are usually based on a sample frame listing the population. With a large population, a sample frame can be very difficult to prepare. For example, it would be impossible to walk around and get a list of every resident in a city. Available lists such as the telephone directory or the election rolls might not be very accurate. Not all people have telephones or have themselves listed in the directory, and election rolls are often incomplete and out of date. The next two techniques provide alternatives.

4. *Area sampling* is an alternative for sampling houses, streets or suburbs. It can be used in large places (for example, a whole town) where it is not possible to get the names of all the residents. Instead, you can sample people at different locations within the town. This means that the sample is a random selection of places rather than people, so you must carefully choose a sample that properly represents all types of residential area.

   You can then go a stage further and sample smaller areas. Initially, you might randomly choose suburbs within the town. Within the chosen suburbs, you can then choose a random sample of streets, and then, of houses within those streets. At each house, you interview the target group (for example, heads of the household, or men and women belonging to a certain age groups). In this way, you would get a representative random sample. This is called *multi-stage sampling* as the sample is taken in two or more stages.

   A simpler type of area sample is *grid sampling*. Here, you number grid point intersections on a map and randomly draw the number of residential locations needed. If maps are not available, you can use aerial photos to identify a sample frame of houses or to overlay a grid.

5. *Cluster sampling* has, as the last stage of the sample, a small group (for example, houses or families) where you try to interview everyone. This overcomes the problem of not being able to identify in advance all the people in the final stage. The final stage clusters themselves should be randomly selected. They should be as similar as possible to each other, as should the members within each cluster.

Sometimes, structured quota sampling is used within the clusters. This is done for practical reasons in situations where: the cluster is too large to interview everyone; it is not possible to identify all members of the population in advance (that is, a proper sample frame); it is important to save time or money; or there are safety considerations in the field. Because quota sampling is not itself random, the methods section of the report should recognise the limitation. If quota sampling is used, it should be very systematic to make sure that the choice of subjects is as unbiased as possible.

Depending on their field location, the type of information that is available about the location and the size of the sample required, you can combine the systematic sampling techniques. Box 5.3 shows an example of how stratified and area samples were used in two surveys in Bangladesh.

BOX 5.3 SURVEY SAMPLING

Household Samples

A household survey of indoor air pollution in 236 households was conducted in areas in and near Dhaka. Household pollution levels were measured, usually for one day per household, during December 2003–February 2004 using 24-hour samplers and real time monitors that measured air pollution at 2-minute intervals.

Household selection was stratified into groups defined by cooking fuel (biomass, natural gas), kitchen type and location, and building construction material.

A follow-up in six regions of Bangladesh randomly surveyed 598 households stratified by urban (174 households), peri-urban (145) and rural (279) locations.

Source: Adapted from Dasgupta et al. (2004).

5.6 Non-response

If too many people in a sample are not interviewed, the study might be invalid because the non-responses might be from people who would give different results. For example, females might refuse to answer questions from male interviewers about sensitive topics. A high level of non-response from women would, in turn, lead to results biased towards men's views. If women did answer the questions, the results could well be different.

The *non-response rate* is the percentage of people in the sample who could not be contacted, had moved, refused to answer questions or could not answer for other reasons (for example, they were at work or sick). A general rule is to try to keep non-response below 20 per cent. In my own experience, about 10 per cent is typical, but the figure can rise quickly and needs constant monitoring.

With a structured quota sample, you can draw a sample larger than needed to have an inbuilt allowance for non-response. For example, you could draw 20 per cent more sample units than required by the sample size estimate. This way the 'replacements' are already randomly drawn.

Do not assume that an acceptable rate of non-response means an unbiased sample. The sample should be tested statistically against the known population parameters to see whether there are any significant differences. If there are no differences, all the sample data can be interpreted as though it fully represents the population. However, if a sample variable does not match the population data on any particular parameter, generalisations should not be made from that sample variable. For example, four crime surveys in Port Moresby, from 2004 to 2007, found imbalances in education levels in half of the 32 site samples taken, and for the city as a whole in two of the four surveys compared to the 2000 Census. These differences were probably because the census data was becoming outdated and tertiary education levels were increasing in the community, but no data interpretation was based on educational levels.

5.7   Weighting

When there are disproportionate samples, the sub-sample data might need weighting to represent the population proportions correctly before data analysis. Box 5.4 demonstrates the principles involved in weighting, using calculations for the disproportionate school

---

BOX 5.4   WEIGHTING SAMPLE DATA

Disproportionate School Sample

Disproportionate stratified sampling can be use in situations where you do not want to get the same sample fraction from all strata. For some reason, the Grade 6 class might have only 10 pupils and a 10% sample would only give a sample of one. You cannot generalise from such a small number, so you might decide to sample all 10 pupils, giving a sample fraction of 100% for Grade 6. In other grades, actual sample fractions might range from 20% to 50%, depending on the numbers in each grade.

Grade	Enrollment	Proportionate sample fraction	Sample number	Disproportionate sample fraction	Weighting	Weighted sample number
1	50	27.8%	10	20.0%	1.67	16.7
2	40	22.2%	10	25.0%	1.33	13.3
3	30	16.7%	10	33.3%	1.00	10.0
4	30	16.7%	10	33.3%	1.00	10.0
5	20	11.1%	10	50.0%	0.67	6.7
6	10	5.6%	10	100.0%	0.33	3.3
Total	180	100.0%	60	33.3%	1.00	60.0

1. Columns 2 and 3 show the total enrolments in each grade and the percentage each grade has of the school's total, which would be the proportionate sample fraction (e.g., Grade 1 has 50 of the school's 180 pupils or 27.8% of them).
2. Columns 4 and 5 show the sample number and the disproportionate sample fraction for each grade (e.g., Grade 1 with a sample of 10, has 20.0% of the grade enrolment of 50, compared to the school average of 33.3%).
3. Column 6 shows weighting, which is the number of times the grade sample number in Column 4 has to be multiplied to give the correct sample equivalent to the proportion in Column 3. The weighting is calculated using data in Column 5. For Grade 1, the calculation is 33.3/20.00 = 1.67.
4. Column 7 shows proportionate sample numbers from multiplying the grade sample number in Column 4 by the weighting in Column 6 (e.g., Grade 1 is 10 * 1.67 = 16.7). Rounded off, Column 7 numbers would be the numbers for a proportionate sample that would represent the school as a whole. The total sample size of 60 is the same as Column 4, but the grade numbers are now proportional to enrolments (e.g., the Grade 1 sample of 16.7 is 27.8% of the sample total of 60, which is the same percentage as Column 3).

Source: Author.

sample discussed earlier. The weighting figure in Column 6 can be used to keep the sample at the original size, or the weighted sample numbers in Column 7 could be multiplied by three to give a school population figure of 180. If you want to weight in practice, use one of the statistical packages rather than attempt to do this by hand for each question.

5.8   Summary

Most research methods are based on samples. A key part of planning the research project is to decide exactly who or what will be studied in order to address the research problem. Usually, researchers study only a small part of the total group in which they are interested.

Justification

1.   All research projects involve sampling a population or the universe.
2.   The main reasons for sampling are efficiency of time and resources, and effectiveness from freeing time to study a situation in more detail.

Sample size

Exploratory studies might only have samples of 30, but usually a survey sample has between 30 and 400 people (see sample size tables and formula).

Sample types

1.   Once the sample size has been determined, the three main types of sampling are haphazard, simple random and systematic.
2.   The preferred pure, one-stage random sampling is usually possible only with smaller populations whose members can be identified individually, which requires a sample frame.
3.   Types of systematic sampling include list, proportionate and disproportionate stratified, area and cluster sampling.
4.   If a sample or a particular sample stage is non-random, the research report must point this out.

Non-response

1. The non-response rate should generally be under 20 per cent.
2. Do not take non-random substitutes.

Weighting

The principles involved in weighting disproportionate samples are demonstrated.

Techniques of sampling are complicated, but that is not an excuse for bad sampling. Sampling should always be carefully done and as random as possible. Research is like a chain. If one link is weak, the chain will break. If one part of the research is done badly, the whole effort will be a waste.

5.9   Annotated references

Sampling is a basic element of all research. The following books contain plenty information about it. University libraries should have many others.

Babbie, E. (2007). *The Practice of Social Research*, 11th edition. Belmont: Wadsworth.

Best, J. and Kahn, J. (2005). *Research in Education*, 10th edition. Needham Heights: Allyn & Bacon.

Cozby, P. (2009). *Methods in Behavioral Research*, 10th edition. Boston: McGraw Hill.

Case Study Method 6

The case study method takes a situation as given and tries to find out what it particularly means to the participants. Commonly, case studies are associated with qualitative research, but often they combine different research techniques. They can illuminate quantitative findings and can incorporate quantitative data.

The method usually involves the examination of one or, possibly, two or three particular cases in-depth and holistically. A case study can take months or even years to complete, which allows mature consideration of the findings, correction of misunderstandings, filling of gaps in the data, investigation of new ideas arising from the data and a longitudinal view. This last feature can be a considerable advantage over surveys and experiments, which typically are one-off methods.

This is a practical and interesting research method that can teach you many different research techniques simultaneously. If you decide to carry out a case study, you could use several of the data collection techniques discussed later in the book, but time limitations on a first research project will restrict your exploration of these techniques. This chapter provides a basis for using many of the later discussed data collection techniques, especially available data, observation and interviews. The chapter will look at:

1. sampling principles that affect case studies and generalisations from them;
2. types of case study;
3. types and location of data; and
4. limitations to case studies, particularly in context of the role of the researcher.

Usually, case studies are selected non-randomly (Chapter 5) and use available data (Chapter 9), observation (Chapter 10) and interviews (Chapter 11).

6.1 Sampling principles

Two different perspectives about case studies exist. In one perspective, the primary interest is a particular theory or issue. The case study is a single example that illustrates the general principle; however, it is too small a sample from which to make reliable generalisations. The other perspective has the case as the primary interest that is important in itself. The case is the research population, but it does not represent other populations and extrapolations cannot be made to them. A sample of one, two or three cannot be fully representative of a larger group. It is not possible to generalise the outcomes reliably from such small samples to the population as a whole. Moreover, a case study is usually a non-random haphazard sample.

Representativeness can be increased by choosing the case systematically. For example, you might look at one particular school to assess student achievement. However, it is not possible to say that all 100 schools in that area would have the same patterns of performance or even know the reasons for them. A sample of 80 would be needed to be fully representative of all the schools (Table 5.1). Realistically, for a sample that size you could only study readily available data, such as public exam results. Of course, understanding the one school would not matter in an action research project, perhaps to identify areas for improvement.

A particular strength of case studies is that they allow in-depth illustration of different examples of the population under study. The more systematically cases are chosen, the more likely they are to illustrate population patterns. For example, the exam results might identify low and high achievement schools. Rather than one case, the study could look at two: a high scoring example and a low one, and investigate the similarities and differences. Does student socio-economic status differ? Do student academic standards differ as a result of their intake? What are the educational philosophies of the schools? Is one school better funded than the other? Do class sizes vary? What qualifications and experience do teachers have? Are some subject areas getting better results than others? What career aspirations do students have? You would be unlikely to get all this data for the entire population of schools, but you could get it for a couple of examples and illustrate themes relevant to the other schools, adding considerable depth to the study. Nonetheless, the report has to be very careful not to claim that findings can be generalised from the two schools to the other 98. More appropriately, individual principals could use the case study findings as a basis for comparison with their own schools.

6.2   Sample of one

In the first approach, as a single example, case studies are an illustration of issues that involve a larger population or universe. The case study is a subset of the whole population. This type of case study has three uses.

1. *Preliminary investigations* can be conducted prior to the main study to identify key variables for further examination using a larger sample. For example, you

want to survey crime, needing to know first what type of crime happens most (for example, property crime or violence) and where it occurs most (for example, in the house, the street or at work) so you can study that situation more closely in the main survey. You might decide to help develop the questionnaire by conducting open-ended interviews in three households in high-, middle- and low-income areas in different parts of the town to learn about the range of household experiences. A preliminary investigation like this will not have the scope of a substantive case study, but will give insights to help shape the survey.

2. *Pilot tests* are another form of a restricted case study that can be undertaken applying techniques used in the larger study, for example, a test of the new questionnaire to see if the people interviewed understand the questions. Here, you might interview in one or two households and then pause to analyse the data, gain further understanding from the households and adjust the question-naire before proceeding on to a full community sample.

3. *Follow-up studies* can be used to examine more deeply particular issues identified in the main survey. Perhaps the crime survey discovers that theft is the most common type of crime. You would now want more information about when and where it occurs, what typically is stolen, who are thought to be the perpetrators and the impact on victims. Similar to the exam example, you might decide on two contrasting case studies: one, of a household that the main survey identified as a frequent victim of theft, the other, affected little by it. Depending on the research problem and the amount of time available, follow-up studies can prove to be very substantial.

6.3   Total population

In the other approach, the case study itself is the research population, the sole interest of research. We want to know the full complexities of a particular situation, but we will still probably face—and must avoid—the temptation to generalise beyond this particular case. This type of case study can have four different focuses.[1]

1. *Individuals* might be the focus, perhaps for psychologists, educationists or social workers, to study, for instance, how people with disabilities fare in mainstream schools. Researchers sometimes conceptualise their study of individuals as biographies and tell their stories as narratives. Other times, autobiographies can provide case study material. For example, the novel and the autobiography by

---

[1] Derived from Weeks (1985), with the addition of projects.

the author, Janet Frame (1961, 1989), in which she wrote of her experiences as a patient in mental asylums, were read widely by psychiatrists. A full research project would normally need to combine a number of individual studies.

2. *Projects* are quite often the focus of policy research evaluations, often by consultant researchers. These can be *formative evaluations* (during the project) or *summative evaluations* (at the end of the project). Project evaluations have case study characteristics because they usually analyse the entire activity and use mixed methods, especially available documents, records and interviews. Box 6.1 has an example from an international aid project in Sri Lanka.

3. *Institutions* can be the focus of case studies when we are interested in the history and nature of particular organisations, for example, a school or a hospital, perhaps to see how it went about implementing a particular policy, programme or project in which we are interested, and how the nature of the organisation influenced implementation.

4. *Communities* can also be the focus of case studies, perhaps where you want to know more about and possibly influence your own residential communities. Alternatively, you might want to research in communities that are new to you

---

Box 6.1   PROJECT EVALUATION AS A CASE STUDY

Summative Evaluation of an Aid Project

1. **Problem:** A Final Evaluation of an Integrated Rural Accessibility Planning Project in Sri Lanka, funded by the International Labour Office, was conducted in 2008. This was a summative evaluation designed to assess the overall effectiveness of technical assistance provided to local and provincial governments to rehabilitate 400 kms of roads. The small project had operated over a 17-month period. It aimed to introduce a set of planning tools to speed definition of priorities.

2. **Data Collection:** The evaluation considered the project's processes and methodology through a desk review of project documents and outputs, discussions with key leaders and five focus groups in selected areas with government officials and community organisations.

3. **Data Analysis:** The evaluation required the reviewers to exercise their professional judgement in assessing the project's effectiveness. The project was found to have provided appropriate planning tools for the government institutions involved. The project would have been more effective if the plans developed had been based more closely on local needs rather than on a standard sector approach. A second issue was that the project produced maps and reports that were usable for planning, but district staff were not trained in producing new ones in future.

4. **Action:** A set of recommendations was made part of the management review processes of the international agency and the recipient government institutions.

Source: Adapted from International Labour Organization (ILO) (2009).

because they face particular issues in which you are interested. Anthropological case studies in other societies are like this. These studies typically use ethnographic techniques, especially participant observation. Box 6.2 has a case study from India that used short periods of fieldwork to understand recent caste conflict in a community.

BOX 6.2   COMMUNITY CASE STUDY

Caste Conflict

1. **Problem:** What was the nature of a rebellion by members of an untouchable caste in a rural village in Rajasthan in 2001? The orientation was to advocate on behalf of the untouchables.
2. **Data Collection:** The case study was based on data that was collected during several visits to the village, being included as part of a human rights fact-finding team. Data was collected through observation, open-ended interviews and review of previous studies.
3. **Data Analysis:** The data allowed the conflict to be described chronologically to establish the setting, the history of caste relationships since the mid-1930s, the current conflict, subsequent developments and the nature of the official response. The analysis showed that rather than castes having developed different but equally valid identities, in this village, caste remained largely hierarchical, imposed by the privileged castes and ruthlessly enforced.
4. **Action:** The fieldwork was part of the human rights fact-finding mission, as well as contributing to this academic article.

Source: Adapted from Bhatia (2006).

Case studies lend themselves to comparative case studies, which systematically compare the features of one case to another. The next study in Box 6.3 compared two teacher training institutions as part of the teacher training study to see how each institution's different educational philosophies influenced their teacher programmes respectively. The study combined several data collection techniques. Sometimes, the *comparative case study* method goes further and holds constant the variables under consideration to make the comparisons more rigorous, for which you can look in more specialised texts for advice.

6.4   Theory and data

Case studies are often criticised for being superficial. Describing a case in detail does not necessarily make it interesting or important, especially if the literature review has not identified themes and issues. The impression from reports characterised by

---

Box 6.3   Comparative institutional case study

Two Teacher Training Faculties

1. **Problem:** The Faculty of Education and Goroka Teachers' College were the only secondary teacher education institutions in Papua New Guinea in the 1970s, thereby constituting the research population. They were both part of the University of Papua New Guinea, but were located in different regions of the country and had quite distinct characteristics. How did their different characteristics influence their teacher training programmes? The literature review had identified a central theoretical theme of professional conflict over the effectiveness of formalistic and liberal teaching styles in Papua New Guinea and this was a key element in analysing the data.

2. **Data Collection:** Data on both institutions was collected from historical reports, in-house files, searches of student records, questionnaires, interviews with staff and from participant observation as a member of both institutions at different times during the study.

3. **Data Analysis:** The data allowed the two institutions to be compared systematically according to their different histories, programme philosophies and structures, organisational arrangements, course composition, staff and student composition and costs. A combination of historical and documentary analysis, quantification of amounts of general and professional education, statistical analysis of questionnaires, qualitative review of interviews and a reflection on my own experiences was used. The data was pulled together using the teaching styles theme.

The pattern that emerged was that the college's lower cost, pre-service sub-graduate two-year diplomas aimed to lay a foundation of formalistic professional training in teaching methods and syllabus content closely allied with the high school situation. The faculty's higher cost, four-year degree programme aimed to lay a broad educational base in arts and science subjects prior to a more liberal approach to professional education. The faculty had more academically oriented staff and higher student intake standards, but the college programmes were a more popular path among comparable students.

4. **Action:** As a subset of the teacher professional acceptability study, this component illuminated the independent variables of teacher general and professional education.

Source: Adapted from Guthrie (1983a: 31–71).

---

endless detail is that the researcher was too close to the data and could not see the bigger picture.

Often, case studies use grounded approaches. They do not start from a formal testing of theories and research hypotheses, but seek patterns arising from the data. This can involve trade-offs. On the one hand, a grounded approach can help keep the mind open to new ideas, which might be overlooked if there is too much obsession with social commitment or a favourite theory. On the other hand, theory that builds on others' experiences in similar situations can help identify patterns that otherwise might not be obvious. A balance lies in reviewing appropriate literature to identify themes of interest, but not having formal research hypotheses.

The teacher training study as a whole tested formal hypotheses statistically, but the comparative institutional case studies were undertaken to understand more fully the institutions that largely determined the nature of the independent variable, which was the teacher training programmes. The literature review nonetheless provided an important theoretical theme about teaching styles. Otherwise, the result could have been a mass of statistics and comments from staff, failing to investigate fully a major difference between the two institutions.

Table 6.1 takes the details further and shows how the themes which were identified during the literature review were illuminated using several data collection techniques. It takes the previous box further by also showing, in the right-hand column, the types of locations where the data was found. The study took place over four years, so there

Table 6.1   Case study data sources

Theme	Data collection techniques	Sources
Institutional histories and relationships	Available data.	1. Public and professional libraries and official archives for Acts, government annual reports, departmental gazettes, official reports and statistics. 2. Historical research articles and theses. 3. Biographies and autobiographies for participant views.
Programme philosophies	Available data, questionnaires, interviews, observation.	1. Professional libraries and institutional files for official statements and background papers to official decisions, e.g., records of academic meetings. 2. Mail survey of staff. 3. Face-to-face staff interviews. 4. Daily work as participant.
Programme structures and course composition	Available data, questionnaires, interviews.	1. Institutional libraries and faculty files. 2. Academic calendars and handbooks. 3. Mail survey of staff. 4. Face-to-face staff interviews.
Organisational arrangements	Available data, observation.	1. University and faculty files. 2. Daily work as participant.
Staff composition	Available data, questionnaires.	1. University and faculty files. 2. Mail survey of staff.
Student composition	Available data.	1. Libraries (especially previous research theses). 2. University and faculty student records.
Graduate output, career choice, attrition	Available data.	Graduate tracer study from university and faculty student records and Ministry teacher files.
Costs	Available data.	University Planning Office papers.

Source: Author.

was plenty of time to do a thorough job. For short first studies, you will have to be more selective in your data collection, but the list takes you closer to the sort of work that your own case study might require and should help generate ideas about where to look for data. It also implies a practical reason for identifying themes in advance. Data for different themes was often collected from the same sources, so having themes saved repeat work.

6.5   Start-up

A case study will use data collection techniques discussed later in the book, but it does have one particular requirement, which is gaining access to the institution or community that you want to study. Some guidelines will help your introduction.

1. Get someone who knows the place to advise you.
2. Discuss the research with community leaders or officials and get their approval.
3. Get introduced around at the beginning of the study.
4. Explain exactly who you are, what you are doing and for whom you are doing it.
5. Have proper identification.
6. Try to appear similar to the people you are interviewing.
7. Explain that all the information will be confidential.
8. Do not be bossy.
9. If people are not available, come back later.

A valuable technique during the introductory period is to draw a sketch map of the institution or community, which can be used in the research report. This will help you see the location as a whole and identify parts which might have been overlooked. Sketch maps do not have to be completely accurate, but they should:

1. have a title, date and author's name;
2. give a direction arrow for north and some landmarks to help orientation;
3. give an indication of size and be to scale as much as possible;
4. use different colours and symbols to make key elements stand out;
5. have a key for the symbols; and
6. be neat and tidy.

Once introduced into the organisation or community, you will be in a position to apply data collection techniques from the later chapters of this book.

6.6   Researcher's role

The biggest potential problem with case studies is not unrepresentative samples, the use of particular data collection techniques or access to communities—it is the researcher. Researchers often establish emotional attachments with 'their' subjects or 'their' community that limit insight. Four role problems arise:

1. Researchers tend to think that they understand the situation better than is really the case. This might limit their minds to the expected. Interviewing is one situation where this can become apparent. After a while, the tendency is to hurry over answers and not use probe questions. This is a sign that quality is starting to suffer because the answer is assumed.
2. Researchers believe that they are testing information more systematically than they really are. Particularly in organisations that are familiar, researchers tend to think they know who to talk to about certain issues and overlook other people with valid viewpoints. In effect, they are starting to carry out haphazard sampling and should slow down to be more systematic.
3. Researchers can overlook routine events. This especially occurs if the work schedule is not arranged to see a community over the full daily, weekly or even seasonal cycles.
4. The more researchers identify with the participants, the greater is the extent to which objectivity, judgement and insight can be lost. It is possible to 'take sides' during data analysis, perhaps to overemphasise one point of view and downplay a competing position to the detriment of balance. Developing themes from the literature review helps counterbalance this tendency.

The chances are that you have chosen a topic on which you hold a personal viewpoint; however, your role as a researcher requires you to suspend your opinions while you collect data against which to test them. Sometimes, it is hard not to become involved in sensitive community situations. Getting involved in conflict is a personal ethical decision for you to make. If you do, know that it could be the end of the research and any long-term value that it might have.

6.7   Summary

The case study method typically involves detailed examination of one, possibly two or three situations in-depth and holistically. Case studies take the situation as given and try to find out what it particularly means to the participants. A case study typically uses a variety of data collection techniques and can take months or even years to complete. This is a considerable advantage over surveys and experiments, which are typically one-off snap shots.

Sampling principles

Case studies are not usually chosen according to strict sampling methods, so we cannot generalise from them reliably.

Sample of one

If the primary interest is particular theories or issues, a case study is an example that illustrates the general principle. As a subset of the whole population, this has three uses: preliminary investigations, pilot tests and follow-up studies.

Total population

1. The research population in the case study can also be the primary interest for research. This type of case study has four different focuses: individuals, projects, institutions and communities.
2. Case studies lend themselves to comparative studies.

Theory and data

Describing a case in detail does not necessarily make it interesting or important, especially if the literature review has not identified themes and issues.

Start-up

1. Careful introduction is needed to the community or organisation.
2. A valuable technique during the introductory period is to draw a sketch map.

The researcher

Researchers tend to think they understand the situation better than they really do, believe they are testing information more systematically than is the case, overlook routine events and overly identify with participants.

Like all qualitative research, properly done case studies are just as demanding as other research. However, they are easy to do badly because the rules of the games are not as transparent as in quantitative research. It is easy to be intellectually lazy and to hide the fact from yourself and others. A careful systematic approach is needed and must be demonstrated in the report.

6.8 Annotated references

Perecman, E. and S. Curran. (2006). *A Handbook for Social Science Field Research: Essays and Bibliographic Sources on Research Design and Methods*. Thousand Oaks: Sage.
This book contains a wide range of guidance on fieldwork, including on data sources, case studies, ethnography, surveys and mixed methods.

Scheyvens, R. and D. Storey (eds). (2003). *Development Fieldwork: A Practical Guide*. London: Sage.
A comprehensive collection on fieldwork in developing countries containing chapters on both quantitative and qualitative research.

Vulliamy, G., K. Lewin and D. Stephens. (1990). *Doing Educational Research in Developing Countries: Qualitative Strategies*. London: Falmer.
Heavily based on practical research experience, which was gathered while conducting case studies in Malaysia, Nigeria, Papua New Guinea and Sri Lanka.

Survey Method 7

The survey method is long-standing in the social sciences, especially sociology and politics. It is used for developing generalisations about populations. The survey method selects a sample that is representative of a larger population and uses the results to generalise about that population as a whole. Its strengths are in collecting demographic and socio-economic data, and in describing people's general perceptions and attitudes.

Surveys are useful mainly for describing patterns in large groups rather than in-depth analysis of individuals' views. Questionnaires, which are the main but not the only research technique used with surveys, usually represent attitudes numerically and, normally, receive only brief written or verbal comment. One-off interviews in surveys are not an appropriate method for collecting information about intensely personal matters.

This chapter will cover:

1. sampling;
2. types of survey and implementation options;
3. survey protocols and management; and
4. reducing non-response.

Commonly, surveys use random samples (Chapter 5), then conduct interviews (Chapter 11) using questionnaires (Chapter 12). Other techniques such as focus groups or observation can give more depth to questionnaire data.

7.1 Sampling principles

Like any other form of research, surveys rely on a very clear specification of objectives and need to collect data specifically related to those objectives. Because surveys aim to generalise accurately from samples to populations, the foundation is reliable sampling. To revise briefly, a survey needs:

1. a clearly defined population;
2. if possible, a simple random sample from a sample frame;
3. otherwise, systematic sampling techniques such as list, stratified, area or cluster sampling; and
4. a sample size usually varying between 30 and 400 people.

Any errors in these matters will be magnified as biases in the findings.

7.2 Types of survey

1. *Censuses* are the most complete type of survey. A census aims for responses from everybody in a population to get basic demographic and socio-economic data for information and planning purposes. This is a large-scale and expensive enterprise that does not involve sampling and can normally only be undertaken by governments, only every five or 10 years. Usually, censuses cover a whole country, but special purpose censuses can target smaller populations.

   The advantage of censuses is completeness and, usually, accuracy. Their main role in survey research is to provide a population baseline against which to test samples. Generally, sample survey data is tabulated, presented as percentages and analysed according to socio-economic variables such as age, gender, education, marital status and income, separately or combined. These *sample variables* should be tested against the equivalent *population parameters* to see if the sample reliably represents the population to check, for example, that the percentage of married people in the sample is not significantly different from the percentage in the population.

   Because of these checks, the survey questionnaire should ask for socio-economic data in the same form as the reference census. Differently put questions might be interpreted variously by respondents; so, any differences from the census might pose an issue of reliability (the different forms of questions) rather than one of validity (a real change in the situation).

   Census data soon becomes outdated, but it is likely to be the best or the only available reference data for sample surveys in the field. If a sample does not match the census, there is a problem. Is the survey unreliable (that is, an inaccurate representation of the population), or is the census data no longer valid (that is, the population changed since the census so that the survey is now correct)? If we assume wrongly that the survey is unreliable, the risk involves incorrectly rejecting its results. If we assume wrongly that the census is invalid, the risk is incorrectly accepting the survey results.

We need to recognise this limitation, but often the objections are not of practical value—it is easier to identify the shortcomings of censuses than to provide better data, so in practice, researchers often have to use them as a reference point because there is no better alternative. We usually have to assume that the census is correct (unless there is independent evidence to demonstrate otherwise) and proceed on that basis. The report should recognise the potential shortfalls and alert readers to any inconsistencies between census and survey findings.

Otherwise, surveys are often based on sample frames using other data sources. For example, educational institutions have enrolment records, which are usually current and can define the population of students or parents to be sampled. Telephone directories and electoral roles are also used, but are often incomplete or out-of-date.

2. *Cross-sectional surveys* represent a particular population at a particular time. Most surveys are like this. This is probably the only type you can consider for a first research project, for three simple reasons. Probably, you will not have enough time to conduct even a small census (unless its a very small unit), to repeat the survey for a longitudinal approach or to conduct a lengthy case study.

There is no point in using cross-sectional studies in an attempt to bring in a time perspective by asking what people used to think as well as what they think now. This is very prone to the vagaries of people's memories and is not reliable.

3. *Longitudinal surveys* repeat cross-sectional surveys. Unless surveys are repeated, they do not give much understanding about how people's views are changing. Three main types of surveys allow serious analysis of how matters change over time (Gall et al. 2006: Chapter 11).

   (a) *Trend studies* take different samples from a general population, for example, first-year students at a particular university. The population of students changes each year, as does the sample. This would not matter if, for example, the aim is to know whether new students' expectations or career intentions are changing over time.

   (b) *Cohort studies* follow the same population over time, for example, all the university's graduates from a particular year. The population stays the same, but a new sample is drawn each time.

   (c) *Panel studies* trace the same sample over time, for example, a particular graduate class to follow their professional careers. Highly accurate coding of respondents and questionnaires is necessary for panel studies so that individual circumstances can be followed. Cohort and panel surveys face reductions of population and sample sizes because it is difficult to trace all members.

With all longitudinal studies, survey techniques and fieldwork protocols need to be the same from one survey to another. If changes were to occur, each subsequent report would have to be qualified by explanations stating changes in results could be due to reliability problems.

This book has many boxed examples drawn from surveys that demonstrate the issues in this section. You should check them systematically.

7.3 Implementation options

The type of data you seek depends on the research problem and your research hypotheses. Be careful not to assume that because you have chosen to conduct a survey, you would necessarily need a questionnaire—chances are that you will, but the decision should not be preconceived. Surveys do not necessarily seek opinions, so various ways of getting information can be considered. For example, organisations might have detailed files. To map a school's student catchment area, a short questionnaire could ask students for their addresses, but obviously the school records would be a quicker and easier (and very boring) data source. Tests can also be used in surveys; for example, of a university class.

If the research problem does require a questionnaire to sample opinion, you will probably conduct a cross-sectional survey. The issue soon becomes delivery of the questionnaires. Do you use them as a means to schedule interviews and interview personally, or use some other means of distribution and let the respondents complete the questionnaire themselves? There are several options, but face-to-face interviews or group administration are likely to provide more reliable results than others.

1. *Street interviews* are a non-random haphazard sample and are not recommended.
2. *Face-to-face interviews* involve going to the place where your respondents are located (at a worksite or, more likely, their residences) and asking them questions. Usually, prospective respondents are notified in advance through a letter, but making contact can prove to be time consuming. Probably, you might conduct an average of less than five interviews a day, and there will be days when you get only one or two. The time problem does not arise so much from the length of the interview, but from the time that lapses in between (for example, four 30–40 minute interviews a day summates to only two or three hours of interviews; however, another five to six hours might be spent waiting for people). Refusals can be emotionally draining, and there will be travel and accommodation costs unless the study is in an area close to home. However, response rates will probably be higher than the alternatives and are more likely to provide a valid study. Interviewing promises marketable work experience as well.

3. *Group administration* is a very efficient option for administering self-completion questionnaires, for example, to school classes or sports teams. Providing the group is a case or a sample unit, non-randomness and non-response are less of a problem.

4. *Mail interviews* seem easy because you mail the questionnaires with a covering letter and a stamped and addressed reply envelope, hoping for the best—and hope and hope. Non-response rates are likely to be high and much follow-up work will be required. The lack of reliability because of high non-response means that valid generalisations might not to be possible from the sample to the population.

5. *Phone interviews* may seem to overcome some of the time and contact problems. However, they are unlikely to be based on representative sample frames (telephone directories). Many abrupt refusals are likely because some people might suspect that you are merely a phone marketeer. In case of high non-response rates, the survey might be invalidated. If you use the phone for business or organisational surveys, the chances of getting through to someone senior enough to give an informed response are bleak.

6. *Internet questionnaires* provide a modern and apparently attractive technological option, but have several disadvantages. They are likely to have inadequate sample frames (where is a list of email addresses that is representative of the population, including people who are computer illiterate or cannot afford a computer at home?). They are often a device used by well-resourced marketeers and might not get any response or, if people open an email, they might not open a questionnaire attachment if they are wary of viruses. Also, if you try to set up an automated system for tabulating questions, you are likely to head your research into solving technical problems rather than getting substantive data.

Phone and emails are much more useful tools for follow-up after rapport has already been established from face-to-face interviews.

7.4 Survey protocols

Having chosen the delivery system, the next step is to develop survey protocols, which are the procedures to be followed. Survey protocols should be included in the research techniques chapter or the appendix to show that the survey was systematic and methodologically correct. A sound guide is that they should be sufficiently detailed to allow a follow-up survey to replicate the same procedures and, thus, not give rise to reliability problems.

Box 7.1 shows the protocols for interviewer training in the crime surveys, but are adapted to show those that apply generally and those that were particular to these surveys. The particular protocols applied to research teams in difficult field environments, but they include many issues (for example, workdays, flexibility, travel, personal safety) that you need to consider for your own study.

BOX 7.1   SURVEY PROTOCOLS

Fieldwork Rules

General Rules
1. Dress neatly and without 'attitude'.
2. Avoid interviewer bias in obtaining quota samples—especially not over-selecting tertiary educated respondents.
3. Interviewees have the right of refusal.
4. Ask household members to leave you alone with the respondent.
5. *Never* gossip about answers or respondents' personal information.
6. Check all questionnaires overnight or on the following day.
7. Lock up completed questionnaires.
8. Photocopy or scan questionnaires if sent out for data entry.

Particular Rules
1. Everyone must follow the directions of the superviser.
2. Fieldwork is normally Wednesday–Sunday.
   (*a*)   Weather might require flexibility.
   (*b*)   Wet days will be made up later.
3. Be at the pickup point on time.
4. Interviewers bring own water, food, hat, sun block.
5. Truck carries small first aid kit.
6. Travel to sites together.
7. Superviser allocates interviewers to clusters/houses.
8. Interviewers must always work in male-female pairs.
9. All interviews must be same-sex.
10. All interviews must be outside in line of sight in front yard—do not go inside.
11. Interviewers must not separate—downtime waiting for partner is ok.
12. During the day, partners check each others' completed forms.
13. Maintain contact with your superviser through phone as necessary.
14. Superviser must be on constant patrol checking teams' progress and safety.
15. Superviser can move interviewers as necessary.
16. Superviser advises interviewers of quota requirements.
17. Superviser calls back at 10% of households to verify interviews.
18. Superviser reviews any issues with the team at end of day.
19. Truck returns interviewers to the pickup point to ensure they are home before nightfall.

Source: Adapted from Guthrie (2007a).

7.5   Managing surveys

A researcher needs to be a good manager. Large-scale surveys require several staff carrying out many tasks. Where you are the only surveyer, you still have to play several roles with different skill sets that require you to review your own work systematically and continually to ensure quality.

1. Survey Director: In this role, you coordinate the survey, write and pilot test the questionnaire, sample, produce maps or other ways of identifying sample units, train anyone helping you and quality assure their work, write and edit the report, solve technical problems as they arise and ensure that field decisions are consistent with the requirements of the method.
2. Survey Manager: The role involves establishing links with authorities, copying and distributing covering letters and questionnaires, arrangement of transport and accommodation, field communications and questionnaire security.
3. Field Superviser: The role entails daily on-the-job supervision of interviewers, including correct identification of the sample units, security awareness, checking completed questionnaires everyday and daily monitoring of interview numbers and quotas.
4. Interviewer: This role is at the heart of the survey if interviews are held face-to-face. It involves gaining access to interviewees, seeking their cooperation, conducting interviews and checking interview forms for completion and clarity.
5. Data Analyst: The roles here are data entry, data checking, table formatting and statistical testing.

The work is quite complicated, but soon settles into a routine, especially if you adapt the stated points to your own survey, turning them into a checklist.

7.6   Increasing response rates

Survey fatigue is a difficulty faced by genuine researchers in many communities. This arises because surveys often are used for marketing and political purposes. Some phone and internet marketeers can be very misleading in using so-called surveys as a device to sell their products. Resultantly, many people become cynical about surveys and do not cooperate. This is their right, but high non-response rates can make the genuine researcher's task difficult.

The following guidelines will help keep response rates high in surveys:

1. Get someone who knows the area to help.
2. If necessary, get approval from community leaders or officials. Get introduced around at the beginning of the study.
3. Explain exactly who you are, what you are doing and why.
4. Have proper identification, preferably with a photo.
5. Try to appear similar to the people you are interviewing. Often, you will be different from them in many ways, but try not to exaggerate the differences. Do not dress with 'attitude' (for example, T-shirts with slogans that might prejudge answers to interview questions).
6. Explain that all the information will be confidential.
7. Do not be bossy.
8. If people are not immediately available, arrange a time to come back later. Give up only after the third visit.
9. Offer feedback on findings.

Finally, there are two other things to remember about non-response:

1. Do not just take any substitute or replacement if the required person cannot be found or a house is empty. This will introduce a non-random element into the sampling.
2. Remember that people do not have to answer any questions. Their right to be non-respondents must be respected.

7.7   Summary

Surveys aim to develop generalisations about populations. A survey selects a sample that is representative of a larger population and uses the results to generalise about that population as a whole. They are useful mainly for describing group patterns rather than in-depth analysis of individuals' views. Unless they are repeated, we do not gain much understanding about changes over time.

Sampling principles

Revise the material on sampling in Chapter 5.

Types of survey

The main types of survey are censuses, cross-sectional surveys and longitudinal surveys (which include trend, cohort and panel studies).

Implementation options

There are several options, the best of which is face-to-face interviews and group administration. Phone, mail and internet are less likely to be successful except for follow-up.

Survey protocols

Survey protocols should be sufficiently detailed to allow a follow-up survey to replicate the same techniques.

Managing surveys

Surveyers combine the roles of a survey director, survey manager, field superviser, interviewer and data analyst.

Increasing response rates

Guidelines are given to help keep response rates high in surveys, but the right of people to be non-respondents must be respected.

Surveys are a mainstream research method in the entire discipline of social sciences. They are complex, but there is much guidance provided in the literature on all aspects of the work. Surveys cannot answer all research problems, but they are the most efficient and effective method of generalising about the views of large groups.

7.8   Annotated references

Babbie, E. (2007). *The Practice of Social Research*, 11th edition. Belmont: Wadsworth.
   Like all sociology textbooks, this one contains plenty of material on survey research and related issues.

Gall, M., J. Gall and W. Borg. (2006). *Educational Research: An Introduction*, 8th edition. Needham Heights: Allyn & Bacon.
   This textbook contains more in-depth material about surveys, included in Chapter 11 on longitudinal studies.

Perecman, E. and S. Curran. (2006). *A Handbook for Social Science Field Research: Essays and Bibliographic Sources on Research Design and Methods*. Thousand Oaks: Sage.
   This book contains a wide range of guidance on fieldwork, including data sources, surveys and mixed methods.

Experimental Method 8

The experimental method is one of the most important scientific research methods, especially in the biological and physical sciences. In the social sciences, it is much less common and is usually restricted to psychology and educational psychology. However, understanding the strengths and weaknesses of the method is important. Experimental concepts demonstrate a major limitation of case studies and surveys, which is that they never have tight control mechanisms to give formal cause-and-effect relationships.

The case study method gives particular data about one or more situations, while the survey method aims for generalisations about populations. Both can indicate associations between variables, but neither can give reliable evidence about causes. The strict demonstration of causation requires rigorous quantitative experimental designs.

This chapter will outline the basic principles of the experimental method, although it will not go far into practical detail because not many students will use it. If you intend to undertake a controlled experimental design in a laboratory or classroom, you must look for texts that have more detail and prepare yourself for some statistical analysis. The chapter will:

1. define key terms;
2. present the logic behind experimental research, including cause-and-effect and control;
3. outline the various types of experiments, including the quasi-experimental designs sometimes used in surveys; and
4. discuss some of the limitations of experiments.

Chances are that an experimental design will use tests (Chapter 13) or observation (Chapter 10) as data collection techniques.

8.1   Attributes and variables

Here, an attribute is defined as a 'characteristic' of something. It is a 'concept' or a 'construct' expressing the 'qualities' possessed by a physical or mental object (the meaning of the quoted terms is similar, but like many terms in this book, you will find from further reading that technical definitions of them vary). A variable uses numerical values to measure an attribute. It is a quantity that expresses a quality in numbers to allow more precise measurement.

1. *Qualitative research* focuses primarily on the meaning of subjective attributes of individuals or groups.
2. *Quantitative research* primarily focuses on the measurement of objective variables that affect individuals or groups.

There are many different types of variables, as Figure 8.1 shows.

1. *Independent variables* constitute the presumed cause. They are introduced under controlled conditions during the experiment as treatments to which experimental groups are exposed.
2. *Dependent variables* are the presumed effect. They are measured before (pre-test) and after (post-test) the treatment to see whether any changes occured.
3. *Background variables* are antecedents that affect the situation prior to the study. They can be observed and measured, but usually not changed.
4. *Intervening variables* are events between the treatment and the post-test measurement that might affect the outcome.
5. *Extraneous variables* are variables that can be observed and which might affect the outcome during the study, but which cannot be controlled.
6. *Alternative independent variables* suggest causes different from the existing independent variable.

Experiments focus on two key variables: the independent variable and the dependent variable. Experimental designs set up conditions (usually in the laboratory or classroom) that allow the introduction of the independent variable as a treatment. Its influence on the dependent variable is measured through a pre-test and a post-test.

An example of an independent variable from educational research would be the introduction of a new textbook. Here, the dependent variable is student performance. An intervening variable is the way different teachers teach their classes. A background variable is student socio-economic status. An extraneous variable might be change of

Figure 8.1   Types of variables

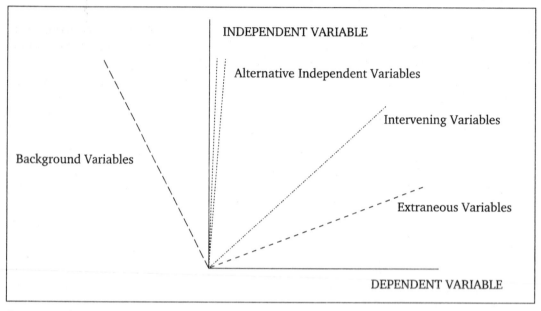

Source: Author.

teachers (some might become sick, for example, requiring use of substitute teachers). These variables should also be measured, where possible, to test for any influence on the results.

Variables must have a very precise operational definition. Research can be *univariate* (studies a single variable); *bivariate* (studies two variables); or *multivariate* (studies three or more variables). However, within each type of study, each variable needs to be *unidimensional* (that is, measures one attribute only). For example, a univariate study of intelligence needs to focus clearly on either intellectual or emotional intelligence. A bivariate study of intelligence can measure both, but must not mix them up.

One way of checking whether variables are clearly defined is to make sure that each end of the variable is described by a *semantic differential* (that is, it is based on polar opposite adjectives such as 'high–low'). If the adjectives are not polar opposites, you are confused. For example, you might find high levels of crime in a survey and write that a 'high' level of crime is 'bad'. However, this actually brings together two variables: a descriptive variable about frequency of crime and an evaluative variable judging crime. The solution is to avoid judgements in writing up data chapters. Report what you have measured, not what you personally think about it.

One of the reasons why scientific reports can appear tedious is that scientists normally first explain the apparently unimportant variables that have to be controlled. Often, we explain methodically the effect or lack of effect of the background and extraneous variables before moving to the independent and dependent variables. Then, having taken up a finding, which identifies the relationship, or a lack of one, between them, we expand upon that information by looking at the intervening variables to see whether they have influenced the finding. Non-scientists might find this boring, but to a scientist the process is necessary to gain confidence in the methods and, therefore, in the key findings when we reach them.

8.2   Cause-and-effect

The demonstration of cause-and-effect requires four types of findings about variables:

1. A statistically significant relationship between the independent and the dependent variable.
2. The independent variable preceded the dependent variable in time.
3. An *experimental group* exposed to the independent variable changed, but a *matched control group* not exposed to the independent variable stayed the same.
4. Alternative independent variables did not determine the result.

In presenting the findings, we need to remember, from Chapter 4, that even tight experiments express results as probabilities and that nothing can be proven absolutely. The report should demonstrate that exposure of the experimental group to the independent variable occurred before the presumed effect on the dependent variable was measured. It should also show whether the result was affected by differences between the control group and the experimental group, which should be matched both in composition and in performance on a pre-test.

One of the limitations of the experimental approach is the tendency to look for one cause and one effect only, that is, take a *unicausal* approach. Our minds should remain open to three other possibilities:

1. There was another true cause. There is an apparently tight result, but was there really a different cause not included in the experiment? To help think this through, you can focus on alternative independent variables. For example, your phone does not work. Does the most likely reason, which is a flat battery, hold true in your case, or were you cut off because you did not pay your bill or is there an error in your phone network?

2. Many causes can have one effect. There might have been many causes or reasons for you to enrol at university: you got enough marks, your friends were going, your parents expected you to and you wanted to be a social worker. This is *multiple causation* or *equifinality*. (Equifinality is sometimes also taken to mean that more than one cause is necessary for an effect to occur. For example, all three conditions have to be met for the phone to work: charged battery, up-to-date account and functioning network.)
3. One cause can have many effects. Completing a good research project can let you pass the course, improve your own thinking, help you get a job and maybe help the participants.

Post-positivist methodologists go further and take the view that everything is interconnected and these approaches to cause-and-effect are all too limited.

8.3   Control

A key element in experimental research is *control*, which means management of the variables so that their effect can be measured and held constant statistically. A very important part of experimental design is ensuring that the control and experimental groups are properly matched, that is, they have the same characteristics, including the ones most relevant to the experiment.

Even if a measurement of the characteristics of two existing groups reveals that they are not significantly different, they might be different in another characteristic not measured. This problem can be dealt with by *randomisation* of the control and experimental groups, that is, assigning individuals to the groups randomly so that their composition is equalised. The assumption in randomisation is that all characteristics, measured or not, will be randomly assigned between the groups and so not have a significant effect on the results.

Control does not only include control groups. The term has an additional meaning relevant to the identification of alternative independent variables. Background and intervening variables can be 'controlled', that is, their effect held constant, if they can be measured and treated systematically as independent variables to test statistically whether they also affect the dependent variable. These variables might be external to the experiment, but three variables within the experiment might need to be controlled as well:

1. Knowledge of subjects that they are involved in an experiment. This is known as the 'Hawthorne Effect' after an industrial experiment in the 1920s. As light

intensity in a factory was increased, production increased too, but when the lighting was reduced again, output continued to increase. The interpretation was that the workers were motivated by the experiment and the attention it gave them. To control this problem in medical experiments, for example, *blind studies* administer some patients with placebos—substitute pills that look like the real thing but contain no medicine. The patients do not know the type of pill they consume.

2. Knowledge of researchers about the experimental protocols. Researchers can bias or contaminate the results, for example, if they know who took the placebos, they might subconsciously influence the outcomes. Experiments can be designed as *double blind studies*, where neither the researchers actually administering the pills nor the subjects know who is getting what treatment.

3. The testing process. If it is suspected that the testing process might influence results, the design can be extended to add groups that are not pre-tested.

8.4   Types of experimental design

True experimental designs require pre-testing and post-testing of randomised control and experimental groups. The 'pre-test–post-test control group design' is the basic true experimental design (Figure 8.2). It has two randomised groups exposed to the same set of influences. Because the groups are randomised, the assumption is that the results will not be influenced by different group composition. Both matched groups are pre-tested. A treatment is introduced to the experimental group, but not to the control group, and both are post-tested to measure any changes. If the control group does not have significantly different performances on the pre- and post-tests, but the experimental group does, cause-and-effect is established because the exposure of the experimental group to the independent variable has changed the group's performance.

Figure 8.2   Basic true experimental design

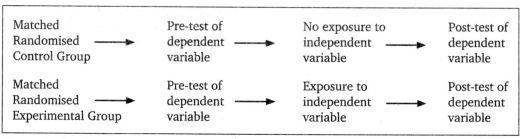

Source: Author.

In their simplest forms, many so-called experiments are not so—they are only pre-experimental or quasi-experimental. The standard classification recognises only three experimental designs as true ones (Campbell and Stanley 1966). Their key features are outlined in Table 8.1. The table includes three less common systematic

Table 8.1   Types of experimental designs

Type of design	Key elements	Comments
Pre-experimental designs		
One shot case study	Single group studied once. Provides a treatment and measures a presumed effect.	Total lack of control. Has only the two right-hand elements shown in the 2nd row of Figure 8.2. Does not measure what performance was previously and therefore, whether it has actually changed. One-off cross-sectional surveys and case studies are like this. Rarely is there prior data about the field situation to establish reliably whether the results show usual or unusual events.
One group pre-test–post-test	Measures performance before as well after introduction of the treatment to a single group.	Carries out all the functions elaborated in the second row of Figure 8.2. No control group, so now unclear if other variables have been at play. Longitudinal surveys and case studies have this problem. They usually do not have ways of reliably measuring background, intervening or extraneous variables and they do not usually have control groups.
Static group comparison	Introduces a control group and measures performance of both groups after the introduction of the new treatment.	Groups not randomised. No pre-test of the groups to see if performance was equivalent to start with.
True experimental designs		
Pre-test–post-test control group	Groups are randomised. See text above.	The basic true experimental design. Has all the elements of Figure 8.2.
Four group	Adds randomised control and experimental groups that are not pre-tested to ensure that testing does not contaminate the results.	Very strong approach.
Post-test only control group	Used where pre-testing is not possible.	Weaker design relying on randomisation of the groups.

Source: Adapted from Campbell and Stanley (1966).

designs that are inadequate for rigorous analysis of cause-and-effect because each one includes only some of the eight elements in Figure 8.2. Most case studies and surveys have these limitations.

8.5 Quasi-experimental and ex post facto research

The standard classification of experiments include quasi-experimental ('as if' experimental) designs. These are not true experiments, but apply experimental logic to attempt to control variables at play in field research. They follow the principles of experimental design except for a key one, which is that randomisation of control and experimental groups is not possible so that they might not be equivalent. For practical action, these methods may provide the best data available even though they do not meet strict scientific standards.

This type of design is sometimes possible with survey research when there are a number of sites and they are surveyed more than once. If the first survey occurred before the 'treatment'—for example, new community health clinics—there is a before-and-after effect. This design is stronger if the clinics are introduced at some sites but not others, which can then be used as control sites.

Ex post facto (after the event) designs reverse the experimental approach by searching backwards from the post-test, case study or survey to infer prior causes logically. A lot of solid research under real-world conditions happens this way when it is not possible to recreate prior events. Many case studies contain detailed research about the present situation and then seek explanations, especially from the participants about how the situation came about. Qualitative researchers often do not conceptualise their case studies this way, but they are doing it anyway.

It is also useful to be clear about *correlation studies*. They are usually surveys that measure associations between variables. They are not experiments and cannot formally establish cause-and-effect, although they can indicate important avenues for follow-up research. If you find a statistically significant correlation in such a study, even a strong multivariate one, be very careful, while writing, not to let your language slide into implying that a 'cause' for the problem has been found.

Table 8.2 shows four of many possible quasi-experimental designs, plus an ex post facto and a correlational design.

The best we can usually achieve in survey research is quasi-experimental design. Table 8.3 shows a design like this for survey research about the introduction of new family planning clinics in Punjab and Sindh provinces in Pakistan. Box 8.1 shows the variables in more detail. The clinics, which comprised the independent variable introduced in 2000–01, aimed to have an impact on family planning needs among poor urban women. Client knowledge of contraception,

Table 8.2 Types of quasi-experimental and other designs

Type of Design	Key Elements	Comments
Quasi-experimental designs		
Non-equivalent control group pre-test–post-test	Groups are not randomised. Pre-testing measures any differences between them.	A common and fairly strong design when randomisation is not possible. Full demonstration of cause-and-effect not given.
Time series	Only one group available, which is repeatedly tested before and after the treatment.	Aims to see if changes remain in place. Reduces the likelihood of random error in test results. If major changes occur, they might be attributed to the treatment, but this is not very rigorous.
Control group time series	Adds a control group that does not get the treatment.	Increases validity by giving a basis for comparison, but still not fully experimental.
Equivalent time samples	Repeatedly gives and withdraws the treatment.	Aims to see if changes from treatment are reversed with its withdrawal. Adds validity.
Other designs		
Ex post facto	Infers causation by working backwards from results to identify possible explanations.	Reverse experimentation. Data cannot provide proof, but logic and inference can give valuable insight. Typical of case studies.
Correlational study	Establishes correlations between variables.	The standard non-experimental survey design. Correlations show association not causation. Stronger results come from multivariate studies. They can indicate the value of further research with greater controls.

Source: Adapted from Campbell and Stanley (1966).

contraception prevalence and unmet needs for family planning were the dependent variables. These variables were pre-tested during 1999–2000, with a total sample of 5,338 married women in two control cities where no new clinics would open and four experimental or study cities where clinics were to open. These six sites were post-tested in 2001–02, taking a sample of 5,502 women after the clinics had been open for 18 months.

Table 8.3 Quasi-experimental survey design

Research design	Locations	Pre-test (baseline surveys)	Post-test (endline surveys)
Control sites	Gujarat and Larkana (one in each province).	1999–2000 survey data.	2001–02 survey data, plus client exit interviews at new clinics.
Study sites	Gujranwala, Sargoda, Hyderabad and Shikarpur (two in each province).		

Source: Adapted from Hennink and Clements (2004).

BOX 8.1 SURVEY VARIABLES

Programme Implementation Variables

1. **Problem:** Were new family planning clinics having an impact on knowledge, contraceptive use and unmet needs for family planning among married women in urban poor areas of Pakistan?

2. **Research Design and Data Collection:** New clinics were opened in 2000–01. Prior to this, questionnaire surveys were conducted using random sampling within clusters in the two control and four study cities. Follow-up surveys in 2001–02 allowed measurement to assess if the clinics were having an impact.

(*a*) Background variables: Analysis of reports about the urban poor and family planning programmes in Pakistan.
(*b*) Independent variable: The new clinics.
(*c*) Intervening variables: Changes in the family planning situation in these provinces might have occurred independently of the new clinics. Two control sites where clinics were not introduced were selected.
(*d*) Dependent variables: Three key variables were measured through the questionnaires: client knowledge of contraception, contraception prevalence, and unmet needs for family planning.
(*e*) Extraneous variables: Possible unmeasured effects such as other new family planning services or campaigns in the clinic locations.

3. **Data Analysis:** Statistical analysis of the questionnaires reflected significant increase in the knowledge of contraception, little impact on the overall prevalence of contraception, but a change in the mix of contraception types and a decline in unmet needs for family planning. 92 exit interviews identified particular groups of clients, some of whom came from outside the immediate area of the clinics.

4. **Action:** An independent report provided feedback to the non-governmental organisation that opened the clinics, showing what impacts the clinics were having and indicating a need for outreach activities.

Source: Adapted from Hennink and Clements (2004).

8.6 Validity of experiments

The extent of the controls needed in experiments usually means that they are confined to laboratories or classrooms. These environments allow very close control of variables so that the research can establish causation more accurately. In education, for example, experiments can test the effect that pupil location in a classroom could have on their performance, which is an easily managed setup.

The drawback of experimental research in a laboratory is a lower level of validity because conditions within this space might be entirely different from the outside world and, hence, the findings will have little relevance when applied there. Psychologists refer to this as a trade-off between internal validity and external validity.

1. *Internal validity* refers to the correctness of the data collected, that is, whether experimental research really made the difference observed. Experiments are often repeated to ensure that results are reliable, that is, that the original result was not just a random error.
2. *External validity* is the extent to which an experiment can be generalised to other situations. Qualitative researchers often question the external validity of experiments. They suggest that laboratory tests may not have relevance outside as the experimental findings might not work in practice. This is also referred to as *ecological validity*—little might be possible in the way of reliable generalisation from the laboratory to dissimilar ecological niches outside.

In terms of the terminology used to discuss research accuracy in Chapter 1, experimental scientific methods in the laboratory can raise the reliability of research, but lower its validity, relevance and generalisability.

8.7 Summary

Identification of cause requires the experimental method, which aims to exclude all those elements that do not affect the outcome. In the social sciences, experiments are usually restricted to psychology and educational psychology. Experimental methods show the limitations of other methods when it comes to causation, and the need to be very cautious in making causal claims except while making them from rigorous experimental data.

Variables

1. Experiments measure carefully several types of variables: independent, dependent, intervening, background and extraneous.
2. Each end of the variable is described by a semantic differential.

Cause-and-effect

1. Demonstration of cause-and-effect requires four types of findings about variables.
2. Researchers need to be open to alternative explanations and situations where many causes can have one effect or one cause can have many effects.

Control

1. Control is a key element in experimental research.
2. Control and experimental groups should have the same characteristics.

Types of experimental design

The key experimental design is the pre-test–post-test control group design, which studies two randomised matched groups. A change is introduced to only one of the two groups, so that any effects caused by that change are apparent.

Quasi-experimental and ex post facto research

Quasi-experimental (partly experimental) and ex post facto (after the event) designs can apply experimental logic in field research.

Validity of experiments

A risk in experimental method is that conditions in a laboratory might be so different that the findings have little relevance when applied in the real world.

Experimental design is complex. The complexity shows how difficult it is to design quality experiments. If you are a psychology or educational psychology student wanting to undertake a controlled experimental design in a laboratory or classroom, you must look for texts which provide further technical guidance. More important for most social science research, the complexity of experimental methods stresses why we should be very careful about making any simplistic causal claims from non-experimental case studies and survey methods.

8.8   Annotated references

Best, J. and J. Kahn. (2005). *Research in Education*, 10th edition. Needham Heights: Allyn & Bacon.
Contains chapters on experimental and quasi-experimental research.

Campbell, D. and J. Stanley. (1966). *Experimental and Quasi-Experimental Designs for Research*. Chicago: Rand McNally.

This work contains the standard classification of experimental designs, which require further study if you are going to conduct experiments. It also shows in detail the various limitations of different types of experimental design.

Cozby, P. (2009). *Methods in Behavioral Research*, 10th edition. Boston: McGraw Hill.

Many psychology texts go into experimental design. This is a good example with several chapters on measurement, various types of experimental design and statistics.

Kerlinger, F. (1986). *Foundations of Behavioral Research*, 3rd edition. Orlando: Harcourt Brace.

A still excellent but very advanced book on the theory underlying experimental design and statistical measurement.

Leedy, P. and J. Ormrod. (2010). *Practical Research: Planning and Design*, 9th edition. Needham Heights: Allyn & Bacon.

Chapter 10 contains a solid discussion of types of experimental design.

Available Data 9

Now we turn from research methods and the principles of research design to research techniques, ways of collecting data.

Often, we do not have to generate data ourselves: it is waiting to be collected. Usually, available data comes as text, as documentary evidence in libraries and archives. Historians frequently examine this type of evidence. Even if available data does not provide the core of a research project, it is often useful in identifying what is known about particular situations and is commonly used as background material to situate the main study, often in combination with interviews.

Available data is particularly useful when the main concern is relevance. If we want to persuade decision makers to use our findings, success is more likely if we use the type of information with which they are familiar.

While you do not have to generate the data itself, collecting and processing it could be time consuming. Therefore, do not assume that available data will save time. It might or might not. This chapter will:

1. briefly discuss sampling principles, then validity and reliability;
2. outline content analysis; and
3. provide approaches to and examples of reporting of textual and numerical data.

Available data is most commonly used in case studies (Chapter 6) to supplement other data collection techniques in surveys (Chapter 7) and often serves as a background in all types of study.

9.1 Sampling principles

Available documentary data often does not meet formal sampling requirements. Identification of the entire population of documents could be difficult. Documents are filed away and it is usually difficult to gauge their completeness. Detective skills are needed in searching for relevant storage areas and repositories (such as archives and libraries) systematically within the given limitation of time. However, the guarantee of absolute success is rare. Historical research is often subject to reinterpretation when new documents surface.

Where files provide lists, sampling can be possible, especially when the lists are complete or nearly so. In such cases, a sample frame exists. If the frame is small, it might be possible to study the total list and not just a sample (otherwise, Chapter 5 on sampling applies). Available data such as addresses or examination results might exist as lists in organisational databases and filing cabinets. Often this data can be treated as primary data, coded numerically and analysed as raw material to test research hypotheses statistically.

9.2   Validity and reliability

A very large range of documents provide many creative possibilities for research projects. Even though the usage somewhat varies, *primary data* usually means interviews and personal reports from actual participants in events. Reports might be found in personal correspondence, diaries and autobiographies, and photos and film.

Additionally, documentation is considered primary data when it is the object of study itelf and is analysed carefully for validity and reliability. This includes documentation often found in minutes of meetings, other records in official files, and data from official statistics and censuses. In schools, syllabuses, textbooks, course notes, student work and test and exam results might all be studied as primary documents and data. In legal systems, as another example, laws, regulations, court decisions and case files are important primary data. In social work, psychology and medicine, case files are also important, but client confidentiality means that a researcher from outside is highly unlikely to gain access to them.

Secondary data is reportage based on others' accounts. Such documents might cover very wide ground, including newsletters, bulletins, catalogues, yearbooks, newspapers, magazines, encyclopaedias and other reference books. Secondary reportage like this has less validity than direct observation, but interviews with eyewitnesses and participants can add to the validity of reportage. Somewhere between primary and secondary data lies others' primary research. Information can be cited from other research, particularly when the subject is little researched and has widely scattered sources.

All documentary evidence is subject to issues of reliability and validity, just as any other type of data is. Are the documents genuine; are they complete? The following issues are up for consideration with data collected from organisations:

1. Incomplete records: This is often unintentional because filing and archiving are low status activities. The tasks are often put on hold, either because they are boring or there are other higher priority tasks at hand. Filing systems are always a work in progress, with a backlog of papers waiting to be filed in cabinets or entered into databases. Misfiling and inaccuracies are, thus, common.
2. Biased data: While bias is not necessarily deliberate, available data is usually collected for organisational and not scientific purposes. For example, aid projects usually collect formative and summative evaluation data, which can be available to independent evaluators. But project administrators are likely to have assumed success without having control groups.
3. Intentional incompleteness: Organisational decisions are usually subject to informal censoring. Written records, such as minutes of meetings, might contain little of the background discussion of issues or the different views that were considered. Decision makers looking to their future might only file material that they think will reflect well on them and destroy anything questionable.

The researcher is responsible for assessing the reliability and validity of available data. Relevant techniques for historical research are external and internal criticism.

1. *External criticism* involves identifying whether data is genuine, which is a validity issue. For most social science research, this is not much of a problem with organisational files. Material in them will probably have letterheads, titles, file numbers, dates and/or official signatures. However, for research about previous periods, external criticism might need to involve detailed technical analysis (think of the controversies about fake paintings).
2. *Internal criticism* involves consideration of the meaning of the data, which relates to reliability. Having established that a document is genuine, we also need to consider what it means, whether it presents the full picture and whether the writer was giving a balanced view. If not, another researcher evaluating different documents might reach different conclusions.

9.3 Content analysis

Using documents requires content analysis, which means the systematic analysis of given information to infer meanings that are relevant to the research problem. The same principle applies whether documents are in the form of historical photos, cartoons containing social comment, newspaper cuttings, children's drawings or artists' paintings.

1. *Classification* is the most basic form of content analysis. Documents can be organised chronologically or into different categories (for example, personnel, student, course and departmental records, etc.). Data within these categories can also be classified. Sometimes, there might be standard classifications, sometimes themes identified in your literature review can be used, other times categories can be developed from the data and you own ideas. If you generate a classification, it should meet the properties of the nominal measurement scale and classify the data into mutually exclusive categories.
2. *Evaluation* takes the analysis of the documents further into the interpretive level. Indeed, there is little point to research unless this occurs, otherwise the mass of 'facts' will have little meaning. A historical chronology, for example, has little value in itself, but needs interpretation to show the meaning of the events that it contains.

Content analysis usually results in the data being presented chronologically and thematically, with section headings identifying key themes. The report will often imply your classification through the logical organisation of the section headings rather than detail its technical basis.

The difficulty faced once evaluation starts is to identify where description finishes and interpretation begins. One way around this trap is to describe the content of documents first, then make separate interpretations.

9.4   Presenting text

Available texts can be brought together for a variety of thematic purposes when writing a report. Box 9.1 illustrates how different types of data can be woven together. It is taken from six pages in the original report about a secondary school inspectorate whose reports were used to measure the dependent variable in the teacher education study.

The citations indicate the scope of the data searches. The historical and organisational documentation was collected from research libraries, the Education Department's own library in Port Moresby, its official publications and from files held in the inspectorate's office. In Box 9.1, the first two citations are of historical research conducted by others. The next two are historical governmental annual reports, followed by papers written by three officials. Then, come five different official documents, including minutes of meetings found in files, gazetted notices and publicly available statistics.

There was nothing sophisticated about the classification and evaluation process. Mainly, it involved writing up my notes, seeing whether the story that emerged about the

---

BOX 9.1 PRESENTING AVAILABLE DOCUMENTARY DATA

Available Text on a School Inspectorate

Inspectorial Beginnings

'Papua New Guinea's inspection system can be traced directly back to innovations introduced in the colony of New South Wales (NSW) in 1848 (Turney 1970: 161–213). ...Queensland was originally a part of NSW. When it became a separate colony in 1859 it inherited NSW's educational practices, including the inspectorial system (Meadmore 1978: 27–34). ...The first examiner of schools in Papua was the headmaster of the European school in Port Moresby, but from 1928 until the start of the Pacific War, Queensland inspectors were brought in each year...The inspector, Mr T. Inglis, subsequently pointed to the need for formal teacher training of Papuan teachers...(Papua Annual Report 1940–41: 40–41). ...After the war a formal inspection system was established...the newly established Department of Education had three divisions, the Chief Inspector being in charge of one of them (Papua Annual Report 1947–48: 26). ...

Changes in the Inspection System

'The 1960s saw steady adaption and expansion of the inspectorial system...[inspectors] were expected to spend 60% of their time inspecting schools and writing reports on teachers (Ralph 1965: 23). ...The description of B.A. McLachlan, who was addressing a Senior Officers' Conference as Chief of Division of Secondary Education, showed that the duties of the district inspector were very wide indeed (see McLachlan 1965). ...The Director of Education from 1966–73, K.R. McKinnon, was well aware of the scope of the district inspectors' duties and of the incumbent difficulties (see McKinnon 1968). ...The legislation which resulted from the [subsequent official review of the education system] Weeden Report...[established] individual chains of professional command...for primary, secondary, technical and teacher training inspections. The Regional Secondary Inspectorate became part of the secondary division, having 12 establishment positions by 1980 (Department of Education 1980a). ...

Organisation and Roles of the Inspectorate

'When this study was carried out from 1979 to 1981, the secondary inspectorate was part of the Provincial Standards Division (Department of Education 1980b: 112). ...Each inspector has responsibility for a 'region'...Table 2.1 [not included] shows for example the inspectorial regions for 1980 (Department of Education 1980a). Twelve inspectors averaged eight schools and 177 teachers between them (Department of Education 1980c). ...The duty statement for inspectors shows a combination of administrative, advisory and evaluative roles...(Department of Education 1975).'

Source: Adapted from Guthrie (1983: 11–16).

---

system made sense against themes from the literature review, and moving information around so that each section dealt with one theme and each paragraph within the section dealt with one main idea. The beginning of the report summarised in Box 9.1 described the development of the inspectorial system and, later, evaluated the system's approach according to the predominant theme of formalistic teaching.

9.5   Using numerical data

Many administrative systems generate numbers that can be classified and interpreted statistically. The obvious example is a census; college grades are another. In policy and action research, the pragmatic point of view is that relevance is increased by using system data, but validity and reliability should be addressed in the report because the research relies on the accuracy of the original recording of the data.

Additionally, ensure that the coding of your own data is accurately done. First, like textual data, ensure that the coding accurately reflects the requirements of measurement scales. Some data is nominal and can be counted and assigned to different categories to generate percentages, for example, identifying student gender. Other data can be ranked ordinally, for instance, examination grades (fail = 0, pass = 1, credit = 2, etc.).

Still other data does not simply involve categorising or classifying, but requires converting text to numbers by formulating ratings (which is what examiners do when they assign grades to research reports). *Ratings* require you to exercise personal judgement in coding, which is more subjective than the gender and examination examples in the previous paragraph. If validated expert judgement is not available from other research projects, researchers can exercise their own judgement. This is called *face validity* and part of the role of research is to test whether or not it is valid.

Preferably, you should ensure that other coders would achieve similar results. The measures for achieving *inter-rater agreement* require that independent and competent judges agree with the interpretation and scoring of the data. You will have to get others to act as judges too. Then look to more advanced texts for statistical measures to test agreement (Gall et al. 2006: Chapter 11, contains a summary of various measures). There are many measures, but a good start is Kendall's coefficient of concordance (*W*), which is a reasonably easy non-parametric correlation with a test of significance.

Carrying the inspectorial example further, Box 9.2 shows how inspection reports that contained text were rated numerically. The report gave an example of the inspection reports and then discussed what they could mean professionally, how they were structured, how reliable the rating process was and how reliable the reports were for their professional purposes.

Your own research projects are unlikely to deal with such large numbers, but similar presentational steps should be followed if you desire a thorough result. If you do not have the time or skills for statistical analysis, your report should be transparent about the lack of formal testing for validity and reliability. You can give your own judgement about the face validity of the data, but should also note that lack of testing poses a limitation to your research.

BOX 9.2   PRESENTING AVAILABLE NUMERICAL DATA

Numerical Ratings From Inspectors' Reports

Three Reports

'The most critical point in understanding inspectorial reports is that although their language is descriptively clear, interpretation and evaluation of the reports is often esoteric...Table 4.1 [not included] lists three reports ...

'The second report was satisfactory, receiving the stamp of "efficient". Teacher B was "good", "adequate", "continuing to improve", prepared "well" and used "a variety of aids" to get "a good student response"...All these comments were average, but ... a number of comments indicate marginal performance: programs were "not annotated", books needed "more regular checking"... As a Teacher In Charge ... the teacher visited his staff irregularly and was not firm with them ... the negative comments were not sufficient to have him rated as unsatisfactory at Level 1, but were certainly sufficient to inhibit eligibility for a Level 2 position...

Format and Language

'A major problem indicated by these three reports is that they contain high inference global judgements and each heading might include several such judgements...Preparation and Planning, for example, might include comments on five points plus adaptation of syllabuses and methods to both students and community...The headings' comments are then reduced to the contents of the Summary, which should be consistent with the seven other headings and not introduce any new material...[For the purpose of this study, the eight headings in reports were rated on a 5-point scale where 1 = very good and 5 = very bad, and analysed with coefficient alpha and one-way analysis of variance]...

Consistency in Interpreting Reports

'Outsiders find inspectors' reports difficult to interpret, but are experts in the system able to agree with their meaning?...The evidence here is that a considerable degree of consistency does exist...[Two statistical tests] on the reliability of the coding [by the researcher, an inspector, and the superintendent of inspections showed that]...inter-judge agreement...and inter-judge reliability were very high...And it is probable that other expert judges would consistently rate reports with a similar level of agreement...

'Is this level of agreement, however, enough? A third measure showed that the level could be improved. This measure was of the internal consistency of inspection reports; the extent to which the coded headings reliably measured teacher performance. Coefficient alpha was .79 for 870 reports. This was well above the .65 necessary to distinguish between groups of teachers (eg., according to their training program), but is not at the .85 necessary to reliably distinguish between the individual teachers, which is the purpose of the inspection system...The levels of consistency in interpreting reports are thus high, but further improvements need to be made.'

Source: Adapted from Guthrie (1983b: 41–47).

9.6   Relevance

Finally, available data can provide a check of the relevance of research. If scientifically strong techniques bear little relationship to how data is used in the real world, research runs the risk of being ignored by practitioners.

Here, an open eye could be useful. While using available data, look for ways in which it is used professionally and see if this provides an independent cross-check. For example, rating, coding and statistical testing of the inspection reports found no significant difference between the performance of the graduates of four teacher training programmes despite the programmes' different lengths, types and costs. Was this an artefact of the method or was the finding consistent with the education system's own treatment of the graduates? A cross-check was made against the 'stamps' given by the inspection conferences. The three stamps showed whether teachers were un-satisfactory and possibly at risk of termination; satisfactory at their existing level; or eligible for promotion. This check found that there were no significant differences in inspectors' promotional decisions about the graduates of different programmes. The result of the triangulation implied that the differences between the programmes were neither statistically nor professionally significant and that the research did reflect professional reality.

9.7   Summary

Usually, available data comes as text, documentary evidence in libraries and archives. It is often useful in identifying backgrounds of particular situations. Additionally, text can provide primary data, and numerical data can be coded and analysed statistically.

Sampling principles

Available documentary data does not often meet formal sampling requirements unless files provide complete sample frames.

Validity and reliability

1. Primary data in historical work means information from participants in events. Direct observation has more validity than secondary reportage, but interviews can add to the validity.
2. Documentary evidence is subject to reliability and validity checks through external and internal criticism of whether it is genuine and complete.

Content analysis

Classification and evaluation are required to interpret the meaning of available data. They should usually be separated in the report.

Presenting text

Text is usually classified chronologically and thematically, according to themes identified in the literature review, the nature of the data and the researcher's own ideas.

Numerical data

1. Text and numbers can both be classified numerically and interpreted statistically. Coding should meet the requirements of measurement scales. Independent and competent judges should agree on the scoring and interpretation of the ratings.
2. If validated judgement is not available, researchers can proceed based on face validity, but the report should note this limitation.

Relevance

Available data can provide independent cross-checks of the relevance of research.

Available data is an important source for a wide range of studies, both for setting of context and as primary data. A potential trap is to assume that because available data is usually presented descriptively, it does not need a disciplined approach. This is definitely untrue, but if you use this source effectively, it will add to the relevance of your research, creating a possibility of the results being applied in practice.

9.8   Annotated references

Babbie, E. (2007). *The Practice of Social Research*, 11th edition. Belmont: Wadsworth.
This text has a chapter on unobtrusive research, including content analysis, analysing existing statistics and comparative and historical research.

Best, J. and J. Kahn. (2005). *Research in Education*, 10th edition. Needham Heights: Allyn & Bacon.
This book contains material on doing historical studies.

Desai, V. and R. Potter (eds). (2006). *Doing Development Research*. New Delhi: Vistaar.
The readings in this book on development research include a section on using existing knowledge and records.

Observation 10

A second data collection technique is observation. Being observant is a skill that applies in all data collection, for example, watching interviewees to see how they respond to questions or reading signs in an organisation to see if it has a library where available data might be found. Observation, as a data collection technique, goes further than this to generate primary data.

Observation is valuable for formal and informal action research. For example, if you are a teacher or are planning to become one, you might conduct action research by observing your colleagues if they will allow you to sit in their lessons. An observer role gives time to learn professional lessons from others; but be careful about how you give them feedback. Make sure you tell them all the positives before mentioning the negatives.

In this chapter, we will look at:

1. different observer roles;
2. validity and reliability issues;
3. structuring observation through recording and sampling;
4. the role of theory; and
5. basic presentation of observational data.

Naturalistic observation is commonly found in case studies (Chapter 6), while structured observation is often found in experiments (Chapter 8). Naturalistic observation typically generates text, while statistical analysis is a usual outcome with data from structured observation. Observation is often used in combination with other data collection techniques.

10.1 Observer roles

Observation relies, evidently enough, on our own skills as observers, but it needs systemisation to be effective. There are two main types. *Ethnography* involves extended periods of observation in natural settings to learn in detail about particular cultures and the meaning of those cultures to their members. Anthropologists particularly use observation for naturalistic ethnographic case studies. *Structured observation* typically uses observation schedules in formal settings, for example, recording of classroom behaviours by educational psychologists.

Observation usually focuses, first, on behaviour and, then, generates ideas about why certain behaviours occur (for example, why interaction occurs between some people but not others, which then leads to an investigation of the cultural explanations for this). It also allows the opportunity for a validity check about whether people do what they say.

The researcher's role is highly critical to the success of observation. Three major roles follow, athough you will find variations and expansion if you read further afield.

1. *Participant observation* means that the researcher takes part in the research situation as a genuine member of the group. This was the situation in my teacher training institutional case studies. Experience over an eight-year period as a member of the two faculties involved in teacher training helped me decide what data to collect, who to interview, how to better understand the written records of the period and how to interpret the competitive institutional dynamics. The role as an observer reflecting on my own experiences was not as systematic as it would have been if observation were the core of the research, but the insights added value to available data, questionnaires and interviews.

2. *Non-participant observation* requires the researcher to be present, but not to participate in group actions. This was the situation when I was observing the work of the inspectorate. I could not be involved in their professional work of rating teachers, but could only observe it as an outsider both in the inspectorate's meetings and on their school visits. Not being an active participant allows the data collection to be more complete because your attention can focus fully on the players and, also, you will be less distracted by your own role.

3. *Hidden observation* occurs when the observer is out of sight (for example, behind a one-way glass observing a classroom), or where the role has not been revealed to the group being observed. This immediately raises the issue of informed consent. In the first situation, parents can give consent. In the second, consent could be gained only from authorities, but I personally do not find this very ethical. Even so, very interesting research has been conducted this way, for example, in prisons or on city streets as one of the homeless.

10.2 Validity and reliability

Observation is prone to reliability and validity issues. Validity issues stem especially from the meanings attached to observed behaviours. You and the participants might infer meanings quite differently. The more complex a situation, the more vulnerable it is different interpretations, so be very careful to limit researcher bias.

The underlying issue is that what we notice is heavily dependent on cultural factors. We tend to filter out what we have learned is usual. Because the ordinary becomes easy to ignore, we often overlook the importance of familiar acts. We also tend to assume that others interpret events just as we do, which can be a considerable mistake, especially in multicultural societies. Observation is easier to use in unfamiliar situations where hold few prior conceptions about what is normal and what is not. Developing observant eyes, even in our own culture, can take time.

Nonetheless, naturalistic observation can increase other aspects of validity, especially ecological validity, by generating understandings where other research methods prove to be superficial. You are more likely to find the cultural meaning of complex events to participants through observation and interviews than through questionnaires, for example.

Risks, however, remain. First, participants might change their behaviour because of the researcher's presence or even mislead researchers. This is one of the issues at the centre of a major controversy, which was generated by Derek Freeman, over allegedly misleading data collected by the famous anthropologist Margaret Mead in Western Samoa. Whatever the merits of either side in this particular debate (you will find plenty of material about it on the internet if you search their names), the strength of the debate is an indication of the importance of validity.

The main ways of improving validity are:

1. *Mixed methods*: This is why ethnographic case studies usually use interviews as well as observation.
2. *Triangulation*: One example of comparing findings from one data source with another is asking participants to comment on draft material. This can greatly add to understanding of the reasons for their reported behaviour.

Reliability issues stem from the risk that other researchers might make different observations. You can easily demonstrate this if you and a friend attempt to tally passing vehicles from the roadside for, say, 30 minutes. You are almost certain to create different categories and to have different numbers.

To increase reliability, two main steps are:

1. Adoption of systematic sampling techniques.
2. Careful recording of data.

10.3   Sampling techniques

A first step in systematising observation is to decide on a sampling method. Like available documents, naturalistic observation poses reliability issues because often it does not meet formal sampling requirements. An *observation* is a unit of data that is a sample of a universe of potential observations depending on time and location, and on the perceptions of observers. That universe is almost impossible to define accurately, especially in naturalistic settings where the next set of events cannot always be anticipated.

Implicitly, this is why naturalistic observation works best in case studies where the objective is to observe the situation over as long a time as possible. In effect, anthropologists living in villages can immerse themselves in cultures for a year or more to observe them as completely as possible, that is, to get closer to observing the universe of data. They use systematic procedures to check the completeness of their work, but there are always limitations. In many cultures, 'secret women's business', for example, will not be revealed to male researchers and vice versa.

Allocating long time frames for data collection is not possible for small research projects, but observation can be adapted to particular settings within people's lives (for example, the life of students in the cafeteria) or used to complement other techniques, such as interviews. This is actually an advantage for smaller projects because a focus on particular features can reduce any tendency for the situation to be overwhelming.

Structured observation can aim to collect extensive data using formal sampling methods and observation schedules, and subjecting the data to statistical analysis. Four options can make sampling systematic:

1. *Time*: Systematic sampling can be undertaken at fixed intervals (for example, every five seconds in a classroom). It is easier to maintain the schedule correctly if this is done at regular intervals rather than randomly.
2. *Location*: Particular locations can be drawn randomly and observation restricted to them, for example, particular seats in a classroom. The observation can also be structured to provide locations of interest to a research hypothesis (for example, seats in the back corners, seats in centre front, etc.).
3. *People*: Individuals can also be sampled to provide units that are more amenable to observation than groups, for example, children diagnosed with attention deficit disorder or pupils new to a class.
4. *Events*: Sampling can focus on particular events at the exclusion of others, for example, recording data from whole of class activities, not from small group work.

These approaches to sampling can also be adapted to naturalistic settings. In a school, for instance, you could observe groups at different times of the day and night, systematically watch particular parts of the grounds, follow particular staff on their daily routines or focus entirely on sports teams at practice.

Systematic sampling provides a more structured approach to naturalistic observation and more confidence that the findings are reliable. The more transparent you are about your methods, the greater the chances that you and your readers will have confidence in them.

10.4   Recording observations

Having decided what to observe, the next step in systematising observation entails deciding the method of recording the observations. The two main types are: relatively unstructured field notes and highly structured observation schedules. They usually accompany naturalistic observation and structured observation respectively.

1. *Field notes*: Field notes record events, usually in notebooks. You already have a lot of experience taking notes during lectures. This is similar except that you record field settings and what people do as well as say.

   Field notes are particularly useful for naturalistic observation because a pen and notebook are easy to carry and use, and participants soon become used to them. Steno pads are good for this because they help keep notes in sequence, but like lecture notes, field notes might be untidy, full of abbreviations and hard to read. An important part of the work plan is to allocate time every day to transcribe your notes while your memory is still fresh. Preferably, the notes should go straight into a computer. The result will be text, so that has to be part of your data analysis intentions, and the computer can be very effective for key word searches in your notes.

   In many field situations, note taking is the only practical choice, but participant observers might not be able to take notes during events. This requires them to make notes as soon as possible after the event as memory is unreliable.

   Assume that if anything can go wrong with technology in the field, it will. Keep field materials as simple as possible so that they do not distract from the main game, which is observing the field situation before you. Collecting observations with video recorders or tape recorders is possible, although I would not recommend either for a first project except if detailed analysis is required. This is because too much time will be required to transcribe the data. Another problem is that the technology might be disruptive (for example, setting up cameras to observe meetings) and make participants self-conscious. More realistic, at least for fast touch typists, is entering the data directly into a computer, although the noise might be disruptive and the battery might run flat. Always have pen and paper as backup.

2. *Structured observation schedules*: Structured observation schedules are the main alternative to naturalistic field notes. They are usually pre-coded sheets with observational categories determined by the research topic, against which behaviours are tallied as they occur. Tallying against pre-coded categories obviously speeds up the data collection process and gives a large amount of data that can readily be statistically analysed. In the main, schedules require two types of judgement:

(a) *Low inference judgements* require little interpretation by the observer in categorising observations. Provided the schedule has been pre-tested and practised, you are unlikely to have to make many judgement calls about whether observations fit in one category or another. To follow the sampling options given earlier, a time sample might record what the teacher is doing every five seconds, with the actions tallied on a predetermined list (for example, talking, listening to a pupil, writing on the board, walking around the room, etc.). A location sample within the classroom might work from a plan showing pupil placement and tallied every time the teacher directs a question to a particular pupil.

(b) *High inference judgements* require considerable judgement by the observer about the actions being recorded. For example, if you try to record whether pupils are concentrating in class or not, you have to make interpretations of internal mental states from their external behaviour. It is quite possible that a pupil who is wriggling is paying attention, while one who is still and apparently attentive could actually be daydreaming. The reliability problem here is that another observer might well make a different interpretation.

If you have a research problem that requires structured observation, look in specialist texts for existing schedules that you can use or adapt.

10.5   Testing theory

Structured observation typically is part of experiments designed to test theories and hypotheses formally. Naturalistic observation is likely to be more open-ended. Much ethnographic research has been strongly based in theory (another of the criticisms of

Margaret Mead was that she set out to prove her theory rather than test it), but plenty is grounded and seeks ideas that arise from observation.

Overly structured hypotheses might blind you to ideas arising within the setting. On the other hand, you run the risk of being superficial if research lacks a theoretical base. The balance lies in solid background reading, clear themes and an open mind about following new leads that appear during observation.

10.6   Presenting observational data

Data gained from tallying on structured schedules can be readily analysed with conventional quantitative techniques. But, how to present data gained from field observation? It can be confusing at first because you will probably have a huge wad of notes. Once writing starts, it is very easy to begin commentating and you quickly have a problem. What is observation and what is commentary? If you are confused, be guaranteed that readers will be too. A basic solution is to follow two simple steps:

1. *Description*: Write out the facts of the situation as observed. This should involve clear descriptive reporting free of adjectival colour. A narrative is usually most straightforward for writer and reader if done chronologically. Do not present everything, only those matters relevant to the themes and the object of study.
2. *Interpretation*: Then present separately your interpretation of the events, picking out key features that identify patterns in the recorded events. This need not be highly conceptual—that can come later when you make a wider analysis of the findings in light of the literature review.

Box 10.1 shows how ethnographic observation data can be presented, being a summary of part of a meeting of a women's micro-credit cooperative group in Nepal.

The first part is straight description of the way in which loans were allocated. The second part from later in the paper is interpretation, highlighting key features about the meaning of the loan group identified from this and other periods of observation.

10.7   Summary

Observation as a data collection technique goes further than just being observant while conducting research for the collection of primary data. Ethnography takes extended

---

Box 10.1 PRESENTING FIELD OBSERVATION DATA

A Micro-credit Programme in Action

'In both groups, the loan access procedure only required women to state the amount that they needed and the names of the friends whose shares they were borrowing. The secretary of the group would write all the names in the register and have the borrower sign or thumbprint the entry. At that point, the borrowers were entitled to receive cash money or a cheque. Manakamana group gave cheques to its members while Chiyabari group just circulated the cash at hand. The following unedited excerpt from my fieldnotes of one of the savings collections meeting shows the vagueness, ease and spontaneity with which the loans were disbursed, "...*Then all the members left, except the ones who were taking loans this month...Nirmala* (all names are changed for confidentiality purposes) *wanted Rs. 24,000 to pay for cement for her house under construction. Another woman, Minu, wanted Rs. 50,000. There were no applications, they just had to sign or thumbprint the register*".

'The fact that members (of both groups) could take the money from up to five shares of other women to add to their loan amounts was also a greatly appreciated feature. This meant that in times of need, the amount of money they could borrow would be substantial....

'From the above narrative, it is clear that the savings and credit programmes are a resource for women, mainly for collecting savings and access to credit. This allowed women in the study to have some amount of "emergency" cash at hand that enabled them to fulfill their household duties, which they regarded as an "achievement". Going to meetings, listening to other women and interacting with them was another significant achievement for most of the members, providing them with an "exposure" opportunity. Women used their membership in the group as a basis for trust, which led to them permitting other women to use their savings shares as loans. The women were also slowly starting to build a network. The feeling of "sisterhood" and potential for collective action that some women mentioned shows that women had used the group as a resource to achieve this network. These perceived achievements are extremely important if we adopt the "generous" attitude that considers any perceived achievement as a contribution to the process of empowerment.' (italics in the original).'

Source: Nepal and Calves (2004: 7–8, 15).

---

periods of observation in natural settings to learn in detail about particular cultures and the meaning of those cultures to their members. Structured observation typically uses observation schedules in formal settings.

Observer roles

Three major types are participant, non-participant and hidden observation.

Validity and reliability

1. The main ways of improving validity are mixed methods and triangulation.
2. To increase reliability, two main steps are adoption of systematic sampling techniques and careful recording of data.

Sampling techniques

1. Naturalistic observation works best when observing the whole situation over longer periods to get closer to observing the universe of data.
2. Structured observation typically samples time, location, people or events.

Recording observations

1. The two main types of recordings are field notes and observation schedules.
2. Structured observation schedules are usually pre-coded sheets. These might require low or high inference judgements.

Testing theory

A balance lies in background reading, clear themes and an open mind about changing direction.

Presenting observational data

1. Data gained from tallying on structured schedules can readily be analysed with conventional quantitative techniques.
2. Field observation requires separation of description from interpretation.

Observation needs systemisation to do well. The depth of understanding that it can generate about particular situations compensates for its vulnerability to other validity and reliability problems. Ethnographic work can take too long for an introductory project, but the techniques can be adapted to small settings. Structured observation typically uses observation schedules in formal settings, but usually commits you to statistical analysis. Either way, you stand to develop a skill that will put you in good stead, formally and informally, in your professional future.

10.8   Annotated references

Babbie, E. (2007). *The Practice of Social Research*, 11th edition. Belmont: Wadsworth.
  A sociology text with chapters on qualitative and unobtrusive research.

Best, J. and J. Kahn. (2005). *Research in Education*, 10th edition. Needham Heights: Allyn & Bacon.
  Contains material on qualitative research, including observation.

Cozby, P. (2009). *Methods in Behavioral Research*, 10th edition. Boston: McGraw Hill.
  This book has a chapter for psychologists on observational methods.

Perecman, E. and S. Curran. (2006). *A Handbook for Social Science Field Research: Essays and Bibliographic Sources on Research Design and Methods*. Thousand Oaks: Sage.
  Contains chapters on fieldwork, including on ethnographic methods and oral histories.

Vulliamy, G., K. Lewin and D. Stephens. (1990). *Doing Educational Research in Developing Countries: Qualitative Strategies*. London: Falmer.
  Several chapters discuss the issues associated with field observation. The headings in the summary above provide leads for using the book's index.

Interviews   11

Interviewing is probably the most common data collection technique in social sciences. It is virtually impossible to do a research project without an interview, even if only informally to get advice about the research design. However, what used to be the staple of social research is becoming more difficult to achieve, not for technical reasons but because of social resistance. Interviewers can be quite annoying. Political pollsters or phone marketeers call and make dubious claims on people's time for research. One result is resistance in many countries to surveys, interviews and questionnaires. This is another reason why you might confine your first research project to your own institution, where people will probably be more sympathetic.

Interviewing is time consuming, but is especially useful because of its flexibility. Interviews can take many different forms and allow in-depth follow-up questions. The style can range from guided conversations to highly structured questionnaires. They are useful for all ages and socio-economic groups and also, for those with language difficulties. They are often used to find out attitudes and perceptions, but they can be a source of factual information too.

The chapter will look at:

1. three main types of interviews and examples of the type of data that they generate;
2. planning and conducting interviews; and
3. interviewer bias.

Interviews are very common in case studies (Chapter 6) and surveys (Chapter 7), and often combine with other data collection techniques. The next chapter will outline the types of questions.

11.1   Unstructured interviews

Unstructured interviews generate qualitative data by raising issues in conversational form. The interviews can go in-depth into a topic and are appropriate for obtaining sensitive information. They are also suitable for one-off situations with someone holding a particular viewpoint or with those who can provide factual information.

If people do not want to talk about sensitive personal topics, interviews can become difficult, even hostile, so rapport is important. A little small talk can help before the start, perhaps about note taking or the tape recorder.

Unstructured interviews require a general plan, but the interviewer asks open-ended questions flexibly to maintain the flow. During the interview, the interviewer should speak minimally. You should present yourself as a tactful, interested but professional person with whom respondents can talk freely. A sympathetic ear will usually generate a flow of comment. Prompt without giving clues or expressing opinions. You are almost a passive observer, quietly taking notes as respondents talk, but keeping the interview on track.

Interviews can give people the opportunity to tell their personal stories to someone who treats them as an equal and takes them seriously, which can be emotionally rewarding for the respondents. Sometimes indeed, it becomes difficult to conclude interviews, especially if they give respondents the opportunity to talk freely, making the interviewer their new best friend.

If you intend to study in great detail the actual words used by participants or if your study is in linguistics, you can record the interview, but otherwise notes will suffice. Verbatim notes are difficult because of the speed of talk, but running notes will do if you are reasonably fast—an indication is whether you can keep up when taking lecture notes. In any case, take notes to improve skill. They do not have to get every word, but should reflect the meaning faithfully and take down distinctive words or phrases that give the tone of the respondent. Ask interviewees to slow down if they are fast talkers, and if necessary, use a small tape recorder to fill the gaps later and check accuracy.

An example of the type of questions and the information gained from unstructured interviews comes from the project manager in an urban safety project.[1] Box 11.1 indicates the type of data that unstructured interviews generate and how it can be used. A footnote with the material indicated how the notes were taken, reflecting the fact that a conversation is often not grammatical: 'comments...are taken from notes in open-ended interviews. They faithfully reflect the substance and much of the phrasing

---

[1] Boxes 11.1, 11.2, 11.3 and 11.4 illustrate interviews and the types of information with examples from an urban safety project called *Yumi Lukautim Mosbi* (YLM), a Melanesian Pisin phrase, meaning 'Let's Look after Port Moresby' (Guthrie and Laki 2007).

Box 11.1   Unstructured interview

Project Background

'In the 2000s, direction began to appear. [In response to a simple open-ended question, 'what was the background to YLM?'] a senior manager…encapsulated developments that gave focus for potential change agents in [the city government]:

> [The city] spent a lot of money on law and order in the 1990s. Perhaps K500 000 a year in grants was given to the police, etc. But it stopped when no impact was seen and funds were abused, for example with police vehicles being misused. So, in the early 2000s…management was asked to make some progress. There was the UNDP program and consultations with interested members of the public. In particular, a Reflection Workshop about [city] functions in 2004 led to the work being brought into [city] functioning. Support came from [the consultative council], which rallied other stakeholders. By that time, [city management] had changed. The project developed a program, the new city management supported it, and the City Manager became Chair of [the advisory committee], which means there is now support.'
> (italics in the original)

Source: Guthrie and Laki (2007: 12–13).

---

of comments, but have been edited and sometimes reordered and paraphrased to make the comments flow more smoothly.'

11.2   Semi-structured interviews

Semi-structured interviews use guides so that information from different interviews is directly comparable. *Interview guides* usually have standard introductions and conclusions, but allow flexibility to vary the order of intervening questions to provide a natural flow. They usually provide coded closed-response questions ('did you report this event? yes/no'). Additionally, they look for opportunities to follow-up with open-ended probe questions ('why?') so that the interviewer can flexibly get a better understanding of the respondents' views. The result is a combination of quantitative and qualitative data.

Usually, interviews are conducted one-on-one, but group interviews are possible too. The most common type is *focus groups*, which is a semi-structured technique derived from marketing and advertising. Here, a group of people is gathered together in a suitable location and the interviewer asks questions of the group. Focus groups typically have non-random membership, but should represent key groups (for example, different interest groups), and have gender and age balance. An attendance list can be circulated to obtain the name and role of group members to acknowledge them in an appendix.

Focus groups can be a highly informative representation of a particular group's viewpoints on a particular occasion, but sometimes, opinions can be affected by group dynamics, so validity is an issue. Often, a dominant person with a strong personality can be a disruptive influence because others do not get enough time to speak. Sometimes, members try to impress each other rather than provide the considered views that you want.

As the researcher, you need the skill to moderate group discussion, following an interview guide, which should use open-ended questions to generate discussion. Box 11.2 shows a guide used with a small six-member group—an advisory committee to the urban safety project. It starts with factual questions and then moves to opinions. Because the researcher is actively involved as group moderator, an assistant is needed to take notes or, preferably, a fast typist to transcribe. In this case, a speed typist transcribed the one and three-quarter hours of discussion, and quotes were used thematically in different parts of the report.

An important role for unstructured and semi-structured interviews is to cross-check viewpoints from different respondents who might have very different perceptions. The first part of Box 11.3 shows an example, summarising the views and some of the pithier comments from one of the focus groups. These reflected professional disagreements

---

Box 11.2   SEMI-STRUCTURED INTERVIEW GUIDE

Key Topics for Focus Group

1. What has been your involvement in YLM? How did you become involved? (for each member to outline).
2. What sort of things has YLM done? (for each member to outline) (check HIV/AIDS, poverty reduction).
3. Has this made any difference to Port Moresby?
4. Has there been an effect on crime? If so, what has the effect been? (including business, street and household crime).
5. If crime has lessened, why?
6. What are the supposed raskols [criminals] doing instead?
7. Have changes in one area affected other areas? (for example, lessened crime there or even increased it if raskols have just moved their activities from their original areas).
8. Are the police or any other law and justice agencies involved in YLM? If so, has it changed community attitudes to them?
9. Are women and girls involved in or affected by YLM?
10. How are youth involved in or affected by YLM?
11. What else could YLM do to improve the situation?

Source: Guthrie and Laki (2007: 61–62).

BOX 11.3   SEMI-STRUCTURED INTERVIEWS

Views on Project Success

'Members of the...committee who participated in the focus group held as part of the impact evaluation, had reservations about some activities. They did note visible successes, especially cleaner streets resulting from funding to community groups; however the musical and sporting activities...received considerable criticism. Committee members did not share the project perception that these were valuable morale boosters. Members considered activities from the perspective of whether they made sustainable contributions to livelihood in the community. One expressed a shared view:

> [Some] of this is froth and bubble...Projects must be sustainable rather than short term because problems will come back again...What use were the musical instruments? What is the sustainability of activities like this? Who replaces broken strings?... (italics in original)

'Not surprisingly, YLM managers took a different view:

> [The] majority of committee members are from formal sector agencies...the concept of community engagement to facilitate agency activity is foreign to them and to this date very few agencies attend the community forum meetings held in each of the target areas...[they] do not see music or sport as having an effect on community and are not involved with the communities who requested such activities as deterrents to crime.' (italics in original)

Source: Guthrie and Laki (2007: 26–27).

---

with the project approach; so, for balance, these views were put later to a project manager in a semi-structured interview, which the second paragraph illustrates from my interview notes.

11.3   Structured interviews

Structured interviews use formal standardised questionnaires. All interviews are conducted the same way to generate reliability using set questions and set response codes. Questionnaire interviews can be used instead of mailouts to increase response rates and decrease 'don't know' answers, with children, or when respondents might not be literate. Trained interview teams can be used to manage large numbers of interviews or when time is limited.

Questionnaires are often used to seek opinions or perceptions. They usually contain large numbers of short questions where answers are coded numerically. In effect, interviewers fill out the form for interviewees. The interviewer also does data coding by ticking boxes or circling numbers to speed data entry. Additionally, qualitative answers come from open-ended questions ('why?', 'can you give me examples?'), but usually gain only short comments that the interviewer writes down.

Structured interviews usually have greater coverage than unstructured ones, but lack their depth. They provide a mixture of quantitative and qualitative data. Statistical testing is often used, but is not compulsory. A basic way of presenting data is to give numbers first, and then quote comments to illustrate them.

The example in Box 11.4 is based on a closed and an open question. Question 5.8d asked, 'has YLM made any difference in your area? (yes/no)', followed by Question 5.8e, 'what are some things that YLM has done in your area?'. The report gave simple percentages for answers, a numerical description of the number of open-ended comments and the percentage breakdown by type. They were followed by brief quotes to show why people gave their answers, keeping to the tone and style of interviewee's language.

BOX 11.4   STRUCTURED INTERVIEWS

Survey Views

'About one-third of respondents thought that YLM had made a difference in their area at the three survey sites of Gordons Ridge/Erima (36%), Nine Mile (33%) and Vabukori (29%) (Q.5.8d). This was about average (33%) for Port Moresby as a whole.

'The most likely explanation of the positive responses outside the trial areas is a perceived public benefit from activities such as street and market cleanups, and reduced street crime. When asked, "What are some of the things YLM has done in your area?" (Q.5.8e), there were 90 responses from the 619 respondents (15%). A majority of these responses (58% or 52%) focused on increased cleanliness, for example:

- *Our area looks clean and tidy...*
- *I can now see that the streets are kept clean and more youths are involved...*

'Another 10% (9 responses) focused on reduced crime, for example:

- *Some parts of the area are clean and no more pocket pickers are around...*
- *Kept the city clean and get youths involved and away from crime.'*

Source: Guthrie and Laki (2007: 25–26).

11.4   Narrative

Even interviews based on simple questions need consideration from a number of perspectives. Box 11.5 is an example of a small but very interesting case study of a six-hour truck trip collecting interview and observational data about transport crime.

The trip allowed an in-depth interview with the driver, and observation of road conditions and crime locations. For this fieldwork, I had a list of topics to ask the driver about (for example, driver involvement in theft, other types of crime) and to observe (for example, road conditions, selling stolen fuel along the roadside). The interview was unstructured, prompted naturalistically by observation along the roadside. Guided by my topics, I asked simple questions about what we saw and the driver talked far more freely than was likely in a formal interview elsewhere.

The material was presented as a narrative to give more of the character of the situation and its meaning to the driver. Indeed, several readers said that this story was far more interesting than the rest of the report, which was a drier mixture of data from documents, standard interviews and statistics, like in the previous box. Even though the presentation of the story appears straightforward, it illustrates a number of other matters.

Box 11.5   Observation and interview as story

Crime on a Highway

'It's 12.20pm on Thursday, the 18th of November 2005 when John [a pseudonym], the driver, wheels us…westwards onto the Highlands Highway … as we go he tells me about particular crime spots, the troubles drivers have, and the sorts of crime they face. He keeps up a running commentary for the rest of the trip and I make untidy notes in my pad as we bounce along. John paints a very similar picture to the company managers and the police but adds the drivers' perspective. Some of the things John talks about happened to him, some he witnessed; others are second-hand from his friends in the [company residential] compound and in other companies…

'I ask about fuel selling on the roadside and over the next few hours John points out features… Part of the problem, he says, is that there is no fuel station between Forty Mile and Kainantu, a gap of some 250km…However, if they open one, John thinks people would still buy black market fuel because it is cheaper…At Fifty Mile, John points to a small bush material shelter where fuel is sold on the side of the road. Soon we pass some 200 litre drum stands with 5 litre plastic containers of fuel for sale on top. It is quite common to see several fuel sellers within a few meters of each other: I soon lose count, but we must pass well over 50 between here and Kainantu. Some have signs. The first one is K8 for a 5 litre container (i.e., K1.60/litre, which is 90 toea a litre cheaper than the bowsers in Lae). As we go along the Highway, prices increase ….

'John, speaking carefully in the third person to distance himself from other drivers, says that they often sell diesel. Drivers earn a lot, he says, but they spend a lot. Some drivers have their families in Lae, and their company pay goes into bank accounts. But, if they want beer on a trip, or if they want a woman, or if they have a village wife too or a girlfriend, they need more money and they sell diesel to get it. Out on the open road he points to some spots where truck drivers stop to sell fuel. They look like they are stopping to relieve themselves, he says, but someone can be buying fuel…'

Source: Guthrie (2007b: 19–24).

1. Mixed methods: In this case, two methods were used concurrently to give a running cross-check.
2. Reliability: The three sources for the driver's stories gave a frame to the interview data, but mostly his personal experiences were reported.
3. Ethical responsibilities: The last paragraph about driver's motives might not be politically correct, but it faithfully reported John's comments without editorialising or making moral judgement.
4. Validity: Observation and interview meant it was possible to fill out information from other sources. For example, many allegations about fuel theft had been made and observation supported them.
5. Triangulation: The driver's story supported management views that drivers themselves committed some fuel theft. A formal interview would have been unlikely to obtain such an admission.
6. Field notes: The bouncing truck meant that many of my notes were nearly illegible, which made it important to put them onto computer that night.
7. Confidentiality: Had the driver been a bit carried away and talked about things that might have got him into trouble with management or other drivers? I cleared the written story with him in case he thought it breached confidentiality.

The variety of perspectives extracted from such a short report illustrate that the more focused a topic, the more likely it is to generate practical research. Short fieldwork can provide a great deal of information if the data is analysed carefully.

11.5   Conducting interviews

All types of interview have common planning elements, which you should follow:

1. Clear objectives: What do you really need questions about? How do they relate to your research problem? Do they help test your research hypotheses?
2. Pre-test: Trial the interview and interview guide.
3. Practice: Do this until you are confident. Record the pilot interviews and expect to be embarrassed when you first listen.
4. Relevance: Prepare questions about which interviewees can reasonably be expected to have knowledge or opinions. Ask only one question at a time.
5. Plain, unambiguous language: Complicated words and jargon will lead to misunderstanding.
6. Reasonable length: About 30–40 minutes is usually within people's concentration spans for questionnaire interviews. Unstructured interviews can vary a lot in

length. Some will only be 10 or 15 minutes if the interviewee is busy or not interested. Others on interesting topics could last well over an hour.

7. Writen fieldwork procedures, especially for selection of interviewees if quota sampling is used.

Similarly, there are common procedures once you meet interviewees:

1. Clear explanation: Explain the reasons for the interview. Be prepared to provide extra assurance if people appear indecisive about being interviewed.
2. Informed consent: Seek this and respect interviewees' right to refuse to participate or to not answer particular questions.
3. Privacy: Do not interview where others can listen.
4. Safety awareness: Does someone else know where you are? Carry a phone (but turn it off during the interview).
5. Completion check: Check the questionnaire or interview guide before the interview is finished and review the notes soon after.
6. Acknowledgement: Thank the interviewees at the end.
7. Feedback: Volunteer a short report. If this is wanted, have a separate sheet on which people can write their addresses so that the anonimity of the questionnaire form is not breached.
8. Confidentiality: Respect the privacy of interviewees, including maintaining questionnaire security.

11.6   Interviewer bias

Interviews are very flexible and can give validity by allowing respondents the chance to explain their views thoroughly, but they are prone to bias from the influence of the interviewer. Here, there are issues similar to those of case studies in general, and participant observation in particular. Several steps can help reduce bias:

1. Dress neutrally and do not talk academically.
2. Be friendly, but professional.
3. Keep the introductions similar in all interviews to provide a common frame.
4. Start with straightforward questions and save more difficult questions for later.
5. Avoid leading questions that imply answers or body language that might convey an attitude. Be alert to 'yea' saying, the tendency for interviewees to say what they think the interviewer wants to hear, especially where the interviewer has higher status.

6. Be comfortable with silence. Wait a little if a response is not forthcoming immediately.
7. Use probe questions to gain more understanding of respondents' views, especially to make sure that you do not misinterpret them in light of your own opinions.
8. Take notes all the time. Respondents might be annoyed if you do not, or start telling you what they think you want to hear because you are suddenly busy writing.

Interviewing can be emotionally exhausting because of constant exposure to new and different people who might talk about major difficulties in their lives. Take a day or two off each week to recharge your emotional batteries so that you can pay full attention.

11.7   Summary

Interviews are a staple of social science data collection. They are especially useful because of their flexibility, but refusals can be a problem.

Unstructured interviews

1. Unstructured interviews can be in-depth. They are appropriate for obtaining sensitive information and for one-off situations.
2. The less the interviewer talks the better.
3. The outcome is qualitative data, which is presented descriptively and can be used as narrative.

Semi-structured interviews

1. Semi-structured interviews are more standardised but retain flexibility, resulting in a combination of quantitative and qualitative data.
2. Focus groups can provide extra insights, but are usually non-random and are prone to the influence of strong personalities.

Structured interviews

1. Standardised questionnaires provide wide data for quantitative analysis but give less depth.
2. Basic reports can give descriptive percentages and brief quotes.

Conducting interviews

Interviews require systematic planning and conduct, including clear objectives, pre-testing, clear language, informed consent, reasonable length and checking procedures.

Interviewer bias

Interviews are prone to bias from the influence of the interviewer, including dress, language, leading questions, body language and personal opinions.

Interviews can collect both opinions and information as words and numbers. They can be very flexible and give validity by allowing respondents the chance to explain their views thoroughly. Many of us are champion talkers, but we need to curb that tendency when interviewing. Interviews need sympathetic but professional listeners who do not intrude on personal views. The questioning and interpersonal skills that you learn while conducting interviews will be well-earned skills, useful in many aspects of your professional life in addition to research.

11.8   Annotated references

Gillham, B. (2005). *Research Interviewing: The Range of Techniques*. Maidenhead: Open University Press.
A comprehensive guide to all types of interviewing.

Kreuger, R. and M. Casey. (2009). *Focus Groups: A Practical Guide for Applied Research*, 4th edition. Thousand Oaks: Sage.
A comprehensive guide to this commonly used method of interviewing, with 13 chapters covering planning, conducting and analysing the results from focus groups.

Kvale, S. (2008). *Doing Interviews*. London: Sage.
This is a readable coverage of conducting and processing interviews.

Questionnaires 12

For the public at large, questionnaires and interviews are a common interface with social science research. Structured questionnaires lend themselves to large quantitative surveys that collect factual data, such as censuses. They are used commonly for perception studies and provide a base for systematic longitudinal studies. Questionnaires are often used as face-to-face interview schedules. They can also be administered efficiently in groups, for example, to entire classes or sports teams rather than individually.

Questionnaires are often equated with surveys. This is wrong. Questionnaires are just one of the techniques that can be used to collect data using the survey method. A sample survey of children can measure age, height and weight, for example, and use tests to assess whether nutritional status is affecting achievement: there is not a questionnaire in sight. Questionnaires can also be used with other methods, which happened in my case studies of the teacher training institutions and the school inspectorate. Because a questionnaire can be unnecessary, make sure before using it that it is the most appropriate technique for collecting data on your particular research question. If you are after factual data, it might be available elsewhere. If you want in-depth understanding, use unstructured interviews.

This chapter will demonstrate:

1. different types of questions, their answer formats and some examples of basic reporting of results; and
2. structure and administration of questionnaires and mailouts.

If you intend to carry out a questionnaire survey, you will also need Chapter 5 on sampling, Chapter 7 on the survey method and, if necessary, Chapter 11 on structured interviews. Chapter 16 will introduce tests of statistical significance. It is important to understand in advance how to analyse your data otherwise you will be in trouble when it comes to writing up the results.

The two main types of questions are:

1. Open response.
2. Closed response.

12.1   Open-response questions

Open-response questions are used when we do not want to limit answers. Skilful open questions are high on validity because they get comprehensive answers in respondents' own words, but are lower on reliability because different interviewers might get different answers.

Fill-in responses provide a space in the questionnaire for the response. For example, two important questions in the crime victimisation surveys were open-ended. They were at the start of a new section of the questionnaire, which had a short preamble for the interviewer to focus the interviewees on a change in direction from the previous section.[1] The underscored words provided a frame for the new questions:

Section 4.   *Now I will ask you some questions regarding the crimes where you or a member of your house was a victim in the* past 12 months. *Concentrate on the crime that you or your household found* most troubling.

4.1   What was the crime? _____

4.2   Why do you consider this crime to be the most troubling? _____

_____

_____

(emphasis in the original)

Open responses need to be categorised and results can be expressed simply as percentages. For example, Question 4.1 answers were later coded manually against 13 categories of crime used elsewhere in the questionnaire, finding that in Arawa, in 2006, the most common troubling crime victimisation was stealing (44 per cent of 75 respondents), followed by assault (19 per cent).

Reporting should include the question number (with the questionnaire included for reference as an appendix), response numbers and the non-response rate. To free the text from clutter, these can be put in a small font as a table note along with any detail

---

[1] The examples of questions on crime used in this chapter come from Guthrie et al. (2007: Appendix D). The questionnaire was developed by M. Findlay, Institute of Criminology, University of Sydney.

on interpretation. High non-response can be a sign of bias, so explanations should cover them. With Question 4.1, the table note was:

Q.4.1. Arawa 2006 N = 75, Non-response = 74%. S.4 answers were conditional upon respondents having identified in S.3 crimes experienced by them or other household members in the previous year. The high non-response rate derives mainly from respondents who gave nil responses to S.3, in part from respondents who did not regard crimes such as petty theft as being troubling, and occasionally from respondents unwilling to discuss traumatic events. The victimisation was not necessarily the most feared one, but the one that the respondent considered the most troubling. Different household members might have considered different victimisations to be the most troubling.

Otherwise, open-ended comments, like from Question 4.2 given earlier, can be quoted in the report along with their numbers, which you saw in Box 11.4.

Tabular responses can be used for factual information, for example:

Please outline your employment history:

Previous Employers	Positions	Month/Year Commenced	Month/Year Finished
_____	_____	_____	_____
_____	_____	_____	_____

For writing up, previous employment might be categorised by type of industry and type of position. The factual data could easily be used to construct relevant indicators, for example, total years of work experience. The dates could provide mean time with each employer as an indicator of employment stability.

12.2   Closed-response questions

Closed-response questions have pre-determined options for the answers. This is less valid than open-ended questions because the choices might be restrictive, but is more reliable because the form of the question and answers is set, so research is more replicable. To increase validity, fixed choice response scales often include the category 'other' and add open-ended *probe questions* seeking further explanation, often with a simple 'why?'.

Categorical responses are the most basic form of closed questions. They give a restricted choice for answers (often 'yes/no' or 'true/false'), sometimes with the addition of 'don't know'. Boxes can be left open for the respondent to tick or they can contain pre-coded numbers for the interviewer to circle clearly. This type of question can be superficial, so an open-ended probe often follows. Three questions illustrate these features:

2.12   Do you think that crimes in your area are most likely to be committed by:

1	People who live in this place
2	Outsiders
3	Both
4	Don't know

4.13 Did you report the incident to the police?

| 1 | Yes | | 2 | No |

4.14   Why? (specify)

_____

Box 16.1 later shows how the response percentages were presented longitudinally for Question 4.13.

Checklist responses provide more choices from which respondents can select or against which the interviewer can code:

8.1   In what ways could members of your community better assist the police?

1	Participate in peace and good order (crime prevention) committees
2	Provide more information to the police
3	Call the police when they see criminal activity
4	Co-operate with the police
5	Be more respectful, and/or
6	Other (specify)_____

Ranked responses have a given series of preferences to rank. For example, in Question 8.1 you could use the first five choices but leave the boxes empty, and ask respondents to write in a number ranging from 1 (the most preferred option) to 5 (least preferred). You then rank order the results according to the mean score for each item. An alternative that is easier for the respondent is to keep the checklist and list the results in a table, rank ordered by the number of responses for each item.

Scaled responses are used mainly for measuring attitudes and perceptions. They provide options to be rated from high to low, with scores in-between. All closed-response questions should have answer choices that are univariate (based on a single-response variable), otherwise the question will be ambiguous and the answers inconsistent.

A common form is the *semantic differential*, that is, answers based on polar opposite adjectives such as 'high–low' or 'good–bad'. One advantage of scales like this is that they are valid cross-culturally.

Likert scales are a common form of scaled response that asks interviewees to respond to a statement by choosing the answer that best corresponds to their viewpoint. The scale has a neutral centre point, 5 or 7-point scales being the most usual, for example, 'strongly agree > agree > undecided > disagree > strongly disagree'. The categories are scored 5 > 1 or 1 > 5 depending on the direction of the statements, which should be divided evenly between positive and negative so that total or mean scores can be compared. For example, the teacher training study questionnaire with inspectors asked them to rate six teacher training programmes:

What do you think of the following secondary teacher training programs? (*To answer questions, please circle the number on the scale which you feel closest represents your opinion.*)

	Very Good				Very Bad
Conversion Course	1	2	3	4	5
Dip S.T. (Goroka) *etc.*	1	2	3	4	5

Forced choice scales with no centre point (and therefore, with an even number of choices) are used particularly in political polls to avoid 'fence-sitting'. The respondent chooses the most preferred option. The results can show the percentage of people agreeing with statements.

Scaled responses are used especially for scoring attitudes, opinions and perceptions by combining the results on a number of questions. Because people do not usually think unidimensionally, about 10 questions are needed for each attitude. There is a large literature on different types of attitudes and how to measure them. Look at this literature before attempting to develop a scale yourself.

Finally, questionnaires often contain *funnel questions* that seek more detail by providing filters that allow respondents without relevant information to skip sub-questions. The crime victimisation questionnaire had over 100 questions, but filters meant that few interviewees needed to answer all of them. The following example starts with a general question and then moves to more specific ones, with Question 6.3 a filter with an instruction to the interviewer that allows some interviews to skip to Question 6.6.

6.1 Do you know where is the nearest police station where you could go for help or to make a complaint?

1 Yes   2 No

6.2   Have you been to this police station in the past 12 months?

| 1 | Yes | 2 | No |

6.3   Have you ever had official contact with the police other than visiting the police station?

| 1 | Yes | 2 | No (*If No to either this or the previous question, skip to Q.6.6*)

6.4   If so, was this as a victim of crime?

| 1 | Yes | 2 | No |

6.5   Did this contact with the police, or your visit to the police station improve your opinion of the police?

| 1 | Yes | 2 | No |

6.6   Do you think the police in your area are doing a good job?

1	Yes
2	No
3	Sometimes
4	Don't know

12.3   Questionnaire design

A disadvantage of questionnaires is the long time it takes to develop and trial a good one. If you can find a questionnaire on your topic that has already has some validity and reliability, use it or adapt it. If you write one of your own, the wording of all questions should be:

1. short;
2. simple;
3. specific;
4. unambiguous; and
5. neutral.

You should include both open- and closed-response questions. For self-completion questionnaires, it is a good idea to have few types of closed-response answer scales so that respondents can follow them more easily.

Questionnaires require many procedural elements similar to those of interviews:

1. Clear objectives. Be sure that each question relates to the research problem.
2. Pilot testing and practice.
3. Questions about which interviewees are likely to have knowledge or opinions.

4. No unnecessary questions, including none that has an answer elsewhere.
5. Clarity, for example, not mixing up issues within a question.
6. Short length (around 30–40 minutes is acceptable for interviews, but mailed questionnaires should be shorter).
7. For interviews, boxes at the beginning and end to monitor completion times.

The form should have enough space for answers, which should be on the same page as the question.

Self-completion questionnaires should look attractive. A common layout rule applies: 50 per cent of each page should be white space (although this is less important for interview schedules with trained interviewers).

The questionnaire should be modular so that sections can be added or subtracted and different sections used with different types of respondents. A typical progression is:

1. A short introduction to ensure informed consent.
2. The first section seeks background information that is necessary and non-contentious to help build trust and to develop a question and answer routine.
3. Middle sections progressively ask questions that might be emotionally difficult for respondents.
4. The final section asks for basic socio-economic data against which you will test variables. This allows a winding down process.
5. An acknowledgement.

The crime victimisation questionnaire had the following sections. Sections 1 and 2 were introductory; 3 and 4 were the most difficult; 5 to 8 progressively less contentious; and 9 was factual:

Introduction
Section 1: Screening Questions and Demographics of the Household
Section 2: General Thinking/Beliefs about Crime
Section 3: Experience of Crime
Section 4: Experience of Nominated Offences
Section 5: Individual and Community Response to Crime
Section 6: Police–General
Section 7: Police Accessibility and Service Delivery
Section 8: Police–Community Participation
Section 9: Personal Demographics.

Each section generally has a short bridging introduction (you saw an example earlier with Section 4 of the questionnaire). Within each section, questions should progress from the general to the specific.

Personal demographic questions are important for testing the reliability of your survey and checking whether a measurable bias resulted from non-response levels. The questions should be in the same form as your population data (for example, the latest census) so that any differences are not due to changing the form of the question.

12.4   Pilot testing

A three-step process can be used to test the draft questionnaire:

1. Have a few fellow students and, preferably, people from the target group vet the draft. They should comment especially on language issues and ambiguities. Interview some to smooth the flow and check the length.
2. Field trial or *pilot test* the amended questionnaire, assessing interviewing techniques, completion time and logistics. Take one or two days with interviewees drawn from your sample.
3. Examine the completed questionnaires for misunderstandings, omissions, layout problems and proofing errors, and amend as necessary.

When piloting, high numbers of queries about the meaning of particular questions, that is, 'don't knows', 'don't understands' and non-responses are all signs that those questions need revision. If the number of changes is small, the trial questionnaires can count as part of the total and absent answers can be treated as non-responses.

The crime survey questionnaire was typical of this process. It mainly received comments in the first stage prior to fieldwork about improving individual items and coding responses by interviewers. The questionnaire was revised prior to a two-day pilot test in the field, which resulted in a few further changes in the layout of coding for the final printed version. These changes did not affect the survey's substance and the interviews were used as part of it.

12.5   Administering mailouts

One-on-one interviews can be time consuming. An alternative is to conduct a mail survey. The following guidance on mailed questionnaires particularly aims to reduce non-response rates. Even so, the rates are likely to be high and might well bias the sample outcome, so think twice before proceeding.

Once the mail sample has been drawn, the next step is to contact members by sending out a letter or card, or email or phone to alert them about a questionnaire on its way, and if possible, to let them ask any questions about the survey.

Two or three days later, send out the questionnaire with a short, courteous covering letter that:

1. explains the reasons for the survey in a way helps motivate respondents;
2. identifies the institution sponsoring the survey;
3. stresses confidentiality;
4. offers a copy of results;
5. gives a return date about 10 days from likely receipt;
6. is signed personally; and
7. contains a stamped and addressed return envelope.

Remember that mailed questionnaires should be short and laid out attractively.

A few days after the return date, send another letter with a second copy of the questionnaire. If you have time, a third follow-up by card might generate a few more returns. If your questionnaires and envelopes are anonymous, mailouts have to blanket the whole sample. You can put tally numbers on envelopes, but include in the covering letter a reassurance that this is only for counting returns and that the actual questionnaires will be anonymous.

12.6   Summary

Questionnaires are suitable for quantitative surveys and perception studies using mailouts or interviews and can be administered efficiently in groups, but be sure that a questionnaire is the most appropriate way of collecting data for your particular research question. Understand in advance how to analyse the data.

Open-response questions

1. Use open-response questions when you do not want to limit interviewees' answers.
2. The main types have fill-in or tabular responses, which need to be categorised. Results can be expressed simply as percentages.

Closed-response questions

1. Closed-response questions have pre-determined options for the answers, often with open-ended probe questions.
2. The main types have categorical, checklisted, ranked or scaled responses underlaid by semantic differential scales.

Questionnaire design

1. Use short, simple and unambiguous questions.
2. Have clear objectives and do not ask unnecessary questions.
3. Use modular sections that go from the general to the specific.

Pilot testing

A three-step process that revolves around a field trial.

Administering mailouts

1. The aim is to reduce non-response rates, but they are likely to be high and might bias the outcome.
2. Contact sample members in advance. Two or three days later send out the questionnaire with a covering letter. If time permits, plan for two follow-ups.

Questionnaires are highly effective, but are not the only way of collecting survey data to help develop reliable generalisations about populations. They are a very common, but sometimes an unnecessary data collection technique. If the data you need is available in some other form, use it, especially where the alternative is a mailout questionnaire with a risk that high non-response levels will invalidate the survey. Nonetheless, questionnaires are a very effective way of gathering survey data. Go for it if you need one, but there are a lot of procedural requirements so make sure you are well organised.

12.7   Annotated references

Babbie, E. (2007). *The Practice of Social Research*, 11th edition. Belmont: Wadsworth.
   This text has a thorough chapter on surveys and questionnaires.

Best, J. and J. Kahn. (2005). *Research in Education*, 10th edition. Needham Heights: Allyn & Bacon.
   Contains useful material on questionnaires.

Iredale, R., F. Guo and S. Rosario (eds). (2003). *Return Migration in the Asia Pacific*. Cheltenham: Edward Elgar.
   A book on migration involving Bangladesh, China, Taiwan, Vietnam and Australia that includes extensive use of questionnaire data.

Fien, J., D. Yencken and H. Sykes (eds). (2002). *Young People and the Environment: An Asia-Pacific Perspective*. Dordrecht: Kluwer.
   This book contains extensive data from a large questionnaire study. It includes a full copy of the questionnaire that uses a number of the types of questions outlined in this chapter.

Tests 13

Because of our prior experience as students, we tend to have a restricted view of tests. We are all familiar with the idea of intelligence testing, and we have had seemingly endless subject tests and exams throughout our formal education. We might also have come across research reports from psychology and educational psychology experiments, but tests do have a wider use. Indeed, often they are not recognised as research method or even as tests.

Informally, teachers use pen and paper tests continuously to assess student progress in the classroom. Although teachers do not usually think of this as research, classroom tests can be both formative and summative evaluation techniques. Additionally, classroom tests can be very useful for action research: is a new teaching method, textbook or curriculum making a difference? The school inspectors' reports measuring teacher performance were also a form of test, this time of the teachers, and were analysed as such during the research project. Testing also occurs outside the classroom. Every time sports coaches click their stopwatches, they are testing athletic prowess.

This chapter will consider:

1. norm and criterion-referenced testing;
2. types of test validity;
3. achievement test questions; and
4. test administration.

You may need experimental or survey designs if you undertake applied research using tests (Chapters 8 and 7 respectively). The previous chapter's guidance on question writing also applies; this chapter focuses more on principles.

13.1   Norm-referenced testing

Norm-referenced tests aim to find out which members of a given population or sample score higher or lower. Half the takers fail the tests in the sense that they come below the mean. Most takers come near the middle and there are few with very high or very low results. The curious will readily find many types of intelligence tests on the internet: IQ tests are standardised against a normal distribution, with a mean of 100 as the centre point and a standard deviation of 15. The range from 85–115, therefore, encompasses 68.26 per cent of the reference population's distribution. Often, norm-referenced results are reported as percentile ranks. You can also work backwards from a score and the standard deviation to find a position using z score tables or tables that give percentile equivalents to z scores.

Test designers aim for 50 per cent pass and 50 per cent fail rates on individual test items because the purpose is to differentiate or *discriminate* between test takers. In education systems, this means that the primary function of norm-referenced tests is selection. Many universities use the American Graduate Record Examination (GRE), for example, as part of selection requirements for graduate admission. The GRE is a standardised norm-referenced test that measures analytical writing with two writing tasks, and uses multiple-choice questions to measure verbal and quantitative skills.

If you are interested in testing, a very large range of norm-referenced tests is available in psychology and educational psychology to measure traits such as intelligence, aptitude and personality, as well as attitudes and perceptions. The extensive literature on norm-referenced tests has many criticisms that you will need to consider.

Writing valid tests is difficult and time consuming, but many university psychology and education departments have libraries of tests that may be used for legitimate research. These tests usually come with full instructions on administration and interpretation. The instructions must be followed very carefully so that the reliability of interpretation against the test norms is not suspect. The literature contains many detailed statistical techniques as well. You will not go far in this sort of research unless you are willing to become statistically competent.

13.2   Criterion-referenced testing

In contrast, criterion-referenced tests aim to show whether students have achieved a given learning objective, with performance on a test item treated as a behaviour that demonstrates learning. Ideally, 100 per cent of students pass each item, thereby showing that they have the required knowledge; but it is equally possible that everyone could fail. In *mastery tests*, the pass mark is usually set at rightly answering 80 per cent of the questions. Students can be ranked by their scores, so criterion-referenced tests can also be used for selection, although that is not their prime educational purpose.

Implicitly, most classroom tests are criterion-referenced, although they might not be written formally against learning objectives. For valid research on student achievement, formal learning objectives are required, they need to be taught and the tests must measure student performance systematically against the learning objectives.

A research project to improve the validity and reliability of classroom tests can be valuable professionally for teachers and teachers in training, especially because tests help determine the future of students, and this is a serious ethical responsibility. Applied or action research could be conducted as a case study of a class, a survey of grade performance or as an experiment to measure the effect of a new textbook.

13.3   Test validity

What tests actually measure is a complex issue. There are three main approaches to measure test validity.

1. *Construct validity*: One approach is to focus on the property that a test measures. The starting point is a theoretical interest in different types of human behaviour and explanations for them. A construct is a concept used to explain a psychological property that we cannot observe directly: we can only see what appear to be the consequences of it.

    Intelligence is a prime example. We cannot see intelligence, but infer it from certain types of behaviour, including test-taking behaviour. Certain people behave in certain ways. Some seem to learn faster and with greater understanding than others do. In western society, intelligence is one of the constructs used to explain this, but a construct is only as good as the theory behind it and intelligence is a cross-cultural minefield. A beginner in research can only ensure that any tests are used within the population against which they are normed.

2. *Criterion-related validity*: A second approach focuses on external criteria, especially how well a test predicts subsequent performance. It does not matter so much what the test measures, as what it predicts. This approach is relevant, for example, to student selection for vocational courses. Who is most likely to succeed with the tasks for which they will be trained? Despite the confusing terminology, criterion-related tests can be norm-referenced.

    Criterion-related validity can be considered in two ways during research design. First, criterion-related validity focuses on identifying independent variables that are the most successful predictors. Second, it reinforces the need to have appropriate dependent variables, to be very clear about what is the appropriate criterion. For example, a common problem with curriculum innovations is that their effect is measured not on student achievement but on teaching style, which is actually an intervening variable.

3. *Content validity*: A third approach focuses on educational achievement and the adequacy with which a test samples particular knowledge. In achievement tests, the subject knowledge to be tested is the universe and the test items are a systematic sample of the content defined by the learning objectives. Sampling

should be stratified proportionate to the learning objectives. If 60 per cent of a geography practical course is on mapping skills, 60 per cent of an end-of-course test should sample them.

Additionally, a course should not teach one thing (for example, mathematical knowledge) but test another (for example, mathematical reasoning). The test items should systematically cover all aspects of the course. In other words, be very careful in your research not to claim that you are measuring one type of content when you are really measuring another, or to teach some content and not test it.

Content validity is achieved by a small group of experts exercising professional judgement. For our purposes, three fellow students or teachers could constitute a panel. Measures for testing expert judgement (*inter-rater reliability*) can be found in specialist texts.

The principles of test development can be applied in a range of subject areas. A study of Total Quality Management (TQM) in Indian industry (Box 13.1) illustrates all three types of validity in developing an instrument for measuring business management.

Box 13.1 INSTRUMENT VALIDITY

Measuring Total Quality Management

1. **Problem**: Did a measure of TQM developed using a web-based methodology have content, criterion and construct validity?

2. **Data Collection**: Ten primary TQM critical success factors were identified from the literature. A survey questionnaire was developed with 75 items measured with 5-point Likert scales. The questionnaire was administered via the internet with responses from 104 TQM-certified businesses.

3. **Data Analysis**: Parametric statistical analysis was carried out using the computer program Statistical Package for the Social Sciences (SPSS).

   (a) Content validity was assessed through a comprehensive review of previous detailed research studies and systematic pre-testing of items. The items were considered to reflect accurately TQM content.

   (b) Criterion validity was assessed statistically, demonstrating that the 10 measures had a high and statistically acceptable level of prediction of businesses' quality performance.

   (c) Construct validity was also found statistically to be acceptable for all factors.

4. **Action**: The article demonstrated that a valid and reliable operational measure of TQM had been successfully developed.

Source: Adapted from Karuppusami and Gandhinathan (2007).

13.4   Achievement test items

The three previous sections indicated two types of realistic first research projects. One is norm-referenced psychological testing using established standardised tests. The other is student achievement tests using criterion-referenced testing based on content validity.

Fortunately, educational achievement testing is an area with a standard classification in place. The classification allows you to focus on the content of any standardised tests that you use or non-standardised ones that you develop. Bloom's Revised Taxonomy of Educational Objectives has cognitive, psychomotor and affective domains that correspond to knowledge, attitudes and skills (as found in the three objectives for this book on the first page of the Preface). Achievement tests focus on the cognitive domain, where there are six levels from lower to higher order thinking: remembering, understanding, applying, analysing, evaluating and creating (Table 3.2). Learning objectives should clearly identify the levels to be taught in a course. These levels should be the basis of both teaching and testing to give content validity.

Particular key words are used for each cognitive level when writing classroom test items. Table 13.1 illustrates a few items from lower order to higher order.

Table 13.1   Classifying achievement test items

Cognitive levels	Learning objective and item terminology	Test items
Remembering	List Name State	List the six cognitive levels in Bloom's Revised Taxonomy of Educational Objectives.
Understanding	Describe Discuss Explain	Discuss the uses of Bloom's Taxonomy in classifying student achievement.
Applying	Calculate Practice Summarise	Write a question testing each of Bloom's cognitive levels.
Analysing	Classify Compare Illustrate	Classify the three objectives for this textbook according to their domain in Bloom's Taxonomy.
Evaluating	Critique Justify Interpret	How would a mismatch between learning objectives, classroom teaching and test questions impact on content validity?
Creating	Construct Design Formulate	Use Bloom's Taxonomy to design an achievement test for this chapter.

Source: Author.

To develop your own items, you can use some of the question types mentioned in the previous chapter. Generally, lower order items are more likely to have closed responses, which are easier to mark as right or wrong (that is, have greater reliability). Open-ended responses for higher order items require numerical rating. You can also look in education texts for more specialised items, such as those used in closed tests.

13.5   Test construction and administration

All tests should meet several criteria (Best and Kahn 2005: Chapter 9):

1. Validity: The construct, criterion or content validity.
2. Reliability: The test should achieve consistent results. Different markers should assign similar scores.
3. Economy: The test should be only as long as necessary and should be easy to administer and mark.
4. Interest: The test should not be boring for takers.

Administration of a test should be the same each time in order to help ensure reliability. If you use an existing standardised test, rehearse the instructions in advance and follow them exactly. Otherwise, have a short set of protocols for your own test. The instructions might need to be written on the test form or given verbally. To administer the test, you should:

1. Have all the test materials.
2. Make sure that the testing location is quiet and suitably arranged.
3. Explain clearly to the students what the test is for and how long they have to answer.
4. Distribute the materials.
5. Read out any directions and ask for questions, if any.
6. Supervise by quietly moving around to check that students are not cheating.
7. Take a note of any disruptions.
8. Allow students to avail the exact length of time.
9. Collect all materials and maintain test security.
10. Provide the results to the test takers.

13.6 Summary

Tests are commonly used for grading student achievement and in psychology and educational psychology research. Classroom tests can be very useful for action research.

Norm-referenced testing

1. Norm-referenced tests aim to separate out the people tested. In education systems, this means that their primary function is selection.
2. A very large range of norm-referenced tests requiring statistical analysis is available for research in psychology and educational psychology.

Criterion-referenced testing

The primary function of criterion-referenced tests is to show whether students have achieved a given learning objective. Mastery tests usually have a pass mark of 80 per cent. Students can also be ranked on the basis of their scores for selection purposes.

Test validity

1. Both types of test can be used for formative and summative evaluation.
2. The three main types of test validity are construct, criterion-related and content validity.

Achievement test items

1. Bloom's Revised Taxonomy of Educational Objectives provides a standard classification for writing cognitive test items.
2. Learning objectives should clearly identify which levels are to be taught in a course. They should be the basis of teaching and testing.

Test construction and administration

1. Tests should be valid, reliable, economical and interesting.
2. Test administration and marking should follow defined protocols.

Research on formal testing is a task requiring statistical work, but informally teachers can use pen-and-paper tests to measure student progress in the classroom. If you are training to be a teacher, you are probably more concerned at this stage with issues such as class control, but action research in this area can lay a foundation for the future. For those of you who are already teaching, action research on assessment could provide a professional challenge to upgrade your skills.

13.7   Annotated references

Anderson, L. and D. Krathwohl (eds). (2001). *A Taxonomy for Learning, Teaching, and Assessing: A Revision of Bloom's Taxonomy of Educational Objectives*. New York: Longman.
This is a fundamental book used in this text at several points to provide a structure for abstracting, testing and, later, for analysing data.

Badgett, J. and E. Christmann. (2009). *Designing Elementary Instruction and Assessment: Using the Cognitive Domain*. Thousand Oaks: Sage.
Provides a readable step-by-step guidance on constructing classroom tests based on Bloom's Taxonomy.

Kline, T. (2005). *Psychological Testing: A Practical Approach to Design and Evaluation*. New Delhi: Vistaar.
This book covers all aspects of psychological testing.

SECTION 3

DATA ANALYSIS

You now have a pile of qualitative and quantitative data, otherwise known as words and numbers. You also have a serious problem. How does all this data get analysed? If you have collected words, much reading, sorting and cross-referencing lies ahead. If you have collected numbers, lots of figures need calculating, cross-tabulating and testing.

Both words and numbers must be analysed carefully. Statistics do not guarantee the rigour of your research, nor does naturalistic inquiry guarantee its meaning.

For those of us without a strong mathematical background—and many social scientists are in this situation—statistics are off-putting. Hence, we tend to look to qualitative data as the core of our research.

However, research is not that simple because the distinction between qualitative and quantitative data is ultimately a false one. All research is stuck with both qualities and quantities—they are two sides of the same coin. Even if we plan a research project that completely avoids numbers, we still have to understand basic measurement principles.

This section of the book will explain measurement principles and give more practical guidance on analysing data, whether in the form of words or numbers. Although measurement scales, in particular, are positioned here because they most closely relate to data analysis, you need to anticipate them early on when defining your research proposal so that you understand in advance how to deal with the data you collect. Otherwise, that pile of data could overwhelm you.

Measurement Principles 14

Here is a proposition: *everything can be measured.*

When I was young, many did not like that idea because we thought it dehumanised us and that some things about people could not be measured anyway.

So, here is a paradox that seems quite illogical: *everything can be measured, including those things that cannot.*

There is a trick of course, and that trick is the use of the word 'measure'. In research, measure has a particular meaning derived from *measurement scales*, which are technically defined methods for classifying or categorising. All information is data (whether represented by words or numbers) that can be categorised as qualities and, therefore, measured as quantities.

We can conceptualise and, therefore, classify things that do not exist because 'things that do not exist' is a category that can be represented on a measurement scale. This comes about because the absence of something is defined in relation to its presence. Only if we can define something, that is, recognise its qualities or attributes (for example, 'things that exist'), can we conceptualise its absence ('things that do not exist'). In both cases, we are categorising and, thus, measuring them on a binary scale.

This chapter provides principles underlying data collection and analysis. Even if you do not intend to do quantitative research, you need to understand these principles. In many ways, these principles make this chapter the most important one in the book and you should keep revisiting it. The chapter will:

1. define some key measurement terms, using examples of the sort that you might find in your own research; and
2. look at some other key measurement principles that underlie all social science research, both quantitative and qualitative, including hypothesis testing, probability and randomness.

14.1   Measurement scales

How are variables measured? A quantity is a quality expressed as a number, which might be as basic as 1 or 0 on the binary scale used to classify presence or absence. For example, we can see the effects of the presence of electricity when we turn a switch on ('1') and its absence when we turn it off ('0'). In a social science research project, we might interview someone and ask if they have been to school (presence of schooling) or not (absence of schooling), which can also be coded as 1 or 0. This is simple, but the approach can be very powerful in practice—it is how computers store data.

Conventionally, four measurement scales are used. These are the nominal, ordinal, interval and ratio scales, but we need to include the usually overlooked binary scale too. Table 14.1 shows that each scale adds to the measurement properties of the

Table 14.1   Measurement scales

Scale	Characteristics	Physical examples	Social examples
Ratio	Mutually exclusive, equal interval, ordered categories, plus: (a) True zero.	Weight.	Age (0/1/2, etc.). Funding ($0/$1/$2, etc.).
Interval	Mutually exclusive ordered categories, plus: (a) Categories differ by equal amounts. (b) Arbitrary zero point, if any.	Temperature (Celsius or Fahrenheit scales).	Opinion scored 1–10 on a response scale.
Ordinal	Mutually exclusive categories, plus: (a) Orders categories logically as greater than > less than. (b) Differences between the categories not necessarily equal.	Height (tall > medium > short).	Level of formal education (tertiary > secondary > primary). Rank order (1st > 2nd > 3rd in class). Attitude (very good > good > average > bad > very bad).
Nominal	(a) Classifies object into different categories. (b) Categories mutually exclusive (object can only belong to one category). (c) No logical order to categories.	Types of object (animal/mineral/vegetable).	Gender (male/female). Marital status (unmarried/married/divorced/widowed). Nationality (Indian/Malaysian/Other).
Binary	(a) Quantifies object as present or absent.	Electricity (on/off).	Schooling (some schooling/no schooling).

Source: Author.

lower order ones. The mathematical properties of the scales imply different types of descriptive and inferential statistics that are appropriate. The further up the scales, the more mathematical information is added, the more precise the measurement and the more powerful the statistical tests.

Most social science research only has data that can be measured on the nominal and ordinal scales. Existing groups are predominantly labelled using the nominal scale (for example, males/females, married/unmarried), or data is collected using the ordinal scale (for example, strongly agree > agree > disagree > strongly disagree).

14.2   Testing hypotheses

In research, measurement scales order data: *(a)* informally to explore patterns arising from the data as we analyse it; and *(b)* formally to test hypothesised relationships between variables. As we began to see in Chapter 4, the logic of hypothesis testing is convoluted.

Research cannot prove correct theories or hypotheses derived from them, it can only prove them wrong (that is, refute or falsify or reject them). A theory leads to a research hypothesis predicting a positive relationship between variables. For testing, the re-search hypothesis must be defined more precisely as an *operational hypothesis*, that is, one with carefully defined measurement characteristics. We cannot prove that the hypothesised relationship exists, so operationally we test for its non-existence using the *null hypothesis*, which is a prediction that no difference will be found. In other words, we do not test the proposition that the research hypothesis is correct (because it can never be proven); we test the proposition that it is incorrect (because we can disprove it).

1. Rejection of the null hypothesis gives a difference predicted by the research hypothesis and the theory from which it derives, which are supported (technically, the research failed to reject them).
2. If the null hypothesis is supported, the difference predicted by the research hypothesis did not occur. In this case, the research hypothesis and maybe the theory are rejected as false.

Box 14.1 shows how formal hypothesis testing and informal searching of data added to the validity of findings in the teacher education study. The box revises how the hypotheses were progressively refined to give operational research, for example, by giving an operational definition of 'professional acceptability' as being measured by eight-item global judgements by inspectors. While the wording of the hypotheses has

---

BOX 14.1 INCREASING THE SPECIFICITY OF HYPOTHESES

Teacher Education Hypotheses

One of the 'research hypotheses' in the teacher education study was:

H_1 Increased amounts of professional training will result in graduates being rated as more professionally acceptable by inspectors.

This was revised to become a more detailed 'operational hypothesis': increased number of years of professional training [in six defined teacher education programmes] will result in graduates being rated as more professionally acceptable using eight-item global judgements by inspectors of teacher performance in secondary schools.

The statistical procedures were defined as an item analysis using coefficient alpha to test whether the data from 870 inspection reports were sufficiently reliable to test scale totals, with one-way analysis of variance testing totals for significance of differences between the programmes with a 0.05 level of confidence.

The 'null hypothesis' was:

H_0 There will be no statistically significant difference in professional acceptability between the teacher education programmes.

Source: Adapted from Guthrie (1983a: 23).

---

quite small differences and seems repetitious, each one refines the previous one to meet the next step in the formal logic of scientific measurement.

The research hypotheses were already quite specific, so the operational hypotheses acted to narrow down the measurement possibilities. For example, professional and general education were measured crudely in years (or parts of years) because apparently more precise options such as numbers of courses or contact hours amongst subjects varied widely in practice and could not be measured accurately. The null hypotheses gave the formal statistical logic.

The result was that the statistical tests did not find statistical differences in the professional acceptability of the graduates from the two different programmes. This part of the research evidence failed to reject the null hypotheses, so the operational and research hypotheses were apparently not supported. However, the programmes themselves were very different in approach, content, length and costs. The longer, more expensive programmes were no more effective than the shorter, cheaper ones.

In fact, the operational and null hypotheses were not provided formally in the report, but were implied in lengthy discussion of their elements in the text. In sociological research, this is usually acceptable, but in experimental research, they would probably be written out.

14.3   Probability

Null hypotheses are tested statistically. Because we cannot be absolutely sure of anything, the test results are expressed as probabilities. In science, we use the probability level to predict the likely occurrence of predicted events. The social sciences usually set 95 per cent as the acceptable likelihood of an outcome occurring. Behavioural sciences like psychology also use a 99 per cent level. Biological and, especially, physical sciences, which are better able to control the variables they study, can go higher.

Statistical analysis does not usually express the outcomes of hypothesis testing as levels of probability (chances of being right), but as levels of confidence (the chances of not being wrong). One provides a balance for the other (a 95 per cent probability gives a 5 per cent level of confidence), but levels of confidence are expressed as decimals (5 per cent is expressed as .05).

A .05 level of confidence expresses the level of confidence we have when we reject the null hypothesis that there is no difference. It shows we have a result with only one chance in 20 of being wrong in finding a difference and, by interpretation, of failing to reject the research hypothesis predicting the difference. A .01 level is a higher level of confidence (despite the smaller number) because it provides only one chance in 100 of being wrong. Thus, with a .03 result, for example, we can say we reject the null hypothesis at a .05 level or greater (> .05).

When we find a statistically significant difference, the interpretive term 'accept' can be used in practice instead of the correct but clumsy 'fail to reject'. Note in the report that you are doing this so that the technical reader knows you understand the difference.

A .05 level of confidence means we are vulnerable to two types of error on 5 per cent of occasions:

1. *Type I errors* are false positive results (that is, incorrect rejection of the null hypotheses).
2. *Type II errors* are false negative results (that is, incorrect acceptance of the null hypotheses).

These are not a result of incorrect use of statistical tests or of mistakes in computation, but are random consequences of the use of probabilities in sampling.

14.4   Randomness

Randomness is a mathematical principle affecting all research. This is true, too, of research that does not involve quantification and statistics. Selection of case studies and use of qualitative techniques do not make randomness go away; they merely make it less transparent and more prone to reliability issues.

Random events are ones where we cannot predict each outcome individually (which is much the same as saying something was an accident). We might know that there is a pattern of events with certain levels of probability, but we cannot know what the next event will actually be. For example, we know that 50 per cent of the time, on an average, a tossed coin will show heads, and the other 50 per cent of the time tails will come up, but we cannot know whether the next toss will be a head or a tail.

The probability levels used in social science are a reflection that statistical testing provides findings that are highly calculated gambles. At a .05 level of confidence, we know that we will be right 19 times out of 20 on an average, but we do not know which one of the 20 occurrences will have the chance error.

If a large number of statistical tests give some unexplained results, random sampling error could be the reason. For example, the possibility of Type I error was a point of reference when sample results from the crime victimisation surveys were synthesised, which Box 14.2 illustrates.

Box 14.2   TYPE I ERROR IN SAMPLING

Sampling Error

The 16 crime victimisation survey samples were each tested against four variables of age, gender, marital status and education using population data from the 2000 Papua New Guinea Census. The level of confidence was set at .05.

Age means and standard deviations for all samples were statistically acceptable, with one exception out of 16 (i.e., 6%, which was 1% above the permissible level of 5% of Type I false positive errors). Arawa, in 2006, had a sample age mean of 30.3 years compared to the census result of 31.8 years for the 15+ population, i.e., there was a slightly lower average age of 1.5 years below the census, and a narrower age range than expected (a standard deviation of 10.2 years rather than 12.4).

Technically the sample should have been rejected, albeit by a very small 1% margin, but it was not, for four reasons. First, the census was taken close to the end of a civil war, and there was no guarantee that it was very accurate. Second, it was possible that the population numbers had changed somewhat as peace developed and the town was resettled. Third, the difference between the sample and the population means was small. Fourth, the age and gender cohorts and all other tested parameters matched the census. The age data was used with appropriate qualification.

However, three of the 16 samples had unacceptable differences in married numbers and three had unacceptably high levels of people with technical/university education. Both marital status and educational level had 19% of null hypotheses rejected, which was well above the permissible 5% level. The reports used population estimates based on age and gender, and did not present data based on marital status or educational levels.

Source: Adapted from Guthrie (2008: Appendix C).

A further complication is that the chances of error apply not only to individual tests, but also to samples as a whole. Not only might the statistical tests be wrong on 5 per cent of occasions, 5 per cent of samples and the results derived from them might be wrong too. This is part of the reason why there is controversy over so many research findings—apparently similar studies can produce different results. The problem can be a result of random sampling error in some of the studies, which is one reason why meta-analyses group studies together to check the distribution of results.

14.5   Summary

Measurement scales define how to classify or categorise. All information is data, represented by words or numbers that can be categorised as qualities and measured as quantities.

Measurement scales

1. Five types of measurement scale are binary, nominal, ordinal, interval and ratio. The further up the scales, the more precise the measurement.
2. Most social science research only has nominal and ordinal data.

Testing hypothesis

1. Measurement scales order research data informally to explore patterns in the data, and formally to test hypothesised relationships between the ordered variables.
2. Research cannot prove correct theories or hypotheses derived from them; it can only prove them wrong.

   (a) If the null hypothesis is rejected, the difference predicted by the research hypothesis occurs so it is not rejected as false.
   (b) If the null hypothesis is supported, the difference predicted did not occur and the research hypothesis is rejected as false.

Probability

1. Statistical results are probabilities. The social sciences usually accept a 95 per cent level.
2. Type I errors are false positive results. Type II errors are false negative results. These are random consequences of sampling error.

Randomness

Random error also affects samples as a whole.

Conducting qualitative research might lead to the false conclusion that measurement is unnecessary. Both words and numbers must be analysed carefully. Just because you have collected words does not make them meaningful, especially if they are presented in a disorganised way. Does some data interpretation—whether of words or numbers— seem confused? Perhaps you are mixing variables or misinterpreting the underlying measurement scales. Even if a research project completely avoids numbers, it still needs an understanding of basic measurement principles.

14.6   Annotated references

Babbie, E. (2007). *The Practice of Social Research*, 11th edition. Belmont: Wadsworth.
    This sociology text has chapters on measurement scales and qualitative and quantitative data analysis.

Cozby, P. (2009). *Methods in Behavioral Research*, 10th edition. Boston: McGraw Hill.
    A psychology text with clear chapters on measurement and statistical principles.

Desai, V. and R. Potter (eds). (2006). *Doing Development Research*. New Delhi: Vistaar.
    The readings in this book on development research include chapters on quantitative and qualitative research.

Scheyvens, R. and D. Storey (eds). (2003). *Development Fieldwork: A Practical Guide*. London: Sage.
    A comprehensive collection on fieldwork in developing countries containing chapters on both quantitative and qualitative research.

Qualitative Data 15

Many of us in the social sciences come from arts rather than science backgrounds and find statistics difficult. Hence, we tend to look to qualitative data as the core of our research. Qualitative data is information that is represented usually as words, not numbers. If you have pages of text before you, recordings of interviews or notes from observation, for all practical purposes you have qualitative data. Nevertheless, words must be analysed as carefully as numbers. Naturalistic inquiry does not guarantee the meaning of your research any more than statistics guarantee its rigour.

In researching people's subjective perceptions, we build up scientific knowledge about their personal knowledge by objectifying their perceptions systematically. However, the actual perceptions themselves do not suddenly become scientific by virtue of having been studied scientifically. Just because our research gives us a better idea of what some people think (and maybe, gives us an emotional attachment to these people and their ideas), it neither suddenly changes the nature of their thoughts nor makes them more important than other people's. Different groups have ethical, social and political rights in consonance with their own culturally meaningful sets of social constructs. However, this does not necessarily mean that these groups have professionally or scientifically informed views, or that their constructs are valid beyond their own group.

Carefully done qualitative research is just as demanding as other research. However, it is easy to do badly, by being intellectually lazy and hiding the fact from yourself and others. The rules of the game are not as transparent as they are in quantitative research. The result can be a weak report that has neither technical nor intellectual rigour. Rather, research reports must demonstrate a careful systematic approach to data analysis.

This chapter will:

1. review the key principles about qualitative data established earlier in this book, including the key hierarchy for presenting data;

2. show how to present observational and unstructured interview data in more detail; and
3. outline some basic techniques for manual and computer analysis of short open-ended questions.

15.1 Qualitative data principles

First, we need to revise some of the underlying principles that apply to qualitative data:

1. Words are data that express qualities and attributes (Chapter 14).
2. Words particularly come from available sources (Chapter 9), naturalistic observation (Chapter 10), unstructured interviews (Chapter 11) and open-ended questions in questionnaires (Chapter 12).
3. Words are most often classified on the nominal measurement scale (Table 14.1).

Although much qualitative research does not analyse data formally using measurement concepts, understanding the principles will often help solve problems that arise during analysis. Does something not seem logical? You are possibly confused about the measurement scale or maybe, the underlying semantic differential is not a polar opposite. Does a paragraph seem jumbled? Are you not sure about where some material belongs? Chances are that you are mixing up more than one variable.

A hierarchy drawn from Bloom's Taxonomy helps present data clearly. First, describe; then analyse; and later, draw conclusions or interpret.

1. ***Describe***

   (a) Write out the 'facts' of the situation observed or heard about in open-ended interviews. This should be clear descriptive reporting, free of adjectival colour.
   (b) Do not present everything. Filter out those matters which are not relevant to the research problem and themes.

2. ***Classify***

   (a) Group the material to identify similarities and differences in the data.
   (b) Break paragraphs when they start getting complex so that there is one main idea in each paragraph.
   (c) Use more headings if you have trouble categorising the literature appropriately. Rather than making the headings more abstract, make them more concrete.

3. *Interpret*

    (*a*) Present your interpretation of the material separately. Pick out key features that identify patterns and keep your mind open to new ideas that arise from the data.

    (*b*) You do not need to be highly conceptual here—that can come later in the concluding chapter with a wider analysis of the findings in light of the literature review.

The aim should be reporting that is clear and analytical. It should work from the data as recorded in observation and interviews to the analysis generated by the literature review, the fieldwork and interviews.

15.2 Presenting available and observation data

How do we present unstructured qualitative data gained from available sources and field observation? This can be confusing at first because now you have large chunks of text, usually written in a note pad. Once writing begins, it is very easy to start commentating, and quickly there is a problem. What is observation or description and what is commentary or interpretation? The answer to the problem remains, first, describe, then analyse and, later, draw conclusions or interpret.

Computers can be used to analyse this data, but for decades, qualitative researchers survived without them. Some manual techniques are quite usable, especially when there are large volumes of text. Computer processing will be faster than manual processing once the text is set up, but the trade-off is that learning to use specialist computer packages and setting up text analysis functions might take more time than you save in processing. For small amounts of data, you can transcribe from your notes into a word processor.

In writing up the material, you have two main options:

1. Narrate it as a chronological story, which is usually the most straightforward for both writer and reader.
2. Analyse it systematically, which will add insight and academic value.

Examples of chronological narration have been given already in Box 9.1 (based on available documentary data about school inspections classified under appropriate headings) and Box 11.5 (using observation and interview about highway crime). You can revisit those examples, so now we will focus on systematic analysis.

The basis for systematic analysis is issues or themes identified in the literature review or grounded in the data. You can either work straight from a note pad (which

I did with the 18 interviews in the highway study) or transcribe the material into a word processing document, which you should do as soon as possible after collecting it. Entering the whole text into the computer is time consuming, but the entry process leads to revision of the material and ignites your thought process about patterns and connections in the data. Then the following steps apply:

1. If a note pad is the source, strike out material in the pad as it is copied. If you have typed up the material, make a backup document and use another copy as a source for cutting and pasting. In both cases, keep coming back to the remaining material.
2. In a new document, insert headings using key themes from the literature review. Use them as destinations to copy different phrases, sentences or paragraphs from the notes or document.
3. If using more than one period of observation or more than one interview as source material, keep a reference to it with each item that is entered. When you analyse the data, you can comment on who said what and how their different perspectives might illuminate the topic under discussion.
4. If source material straddles more than one heading or does not fit under an existing heading, consider making up a new one.
5. If something still does not fit, perhaps it is of minor importance and can be omitted, but do not leap too quickly to this conclusion. The minor elements might actually be important and the problem is that you have not woken up to this.

To clarify the data, follow the describe/classify/interpret steps given in the previous sub-section. Box 15.1 shows an example, being a summary of two days observing a school inspection visit during which I followed the inspector and took detailed notes. The first part, taken from eight pages of the original report, is a straight chronological description of the inspector's day and his interactions in the school. However, the description reports only his activities and filters out other aspects of the school that were secondary to this (for example, details of lessons observed). The second part is classification of the events to show themes, being key summary points cross-referenced back to parts of the observation. Broader academic and professional interpretation about the nature of inspections in a formalistic education system was saved for the concluding chapter.

15.3   Presenting open-ended interview data

The techniques for presenting long pieces of data from unstructured interviews are similar to unstructured observation. Once you have notes or text, you can describe, classify and interpret it using the five steps listed earlier.

Box 15.1   Presenting observation data

A School Inspection Visit

An Advisory Visit

'7.50am. The Inspector arrived at the school, met the Headmaster and introduced the researcher. Arrangements for the day were discussed and the timetable checked.

'8.40. A second teacher interview began...The Inspector went through the eight Inspection Report headings...then the Inspector went over a lesson observed the previous day...

'10.30. The Inspector and the researcher walked down to the Social Science office to interview the Subject Master of Expressive Arts and Social Science. The Inspector first checked teachers' timetables and whether there was an Expressive Arts syllabus, a problem raised by the third interview. He then checked how many subject meetings had been held...[and] checked the availability of Expressive Arts materials...He then turned to Social Science duties...

'8.50 [the next morning]. A grade 8 Agriculture class lesson on picking coffee cherries was observed until 9.10 when note-taking from the blackboard began...

'11.10 The staff meeting now started ... The Inspector said that there would be ten points in his address...The first point concerned assessment...The Inspector's next point covered the value of applying for in-service courses...For his fifth point, the Inspector discussed school maintenance...and praised the improvement in classroom displays...

Several features were apparent from this visit.

'The first feature apparent was the volume of work covered. The first day spanned about 10 hours, the second 9½ hours...

'A second and constant feature of the two days of the visit was an emphasis on quality, broadly defined: the "tone" of the school, the need for thorough preparation and planning, the need to challenge and extend students...

'A third feature was the close interrelationship between the three inspectorial roles [advice, evaluation and administration]. Within the space of a few minutes in an interview each role was frequently encompassed...Although it is easy in principle to draw a distinction between advising and evaluating, in practice it is somewhat more difficult...

'The intermixing of roles parallels a fourth feature of the visit: the Inspector was the system-defined expert on everything...This was particularly evident in the meeting held with all the staff...

'Finally, a seventh feature of the visit was the thoroughness of the investigations and the thoroughness of the cross-checking...'

Source: Adapted from Guthrie (1983b: 19–27).

Box 15.2 has reporting from an investigation of science teachers' experience in the Philippines. It reports a trainee teacher's narrative about the difficulty she had in relying only on a textbook that contained information contradicted by local knowledge. The article from which this story is taken then analysed the situation in more detail, bringing to bear further narrative about the teacher's life experiences to show how they provided meaning for her teaching career and how that

---

BOX 15.2   REPORTING UNSTRUCTURED INTERVIEWS

A Teacher's Experience

'I'm a student teacher of grade 1. As a teacher in science, there are times when unexpected situations will occur inside the classroom which create dilemmas. My dilemma is not really a big one, but when you look at it deeply, such a dilemma can create a serious situation that is hard to deal with in science teaching.

'One day, I taught a lesson about places where plants grow. I first presented places where specific plants grow—in soil, water, air, wet and dry places. The plants I used as examples were taken from the science book that we were using in class. The pupils were confused about whether the water and wet places were the same? In real life situation there are plants that can grow in both places—in wet and aquatic places. On a test, I asked students to list two examples of plants that grow in soil, water, air, dry and wet places. One child wrote "Kangkong" plant under "wet" places; I marked it wrong because the book implied that Kangkong would be an "aquatic" plant since it grows in water.

'The mother of one of our pupils came to the school. She had a correction for an answer her child had written that I had marked wrong. The mother protested saying that Kangkong can grow also in wet places. Because I followed what is written in the book, I marked it wrong. Besides, most of my pupils believed that the book is the source of knowledge. So, if I checked or accepted other answers that are not found in the book pupils will conclude that books can't be trusted.

'Actually, I believe that books are not the only source of knowledge. You can gain knowledge from other people, and also from real life situations. Answers that can be found in the book are also correct, but they are limited in the sense that other answers can also be found in other books.

'My problem is: Am I going to stick to the book or consider other answers which are based on real life situation? What will happen if I stick or depend only on the book? What should I do to help my pupils understand our lesson?'

Source: Arellano et al. (2001: 214–15).

---

fitted in with her social background. The researchers also commented on the role of English-language textbooks that might contain information conflicting with indigenous knowledge. These layers gave greater depth to the study.

15.4   Computer analysis of text

We now turn to an analysis of short pieces of data from open-ended questions and semi-structured interviews. The individual answers might be short but there are likely to be a large number of them so that manual coding is a burden. Computing is the path to follow.

Your choices are to use whichever package is available on your computer system, buy a programme and obtain manuals and textbooks that teach how to use it, or use a spreadsheet. Several software packages are available for text analysis with large volumes of data, for example, ATLAS.ti, HyperRESEARCH and NVivo. Computer packages can allow audio, video and photo analysis as well, which are beyond the scope of this book. In general, the more powerful and flexible a package, the more time required to learn how to programme it. This can divert time from the primary purpose, which is the research report.

Instead, you can use word processing and spreadsheet packages with which you are already familiar. They are not as good as the specialist packages for advanced analysis, but they can still go a long way. Despite being primarily for quantitative analysis, Excel and other spreadsheets have basic functions that allow text analysis too. This section gives you some procedures for searching individual questions using Excel and Word 2003. Despite being elementary, they were sufficient for the text analysis in the 16 crime surveys and they will suffice for many other projects.

First, enter each item of text into a spreadsheet cell. The shorter the text units, the easier this is. With a structured or semi-structured questionnaire, column headings should be the question numbers that contain open-ended responses. Row names should be the questionnaire code numbers. If there are 10 open-ended questions and 50 interviews, there will be 500 cells, but 'no answers' on questionnaires will mean that many cells do not contain text. Those with text will usually contain only a few sentences of comment from each interviewee, which is quite manageable with this process.

The next steps involve using the count functions to tally numbers, word search functions to list cells that contain key words and pasting the table text from the spreadsheet to the word processor document. Table 15.1 gives procedures for pasting answers to individual questions direct into the word processor. There you can further cut and paste the items to give the data a logical flow.

Table 15.2 uses a commentary to illustrate further the procedures. This example comes from the 2006 crime surveys in Bougainville, reporting on people's comments on reasons for changes in crime levels that were found in responses to an open-ended question. The result was a mixture of descriptive quantitative data (the number and frequency of responses) and qualitative comments in respondents' own words.

You can also use the Excel 'Edit' > 'Find All' function to search the whole spreadsheet for a key word that might have come up in answers to different questions. However, the copy function for the search results is extremely cumbersome, so you have to do a manual selection of individual quotes from the search results in Excel and copy them one by one into the categories in the document.

Table 15.1   Text analysis guidance using spreadsheets

Task	Operations
Enter text in spreadsheet	Columns = questions, rows = questionnaire IDs, cells = responses.
Add number of responses	COUNTA(...) underneath first column of data > 'Copy' formula to other columns.
Copy responses to Word and format	Highlight all data cells in a column > 'Copy' > 'Paste' cells in word processor > set 'Paste Options' drop-down box to 'Keep Text Only' > format to document quotation style, e.g., bullet points, indented, italics.
Classify text	Inspect text > cut and paste like items to adjacent lines > count number of items in each group and calculate percentage of COUNTA total > cut and paste groups in order from largest to smallest > the final classification is 'Other' for items that do not fit previous categories.
Comment on classifications	Write brief commentary describing each classification, including number and percentage of total cells (from COUNTA).
Delete extraneous text	'Delete' repetitive items. Retain number of comments in each classification in proportion to percentage of total.

Source: Author.

15.5   Summary

Qualitative data is information that is usually represented as words, not numbers. Both must be analysed carefully.

Qualitative data principles

1. Words are text data that express qualities and attributes.
2. This type of data comes particularly from available sources, naturalistic observation, unstructured interviews and open-ended questions.
3. Words are usually classified on the nominal measurement scale.
4. To help present text clearly, follow a hierarchy drawn from Bloom's Taxonomy: describe first, then classify and later interpret.

Presenting available and observation data

1. Some manual techniques are quite practical, especially for small volumes of text.
2. In writing up the material, the two main options are narration as a chronological story or systematic analysis.

Table 15.2   Annotated text analysis

Text	Commentary
'Open-ended responses to Q.2.2 expanded the reasons for the changes in crime levels that were believed to have occurred…In Buka, 36 comments were made. The largest number (47% or 17) was on reasons for peacefulness, for example:	1. The open-ended responses were typed from the questionnaires into the spreadsheet, taking similar time as any other package.
• *As soon as a problem arises, the community holds meetings to solve it.* • *People are behaving.* • *This is a mission area and people respect it.* • *The new Task Force is doing its duties.*	2. Q2.1 asked, 'Do you think the level of crime in your area has changed since the last survey 12 months ago?'. Q.2.2 was a followup, 'Why'. 3. Searching Q.2.2 following the process in Table 15.1 found 36 comments using the COUNTA total.
'Two of this group thought alcohol was under better control, for example:	4. The responses column was copied to the text document and formatted. Blank lines were deleted. The remaining responses were categorised manually into two small groups (reasons for peacefulness, including alcohol-related) and problems (including alcohol, youth and guns).
• *No drinking in public is helping a lot.*	
'Of the comments on problems, 17% (6) related to alcohol, for example:	
• *Drunkards are getting worse.*	5. The groups of comments were put in order from the largest with 17 to the smallest with 2. Repetitive comments were deleted.
'Five comments (14%) related to youth, for example:	7. Linking text was written at the start of each group.
• *A lot of youths don't have a job.* • *Youths are still causing troubles.*	8. Later, in the conclusions chapter, themes were taken up about community responses to crime and the perceived influences of alcohol, unemployment and guns.
'Two commented on guns still being in the community.'	

Source: Adapted from Guthrie et al. (2007: 22).

Presenting open-ended interview data

The steps for presenting data from unstructured interviews are similar to observation.

Computer analysis of text

Large volumes of short text from open-ended questions and semi-structured interviews usually require computing. Techniques are provided for systematic analysis using spreadsheets.

Analysis of qualitative data is deceptive. Just because the data are words does not mean that they would fall easily into place. Text from naturalistic observation and interviews does not automatically provide meaningful results. Research reports must demonstrate a careful and systematic approach to analysis so that the report has both technical and intellectual rigour. Do this well, however, and you should end up with an interesting, meaningful and accessible report that is a pleasure to read.

15.6 Annotated references

Babbie, E. (2007). *The Practice of Social Research*, 11th edition. Belmont: Wadsworth.
This sociology text has chapters on both qualitative and quantitative data analysis.

Best, J. and J. Kahn. (2005). *Research in Education*, 10th edition. Needham Heights: Allyn & Bacon.
There is plenty of material in this book on qualitative research and data analysis.

Scheyvens, R. and D. Storey (eds). (2003). *Development Fieldwork: A Practical Guide*. London: Sage.
A comprehensive collection on fieldwork in developing countries containing chapters on both quantitative and qualitative research.

Vulliamy, G., K. Lewin and D. Stephens. (1990). *Doing Educational Research in Developing Countries: Qualitative Strategies*. London: Falmer.
This book is heavily based on practical research experience using qualitative approaches in Malaysia, Papua New Guinea, Sri Lanka and Nigeria, including extensive discussion of data analysis.

Quantitative Data 16

Even the most basic social science data can be expressed numerically and tested statistically. This understanding sees many areas of qualitative research that historically contained very little quantitative data or analysis (anthropological case studies, for example) now, sometimes, using statistical tests.

A strength of quantitative research is that detailed rules encourage care. The rules get very complicated, but every statistical test has procedures that others can replicate. This provides an intellectual discipline that encourages accuracy. If we pay careful attention to the procedures and rules, the work will be systematic and thorough. Many researchers, including myself, are without a strong mathematical background and find that statistics are difficult. This is not a reason to avoid them; it is a challenge. There is a steep learning curve, but you can become quite proficient if motivated. The first data chapter in my first major research project took two months to write because I had to teach myself statistics; but the last one only took two days.

Care with the maths does not necessarily make the research strong. Overdoing sophisticated statistics to make minor studies appear important is merely statistical overkill. A statistically significant relationship between an independent and a dependent variable is only as useful as the underlying analysis. If we are intellectually sloppy and overlook valid alternative variables, our research is of little value despite the statistics. In other words, statistical analysis can add to the reliability of our research, but we need to establish validity too: we need analytical rigour as well as technical strength.

This chapter will:

1. review the key principles of quantitative data established earlier in this book; and
2. outline some basic techniques for manual and computer analysis of descriptive and inferential statistics.

With a few exceptions that demonstrate some key principles or help with spreadsheets, the chapter will not go far into the definitions or mathematics. If you are going to do some quantitative analysis, find a textbook on statistics that is appropriate for your level, and make good use of the internet.

16.1   Quantitative data principles

Like qualitative data, measurement principles will often help solve problems that arise during analysis. Does a table seem too complicated? Not sure where some material belongs? Just like words, the chances are that an answer lies in confusion over multiple variables with different measurement properties or underlaid by inconsistent semantic differentials. The underlying principles that apply to numbers and tables are:

1. Numerical data expresses quantities and variables (Chapter 14).
2. Numbers come from some types of available data (Chapter 9), structured observation (Chapter 10), questionnaires (Chapter 12) and tests (Chapter 13).
3. Numbers can be classified on all measurement scales, but in social science we mainly use the nominal and ordinal scales (Table 14.1).
4. The further up the scales, the more mathematical information is added, the more precise the measurement and the more powerful the statistical tests that can be used to test null hypotheses (Chapter 14).

The basic numerical steps to be followed for quantitative data are the same as for qualitative data. First, describe; then, analyse; and later, draw conclusions. Two types of statistics do the description and analysis:

1. *Descriptive statistics*, such as percentages and means, summarise the numbers and can be represented in graphs.
2. *Inferential tests* analyse statistical significance for testing hypotheses and drawing inferences about the strength of the findings.

An inferential test with a probability (p) greater than .05 (for example, .01) shows a significant difference. This is useful when we are predicting differences. However, if we are not looking for a difference, a result between $p = .99$ and $p = .06$, is the desired outcome, for example, because it shows the sample is not significantly different from the population from which it was drawn.

One technical issue is the choice of test types. Inferential tests further divide into two types. *Parametric tests* are based on an assumption of a normal distribution in the data and, technically, they are based on the mathematical properties of interval or ratio data. *Non-parametric tests* do not make an assumption of normalcy and, thus, are especially useful with small samples that are not normally distributed and with lower level data. Non-parametric statisticians have argued that tests designed for data at the higher interval and ratio levels should not be used with the 'weak measurement' provided by the lower nominal and ordinal levels typically found with social science data. Subsequently, the proponents of 'strong statistics' demonstrated that the mathematical assumptions of many common parametric statistics are strong enough to allow their use to extract more information on statistical significance from nominal and ordinal data than is available from non-parametric tests.

The effect is that many statistical tests based on higher measurement scales can use data from lower scales. Nonetheless, the results should be interpreted according to the underlying scale. For example, ordinal data remains ordinal even if tested with a measure originally designed for interval data. Just because the test gives a significant result does not mean that the ordinal data now shows exact intervals. It still continues to show results that are greater than or less than, but not by any particular amount.

Additionally, underlying the use of inferential statistics is an argument that goes back to the methodological issues in Chapter 4. Post-positivist researchers object that parametric statistics reflect the law-seeking normative assumptions of positivist research, and that this is contrary to the effort in naturalistic research to emphasise the uniqueness of participants. They will often admit non-parametric statistics, which do not assume normalcy and are useable with small non-normal samples.

The first step in choosing which statistics to use is to identify the data's measurement scale. Table 16.1 shows some descriptive and inferential statistics that can be used with the key measurement scales. For example, binary data should use the mode (the most common score) as the measure of central tendency, which can be illustrated with column graphs. The binomial inferential test can be used to test significance. In fact, there are scores of statistical tests for all five measurement scales, but this book only identifies a few basic ones that are commonly used with nominal and ordinal data and are acceptable for much basic research. The table shows non-parametric (NP) statistics as well as common parametric (P) ones, which can be used with the lower data levels.

For computer analysis of numbers, there is the same choice as for words: use whichever package is available on your system, buy a programme and learn how to use it, or use a spreadsheet. Common statistics packages include BMDP, SAS and SPSS, but they are complex. Spreadsheets are a practical, but sometimes clunky alternative. I will use examples from Excel 2003, which has extensive capabilities for both descriptive and inferential calculations. To use them, make sure that the statistic functions are activated at 'Tools' > 'Add-Ins' > 'Analysis Tool Pak'. This will activate a 'Data Analysis' command in the 'Tools' menu, which will give some of the statistical tests available. You can also use the Excel search function and search 'statistical analysis', 'function' and 'formula' to get overviews, and make use of the 'Help' function to search particular

Table 16.1 Basic statistical measures

Scale	Descriptive statistics	Function
Binary	1. Mode (NP)	1. Most frequent score
	2. Column graphs	2. Visual comparison
Nominal	1. Median (NP)	1. Centremost score
	2. Mean (P)	2. Arithmetic average
	3. Standard error of the mean (P)	3. Statistical error in the sample mean
	4. Column graphs	4. Comparisons
	5. Line graphs	5. Trends
	6. Pie charts	6. Proportions
Ordinal	1. Mean (P)	1. Arithmetic average
	2. Standard error of the mean (P)	2. Statistical error in the sample mean
	3. Histograms	3. Comparisons
	4. Pie charts	4. Proportions
	Inferential statistics	*Function*
Binary	Binomial test (NP)	Sample vs population proportions
Nominal	1. Chi square (NP)	1. Observed vs expected frequency
	2. Contingency coefficient (NP)	2. Correlation between two variables
	3. *t* test (P)	3. Two sample means
	4. *F* test (analysis of variance or ANOVA) (P)	4. Three-plus sample means
	5. *z* test (P)	5. Sample vs population means
Ordinal	1. Chi square (NP)	1. Observed vs expected frequency
	2. Spearman rank correlation coefficient (NP)	2. Correlation between two rankings
	3. Kendall coefficient of concordance (NP)	3. Correlation among three-plus rankings
	4. *t* test (P)	4. Two sample means
	5. *F* test (ANOVA) (P)	5. Three-plus sample means
	6. *z* test (P)	6. Sample vs population means

Source: Author.

Note: NP: non-parametric; P: parametric.

measures such as 'mean' or 'chi square'. 'Insert' > 'Function' > 'Statistical' also lists the available functions.

The first step is to input the data into spreadsheet cells. Beforehand, set up a check of data entry mistakes at 'Data' > 'Validation', which will alert you to any entries outside the data range, but check entries anyway as this tool will not alert you to mistakes within the permissible range. With a questionnaire, column headings should be the question numbers that contain numerical responses. Row names should be the questionnaire code numbers. Perform statistical functions on columns (which now contain all the answers to particular questions) at cells underneath each one.

16.2   Descriptive statistics, tables and charts

Now you are ready to find out what the data says. The following list has several ways of using descriptive statistics to summarise data. Each of these adds more information, so check the data against each one:

1. Central tendency or 'average' (mean, median or mode).
2. Distribution or indicators of the spread of the data (standard deviation, quartile deviation).
3. Outliers or extremes (the topmost and bottommost scores).
4. Range (the difference between the top and bottom scores).
5. Non-conforming cases (data that appear not to fit the pattern).

Table 16.2 has Excel functions for common descriptive statistics.

Table 16.2   Guidance on descriptive statistics

Function	Purpose
AVERAGE	Arithmetic mean
CORRELATION	Correlation between two sets of data
COUNTIF	Tallies cells with data meeting particular requirements
FREQUENCY	Tallies cells containing particular numbers
MEDIAN	Middlemost number
MODE	Most frequent number
PERCENTILE	Percentile values
PERCENTRANK	Percentile ranks
QUARTILE	Quartile deviation
RANK	Ranks
STDEV	Standard deviation
SUM	Totals
'Data' > 'Filter'	Identify particular values
'Data' > 'Sort'	Order data alphabetically or numerically

Source: Author.

Next, use appropriate summary statistics to set up tables in the word processor and then use the table data to create graphs. Tables and charts are equivalent to paragraphs. Just as a paragraph deals with one main idea, so does a table or a chart by presenting data about one particular aspect of the research. Usually, a table will present numbers set out in rows and columns. A chart or figure will present ideas in a systematic form such as a diagram. Normally, each of these will require one or two written paragraphs of explanation. The following list will help improve the quality of tables and charts:

1. Avoid too much information in each one; if necessary, split data or ideas into smaller units and present them in two or three tables.
2. Identify each table, chart or figure.

   (a) Number each one.
   (b) Use a clear and accurate title.

3. Label each row and column accurately, and show the units used in each row and column in the table (for example, per cent or No.).
4. Space out tables and figures—avoid clutter.
5. Keep tables on one page.

   (a) Do not split tables, figures or charts over more than one page. If they are longer than a full page, divide the data into two tables.
   (b) Start tables straight after the end of the paragraph that first refers to them if they fit on that page. If not, place them after the paragraph that carries onto the next page.

6. Cite sources: cite the sources for your information in a table note, including your own research.

Table 16.3 demonstrates these points.

Table 16.3   Reporting of most troublesome incident to the police

Reported	Arawa 2004 (%)	Arawa 2005 (%)	Arawa 2006 (%)	Buka 2004 (%)	Buka 2005 (%)	Buka 2006 (%)
Yes	16	15	35	23	18	19
No	84	85	65	77	82	81
Total	100	100	100	100	100	100

Source: Guthrie et al. (2007: 55).
Note: Q.4.13. Arawa 2004 $N = 106$, Non-response = 66%; 2005 $N = 106$, Non-response = 65%; 2006 $N = 75$, Non-response = 75%. Buka 2004 $N = 125$, Non-response = 57%; 2005 $N = 94$, Non-response = 68%; 2006 $N = 74$, Non-response = 75%. The high non-response rates derive mainly from respondents who gave nil responses to S.3.

The safest Word graph types are:

1. Clustered column (to compare scores).
2. Line (for trends).
3. Pie charts (for proportions).

For graphs, take time and explore fully the options for each type, setting up the first graph very carefully. Thereafter, you will have the style you want, into which you can cut, paste and input new data. This way other such graphs will be much easier to prepare. You can use Excel to set up the graphs and insert them from Word using 'Edit' > 'Paste Special'. Or, you can use the Word graph functions, which are quite advanced. With Word, copy the table data into the datasheet, accept the graph provided, then right click on it to change and/or edit it with 'Chart Object' > 'Chart Type' > 'Edit'. Then, right click the graph again and use 'Chart Options'.

Use distinct colours if your printer supports them, but it is easy to be carried away with other options. Some graph types are better for public relations than for research. In particular:

1. Do not use three-dimensional graphs. They use depth, which implies volume and distorts the visual perception compared to, say, a bar graph.
2. Set up all vertical axes so that they start at zero and do not distort rates of change.
3. Use logarithmic line graphs to show rates of change.

16.3   Inferential statistics

Inferential statistics allow inferences to be drawn about the similarities or differences between the sample and the population, or between samples or between subsets of a sample. Testing can use:

1. Means (for example, t and z tests).
2. Variance (for example, analysis of variance or ANOVA).
3. Distribution (for example, chi square).
4. Correlations (for example, Spearman rank correlation coefficient).

An important point to note is that a *correlation* measures a relationship between two variables, usually on a scale that ranges from +1.00 to –1.00. A high positive correlation means the variables change in the same direction; a negative correlation means that they change in opposite directions. Some correlation coefficients can be tested for significance and correlations can be used for prediction (if Variable A changes, so too does Variable B). However, this describes an *association* between the variables and does not establish cause-and-effect unless measured as part of an experimental design. The changes could be coincidental. For example, a significant positive correlation might be found between smoking and alcoholism, but smoking does not cause alcoholism. Generally, negative correlations occur between health and education, on the one hand,

and financial poverty on the other. But lack of health and lack of education do not cause financial poverty; lack of money does.

Key issues to be considered while choosing a significance test or a particular version of a test are:

1. The measurement level (binary, nominal, ordinal, interval, ratio).
2. Number of sample cases (one sample, two sample, or k (three-plus) samples).
3. Sample type (related or independent).
4. Sample size.
5. Direction of hypothesised difference (one-tail or two-tail).

Statistical tests can be extremely complicated and require algebra to be understood. However, many of the basic statistical tests are quite straightforward and can be calculated with Excel (Table 16.4). Study carefully the 'Help' material on each function because it is written in mathematic language. You will also have to calculate and enter degrees of freedom to get test results (I would like to be able to explain what they are, but like many, I have failed to understand the numerous definitions. Have faith and just do what the textbooks say!).

Table 16.4 Guidance on inferential statistics

Function	Purpose
CHIDIST	Chi square statistic
CHITEST	Chi square significance
CORREL	Correlation coefficient
CRITBINOMIAL	Binomial test
FDIST	F test statistic
FTEST	F test significance
NORMSDIST	z score
TDIST	Student's t statistic
TTEST	Student's t test significance
ZTEST	z test significance

Source: Author.

16.4 Presenting data

The steps in quantitative data presentation are similar to those used for qualitative data:

1. Describe the numerical results (with descriptive statistics in the data chapters).
2. Analyse (with inferential statistics in the data chapters).
3. Interpret (with written interpretations later in the conclusions chapter).

Clarity and brevity are important, as is neutrally toned language.

Box 16.1 is an example combining many of the features discussed in the previous section. This is a synthesis of results from 16 crime surveys on one particular indicator for levels of reported property crime.

1. The first sentence in the box describes the indicator by defining the terms.
2. The second sentence states the importance of the indicator.
3. The first dot point is a brief analysis using statistical significance. Chi square was used to test whether or not there was a common national level of the crime, which the result showed was not the case; the point being that normalcy was tested, not assumed.
4. The second paragraph briefly summarises the data shown in the graph, identifying the top, middlemost and lowest ranking towns to express both the average and extreme cases, and then states the national mean. The third sentence comments on exceptions and patterns.
5. The graph presents the data. The heavy line shows the national mean, with the columns showing the towns relative to the mean and to each other. The graph was edited to insert the raw percentages at the top of each column so that a separate table was unnecessary.
6. The paragraph following the graph discusses an issue that arose, and then briefly expresses what it meant to the respondents by quoting some of their comments, thus adding qualitative data to the quantitative. With other indicators, tables were used to present the data for the top, middlemost and lowest ranking towns to demonstrate the amount of variation.

16.5   Summary

The most basic social science data can be expressed numerically and tested statistically. A strength of quantitative research is that its detailed rules encourage intellectual discipline.

Quantitative data principles

1. Numerical data expresses quantities and variables.
2. Numbers particularly come from some types of available data, structured observation, questionnaires and tests.
3. In social science research, quantities are usually classified on the nominal and ordinal measurement scales.
4. Inferential statistics are used to test null hypotheses. Parametric tests are based on an assumption of a normal distribution in the data. Non-parametric tests do not make an assumption of normalcy.

BOX 16.1   COMBINING TYPES OF ANALYSIS

Levels of Property Crime

'The…indicator for particular types of crime victimisation was the mean percentage of households that had a member who was a victim of stealing property (Graph). In all the surveys, theft was the most common type of crime victimisation reported.

- The differences from the national mean were highly significant ($X^2 = 111.5$, $df = 15$, $p > .001$), ie. the towns had very different levels of victimisation involving theft.

'The highest rate was in Kainantu, with two-thirds (67%) of households in 2008 being victims. Port Moresby in 2004 was the middlemost town, with 38%. Arawa in 2006 had 8%. The national mean was 38.3% of households being victims in the previous 12 months. Notable was the relatively high rate for Kokopo, and the declines in Arawa and Buka from 2004 to 2006, which were statistically significant (Arawa $X^2 = 17.8$, $df = 1$, $p = .001$; Buka $X^2 = 12.5$, $df = 1$, $p > .001$).

Graph: Household the victim of stealing

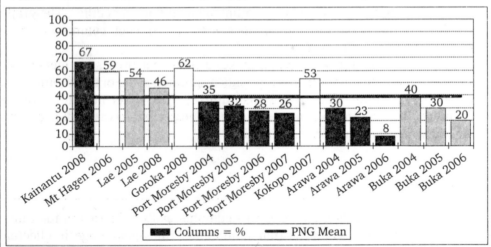

'During the surveys, informal comments were made occasionally to the researchers that petty theft was not a "real" crime: either it was a traditionally derived behaviour because private ownership was not a feature of tribal life; or it was so common as to be part of daily life and not really a crime. However in all the surveys, comments in the interviews about the most troubling crimes that had occurred to respondents in the previous year showed that stealing was a constant irritation… For example:

- *I paid a lot for the bicycle.*
- *We paid a lot of money for that generator.*
- *Those bags of dry beans were worth K1000…*
- *When I recovered the property it was damaged.*
- *They stole our clothes on the line.*
- *Truck parts are really expensive today. People lack respect for others' belongings.*'

Source: Adapted from Guthrie (2008: 30–31).

5. The mathematical assumptions of many common parametric statistics are robust but the results should still be interpreted according to the underlying measurement scale.

Descriptive statistics, tables and charts

1. Summarise data using central tendency, distribution, outliers, range and non-conforming cases, as appropriate.
2. Tables and charts present data about one particular aspect of the research. Simple column, line and pie charts are the most useful graphs.
3. You should: *(a)* not put too much information into each table, chart or figure; *(b)* identify each one; *(c)* accurately label each row and column; *(d)* space out tables and figures; *(e)* keep tables on one page; and *(f)* cite sources.

Inferential statistics

Key issues in choosing a test or a particular version of a test are the measurement level, number of sample cases, sample type, sample size and direction of hypothesised difference.

Presenting data

Describe the numerical results with descriptive statistics, then analyse with inferential statistics, then make written interpretation. Clarity and brevity are important, as is a neutrally toned presentation.

To repeat a key point, just because we are careful with our math does not necessarily mean that our research is strong. If we are intellectually sloppy and overlook valid alternative variables, the research is of little value despite the statistics. In other words, statistical analysis can add to the precision and reliability of our research, but we need validity too. Both analytical rigour as well as technical strength are essential.

16.6   Annotated references

Cozby, P. (2009). *Methods in Behavioral Research*, 10th edition. Boston: McGraw Hill.
  A good clear psychology text with chapters on statistics.

Gaur, A. and S. Gaur. (2009). *Statistical Methods for Practice and Research: A Guide to Data Analysis Using SPSS*, 2nd edition. New Delhi: Response.

This book takes you through using the SPSS package for the types of test outlined in this chapter and much more.

Israel, D. (2008). *Data Analysis in Business Research: A Step-by-Step Nonparametric Approach*. New Delhi: Response.

Contains the major non-parametric statistical tests that can be used with small samples in all social science subjects, assuming little knowledge of statistics.

Kanji, K. (2006). *100 Statistical Tests*, 3rd edition. New Delhi: Vistaar.

This book covers the most commonly used statistical tests, both parametric and non-parametric. For each test, it describes the purpose, limitations and assumptions, a worked example and the calculation.

An internet search will help you obtain much guidance on using Excel for data analysis. There are also several books in the market showing how to use it.

SECTION 4

ACTION

Action can have a wide variety of intents.

Writing the report is actually a limited form of action. In effect, research does not exist unless it is written up for others to read and perhaps to act on. An important part of this is writing well-organised reports with clarity that helps generate credibility for the findings.

Writing up can also be a major form of action for our own intellectual development. This is because judging our own work can be very difficult. We invest a great deal of time, effort and emotion in our study and, often, it is hard to look at it objectively. Learning to do so is one of the major benefits of undertaking research. We learn, often for the first time, to break down our ideas into their logical components and assess their quality. Improving our ability to think clearly is a major benefit gained from learning how to do scientific research, one that will remain with us for the rest of our lives whether or not we continue to do research.

Beyond ourselves, we have the ethical obligation to give feedback to the participants in our research. If the orientation is towards practical, problem-solving research, we will want to ensure that our findings reach decision makers. We might even want to use them as the basis of social action. All these things are quite legitimate, but the difficulties are considerable.

The focus of attention in this section will be report writing but it will also briefly discuss broader forms of action and their advantages and disadvantages.

Social Science English 17

More than anything else, the quality of your research will be judged by your final written report. Obviously, a good report must be based on good research, but a poor report will reduce the credibility of the research no matter how good the research design, the data collection techniques and the data analysis.

There are two broad styles of English writing. One is literary prose. In writing for literary purposes, much emphasis is placed on demonstrating the author's power with language. A wide vocabulary, literary allusion, deliberate ambiguity, metaphor and simile and long, well-controlled sentences are often taken as signs of good prose. In scientific writing, on the other hand, quality is assessed by accuracy and lack of ambiguity. There should be no doubt about the writer's intent. Short sentences, concise words and clear meaning are signs of good report writing. The language is used to convey a message, not, as often in literary prose, to demonstrate the power and beauty of the author's writing. The task is to write clear, direct and correct English.

This chapter will proceed from the perspective of an editor rather than a grammatician or linguist in a building-block fashion through:

1. words;
2. sentences; and
3. paragraphs.

Then, it will consider how all this adds up to style (and the next chapter will discuss the organisation of a report into sections). While the focus is on reporting social science research, the guidelines are just as relevant to similar kinds of academic writing, such as essays, research proposals, book reviews or articles.

17.1   Words

There are four basic things to remember in selecting words around which to construct sentences.

1.   Words should be *short*. Short words are better than long. A frequent but misplaced belief is that long words are a sign of scientific knowledge. This may be true, but only if the words are correctly used. If they are used incorrectly, the author will seem ignorant. It is better to use short words that you know are correct than to use longer words about which you are unsure.

   A useful practice is to go through a report and identify all words with four or more syllables. For each such word ask yourself, is there a shorter word that means the same thing or which more closely represents what I want to say? If there is, then use the shorter word. If there is not, you can feel more confident that your choice of the long word is a good one.

2.   Words should be *accurate*. Accuracy is essential in scientific writing. The words must mean what you intend. One common practice is to use a thesaurus to find synonyms for words used frequently in a report or to give the appearance of a large vocabulary. In scientific writing, this is often not a good practice. The reason is that in all the sciences words have very precise definitions. The thesaurus might not use words in exactly the same way.

   At the other extreme lie slang words. Avoid these, especially because they often have many rapidly changing meanings. Similarly, use words from other languages only when there is no exact or accepted translation.

3.   Words should be *unambiguous*. Avoid ambiguity. You might be intending to use a word accurately in one of its correct meanings, but this is not of much use if the reader thinks you intend one of the word's other meanings.

   A major problem with writing in the social sciences is that many words used in everyday speech have special scientific definitions. Examples of such words are 'significance', 'domain', 'class', 'values' and 'systems'. When writing reports, try to use such words only in their scientific sense. When you do use them, make clear that you are using them this way. Normally, either define the word or write it in combination with an adjective that reveals the scientific emphasis (for example, with the words just indicated, 'statistical significance', 'intellectual domain', 'social class', 'personal values' and 'systems theory'). Also, avoid using technical words in non-technical ways (for example, using 'significant' to mean 'important').

   Use a dictionary if you are not sure about the correct spelling of a word. When unsure about the scientific meaning of a word, use specialised dictionaries such as a dictionary of geography or sociology. Spell all words in full. Generally, avoid abbreviations. Exceptions are for commonly used proper nouns or technical terms, where the first letters might be used (for example, UN for United Nations). When you do use such an abbreviation the first time, present it in brackets after having provided the full spelling. Some very common abbreviations do not require this (for example, e.g. and i.e.).

4. Words should be *necessary*. Finally, use only necessary words. Omit needless ones (for example, 'however' is a much overused word in academic writing). This does not mean that all sentences should be short or that details should be omitted, but it does mean that every word in the research report should have a definite purpose.

17.2   Sentences

Sentences put words into a meaningful order. As with the words themselves, the main consideration in writing sentences is to keep them short, accurate and unambiguous. Here, there are a number of techniques:

1. Use the active voice. For example:

   Better: Use the active voice.
   Worse: The active voice should be used.

2. Be direct. Address yourself to your reader. Do not use unnecessary words. For example:

   Better: Be direct.
   Worse: Your writing should be direct.

3. Keep related words together. One of the most difficult parts of writing is to know where to put modifying words and phrases. When in doubt, refer to a book on grammar. A useful general rule is to put modifiers as near as possible to whatever they are modifying:

   Better: You are better to use short words 'that you know are right' (modifies 'short words') than to use long words 'about which you are unsure' (modifies 'long words').
   Worse: You are better to use short words than long words 'when you know you are right about the one and are unsure about the other' (does 'one' modify short or long words?).

4. Use the past tense. Your report describes events that have already taken place. The correct tense is therefore the past tense. Sometimes anthropological research, in particular, is written in the present tense when describing observations in the field that are thought to be normal life or to continue into the present. Such a practice makes doubtful assumptions about lack of change.

5. Break all the above guidelines on occasion. If all the above techniques are followed strictly, your writing will get boring. Treat the techniques as a guide to better writing, but do not regard them as fixed rules. However, use this practice consciously. In other words, you should break the other guidelines as a deliberate technique to create greater interest, not because you are ignorant of them.

17.3   Paragraphs

Paragraphs place sentences into a meaningful order. Each sentence should have a relationship to the previous one and to the following one. Do not jumble up your writing.

Each paragraph should deal with one main idea. A new paragraph should signal to the reader that a new idea will now be discussed or that a new step in the logic of your argument will be made. If a paragraph is unclear, there is usually one of two problems. One is that there are too many ideas in the paragraph. The other is that you have omitted some step of logic in the argument. In both cases, part of the solution is to break the material up into more paragraphs.

This means that paragraphs should normally be quite short. If you do have long paragraphs (that is, over about quarter of a page in length), chances are that there are too many ideas in each paragraph, and that would confuse both the writer and the reader. Some useful guides to structuring paragraphs are:

1. The most important sentence in a paragraph is the first one. It should express the main idea that the paragraph will deal with. As clarity is so important in scientific writing, you do not want the reader to be confused. Putting the main idea in the first sentence lets the reader know where you are going.

2. The second most important sentence in the paragraph is usually the last one. Normally, this sentence either emphasises the idea expressed in the first sentence, or expresses some limitation or development of that idea and leads the reader to the next paragraph where this point will be discussed. Like the first sentence, the last one should be clear and direct.

3. The sentences in the middle should expand upon the main idea. The middle sentences should deal with the core idea in such a way that the reader has a

better grasp of its meaning and limitations. These sentences will be the ones that most frequently break the rules expressed in the previous section on sentences, doing this in order to create greater variety and interest for the reader. Avoid too many rule-breaking sentences in a row or it will look as though this is your normal writing style.

Tables and charts are equivalent to paragraphs in that they should deal with one main idea.

17.4   Writing style

There are two aspects of style. The first aspect deals with the question of good writing. Unfortunately, good writing is difficult to define, partly because it depends on the purpose which it aims to serve. What is good literary prose is not necessarily good social science prose. The best way to learn good style is to read authors who write as clearly as the subject matter permits. Some fiction authors write the type of clear, direct English that makes good scientific writing—try Ernest Hemingway.

A useful practice is to read drafts aloud slowly to yourself. Good prose is like good formal speech (for example, the sort of speech used in news bulletins on radio and television). Would your draft make a good speech? Or, do you get tangled up and have to breathe in the wrong places? If so, your sentences are too long or are punctuated in the wrong places. Do you lose track of your argument? If so, your paragraphs are too long or contain too many ideas.

An important aspect of style is symmetry. If you raise an issue then you should deal with it subsequently. Often, an introduction will raise a number of general issues that frame the research. If so, your conclusion should refer back to these issues to establish whether your findings help resolve them. Do not leave issues unresolved.

The second aspect of style concerns detailed rules of spelling, punctuation, citation and layout. Academic writing is a pedantic mess in this regard because there are so many different conventions. Three general rules apply to deal with this situation:

1. Be consistent. It does not really matter which style you use, providing you use that style systematically. The simplest method of citation is based on the Harvard system. Under this system, publications are referred to in brackets in the text (by author, year: page), with details listed at the end of the report. Whatever system you use, use it with 100 per cent accuracy. If you get small details like these wrong, the reader will assume that the rest of your research was also inaccurate.

2. Do not make up your own rules. There are numerous guides to follow. Some university departments also issue their own guidelines. If that is the case, follow them for any assignment for that department. If you are writing for a journal, follow the publication's own guidelines, using one of its recent issues as an example. Different scientific disciplines have different requirements, especially for citations. Familiarise yourself with the ones used internationally in your own discipline.

3. Avoid footnotes except for citation. Footnotes are often a sign of sloppy thinking. If something is important enough to write, put it in the text. If it is not important enough to be in the text, put it in an appendix. If it is not important enough for an appendix, omit it. The exception to this is when writing primarily for non-academic audiences, in which case technical commentary can be consigned to table notes and footnotes to maintain the flow of the main text.

Most computer word processing packages have spelling and grammar checking tool. Use them, but double check the results. A spell checker will accept correctly spelled words even though they might not be the ones you intend (for example, *this* is correctly spelled, but you intend *thus*). Computers often oversimplify grammar, so do not accept their suggestions without consideration.

17.5   Summary

More than anything else, the quality of your research will be judged by your final written report. The scientific task is to write clear, direct and correct English.

Words

Words should be short, accurate, unambiguous and necessary.

Sentences

Sentences put words into meaningful order. Sentences should: *(a)* use the active voice; *(b)* be direct; *(c)* keep related words together; and *(d)* use the past tense.

Paragraphs

Paragraphs place sentences into a meaningful order. They should not normally be very long: *(a)* the most important sentence in a paragraph is the first one; *(b)* the second most important sentence in the paragraph is usually the last one; and *(c)* the sentences in the middle should expand the main idea.

Writing style

1. Three general rules apply to spelling, punctuation, citation and layout: *(a)* be consistent; *(b)* do not make up your own rules; and *(c)* avoid footnotes.
2. These guidelines are a good foundation for clear English writing. Break all of them on occasion to elevate interest.

In modern English, scientific or otherwise, there is no one standard or model that governs the style of writing. Adapt these guidelines to whatever subject, publication, purpose or university department you are writing for. Unfortunately, their requirements vary, especially on matters like formatting and citation, and it is impossible to anticipate them all. When in doubt, find a good example of what is required and follow it.

The end product of your research is the report. The research will be judged to a very considerable extent on the quality of your written presentation. Many reports are not read because they are too long or are badly written. As your writing develops, your style will become more complex than the one explained in this chapter, but you will not go far wrong if you start from here.

17.6   Annotated references

Babbie, E. (2007). *The Practice of Social Research*, 11th edition. Belmont: Wadsworth.
   Like all social science textbooks, this one contains material on writing up research.

Billingham, J. (2005). *Editing and Revising Text*. New Delhi: Oxford University Press.
   A short guide to improving written text.

Strunk, W., Jr and E.B. White. (2000). *The Elements of Style*, 4th edition. Needham Heights: Allyn & Bacon.
   First written 80 years ago, this book is still one of the best books available on the style of English writing. More importantly, it practices what it preaches—keep it simple.

An abundance of books provide guidance on correct English writing and on academic writing. A search of your library should find plenty of examples.

The Report 18

Research constantly involves interaction between the four stages, with continual iterations and adjustments. The write-up completes this exercise, but it is a formal logical presentation of the research, not a history of the project as though it proceeded in a linear path planned from beginning to end.

One of the reasons for leaving plenty of time for write-up is to check all aspects of the research for completeness and consistency. The report should show that you have carefully thought about all the elements as you went along, made appropriate adjustments and recognised mistakes. The write-up will proceed faster if you drafted material as you progressed, but now is a very important opportunity to improve the quality by paying careful attention to detail and analysis. Thus, 'writing' in the academic sense is not just about grammar. More importantly, it is about clarity and logic.

Most teachers of writing and research advocate detailed plans in advance. I never work this way myself. While a general plan is in mind, it does not go further than chapter titles. The text is grounded in the ideas and the data as I write. You must do whatever works best for you, but in either approach, a formal or an informal plan is something to be modified and adapted as the writing progresses.

This chapter will consider:

1. how to improve quality by becoming objective about our own work;
2. report structure;
3. progressively drawing conclusions from the data; and
4. persistence.

18.1   Improving quality

Writing up research can be a major form of action for our own intellectual development. This is because judging our own work can be very difficult. We have invested a great deal of time, effort and emotion in it. Often, it is hard to stand outside this process to be objective about our own work. Learning to do so is a major step forward.

I always tell students who ask me to supervise their research that I will do so if they are prepared to invest their egos in making their work better, not in defending it. To write, we have to have ego: we must believe that we have something to write that others should read. However, ego can be counterproductive if we treat professional criticism (whether from supervisers, examiners or friends) as a personal attack and angrily defend what we have written. The ego has to be invested in making our work better. Students usually take the point and we have a productive working relationship.

To improve the quality of our work, we need to objectify it. We must learn to regard our words as data, as objects to be manipulated to make their message clearer and more complete.

1. The best approach is to stand back from your own material and read it as an editor, not the author. This is similar to teaching. When teaching, it is difficult to judge your own performance, but if you observe other teachers' classes, it is easy see their mistakes and apply the lessons to your own work. Similarly, trade essays with friends and practice editing each other's. The editor's job is to stand outside the author's work and judge it professionally to improve it. Learn this role with respect to your own work too and you will judge it more easily, thereby improving it faster and painlessly.

2. Word processors make the task of objectifying your work much easier. Those of us who are not good typists have to go over the work several times to correct the spelling mistakes. Usually, we correct the spelling, improve the word selection, modify sentences and move them around. In effect, by the time the spelling is correct, we have already edited the work several times.

3. Another step in objectifying work is to let some time pass before reading drafts afresh. Mistakes become more obvious then because what we wrote is partly forgotten. Blemishes in logic also stand out more clearly.

4. Proof reading is also important, but it becomes progressively more difficult because it is boring. When we have already word processed something several times, we keep leaving mistakes because we no longer see what is actually there. Rather we see what we expect should be there. One good trick for proof reading is to read passages backwards occasionally, because this forces you to slow down and actually look at the printed word. Otherwise, trade your work again with a friend. Once it is returned, proof read your corrections because if you hurried too much, they will also contain mistakes.

A frequent worry is whether something belongs in the report or not. If the science requires it, it belongs; but if it is more in the nature of comment, or additional detail that adds little to the overall interpretation, the rule of editing thumb is: *when in doubt leave out.*

We cannot expect to attain a perfect report. The deadline decides the amount of time that we can invest into making improvements. After that, wave the work goodbye and move on to the next one.

18.2   Sections

Although different titles can be chosen for each section, research reports will include some or all of the following:

1. Title: The name of the project with an optional subtitle to identify it fully.
2. Contents.
3. Acknowledgments.
4. Abstract: A short synthesis of the study.
5. Introduction: This first section introduces the research, showing why the topic was selected, how the research problem was defined and what any research hypotheses were.
6. Literature Review: The analysis of relevant literature that helped to define the research topic and methods.
7. Methods: The methods used for data collection, including the type of research techniques used, for example, the universe, sample selection, data collection instruments, fieldwork procedures and timing.
8. Results: This section describes the data obtained, how it was analysed and what the results were. This section will contain more tables than any other. If there are too many tables to follow easily, place them in an appendix and refer to them in the text.
9. Discussion: Now, discuss the theoretical and practical implications of the findings.
10. Recommendations: If recommendations are appropriate, these should be clearly listed and cross-referenced to supporting evidence in the report.
11. Appendices: This material can include supplementary information (such as details of data collection and data analysis techniques, data collection instruments and tables of results) that would clutter the main text if included in it.
12. References: Cite any material referred to in the text or used in developing the project. Reread Section 3.7 of Chapter 3 to remind yourself to be thorough about this.

18.3   Drawing conclusions

The report presents the detailed findings, but we also draw conclusions from the findings. We need to be careful where to do this. Whether with quantitative or qualitative data, the report should clearly separate the evidence and our interpretation of the evidence. This requires a logical development from data to interpretation that progressively filters out details and side issues.

1. The results chapters should each present the data, and only the data, which has been collected in the research project.
2. A conclusion at the end of each results chapter should summarise the key points, but not make any judgements about them.
3. The concluding chapter can bring together the summaries and relate them to the theoretical framework of the research.
4. Then, you can draw conclusions about your theory (or the absence of theory if you took a grounded research approach), and draw out any findings that can be generalised.
5. You can now comment on the importance of those findings and use them as the basis for recommendations for further research or practical action.

18.4   Evaluation checklist

The following checklist (adapted from Maxwell 1992: Appendix E) will help you judge the quality of your report. Examiners are quite likely to have a similar list.

Content

1. Purpose of Study

    (a) Purpose is clearly indicated in a problem statement where the main thrust is recognised.
    (b) A problem is formulated as a number of questions or hypotheses that the researcher intends to examine.

2. Background or Context of the Problem

    (a) Is clearly described.
    (b) Is related to the relevant literature.
    (c) Literature review is comprehensive, well organised and critically discussed.
    (d) Literature pertinent to various aspects of the problem is not neglected.

3. Significance of the Study
    The problem selected is shown to be researchable and its importance for the area chosen is indicated.

4. Research Methods

   (*a*) Methods are explained in detail.
   (*b*) The type of data collected is appropriate and justified.

5. Assumptions and Limitations

   (*a*) Assumptions and limitations are recognised and stated.
   (*b*) The delimitations are reasonable.

6. Definitions

   (*a*) Key terms are defined.
   (*b*) Definitions have a basis in the literature.

7. Description and Analysis of Data

   (*a*) Description and analysis are thorough and detailed.
   (*b*) Description and analysis are clear and concise.
   (*c*) Relationships or arguments are logical and perceptive.

8. Conclusions

   (*a*) Relationships and/or arguments are justifiable and related to main findings.
   (*b*) An effort is made to draw together arguments and findings.
   (*c*) Practical implications, if any, are identified.
   (*d*) Implications for further research or problems the study has generated are indicated.

Presentation

1. Organisation

   Order of chapters and sections is appropriate and logical.

2. Style of Writing

   (*a*) Style is simple, clear and readable.
   (*b*) Arguments are logical.
   (*c*) Assertions and generalisations are well founded and supported by evidence.
   (*d*) Report and chapter titles are appropriate and succinct.
   (*e*) Sources of information or ideas have references.

3. Technicalities

    (*a*) All sources referred to in the text are noted in the references section.
    (*b*) References include all the required details and are in the appropriate format.
    (*c*) The abstract is comprehensive but concise.
    (*d*) Grammar, punctuation and spelling are correct.
    (*e*) Figures and tables are clear and appropriate.
    (*f*) Table of contents indicates pagination correctly.

18.5   Persistence

Research reports are completed by doing one thing after another. Whether or not you complete yours depends on many factors. Brains obviously help, but confidence and determination are more important.

Sometimes when reports are not getting finished, we start to use the label writer's block. This is often a cop out expressing lack of confidence, or is a result of focusing too much on one writing problem. If you are at a dead end, do not stop or give up, turn to another part of the project, type some words and let them build. Let your subconscious work away at the initial problem and come back to it later.

Writing does not create instant perfection. It works by putting one letter after another, then one word after another, then by rereading and changing them. If your topic is one on which you have written essays previously, you can also cut and paste material from them to give a start for editing. When you reach a dead end or get bored, leave a gap and came back to it later, or turn to another chapter so that two or three progress simultaneously. Constantly revisiting earlier material to edit and correct it is good practice too, not only to correct mistakes but also to avoid writer's block. I wrote this book using all these techniques.

This approach means that the big problem that can seem beyond us, always giving us a sense of impending failure ('This is too hard. I will never finish the report'), can be broken down into little problems where success is easy and psychologically rewarding ('The last paragraph is better. Now I am making progress'). Lots of little successes build a positive attitude to completing the final report.

I have seen many distinction and high distinction coursework students drop out of research degrees. Clearly, they had the ability but lacked confidence and determination. Students with lesser grades often prevailed because they did not give up. Research is very demanding, but do persist. Grind your way through it. You might be put off by the many reports making difficult research appear easy, but do not forget that reports are formal presentations, not blow-by-blow histories of projects. Those pieces of research were hard work too.

18.6   Summary

Research constantly involves interaction between the four stages that constitute it and its ongoing iterations and adjustments. The write-up completes this exercise, but it is a formal logical analysis of the research, not a history of the project as though it proceeded in a straight path from the beginning to the end. The report should show that you have carefully thought about all the elements, made appropriate adjustments and recognised mistakes.

Improving quality

1. Put your ego into making the report better, not defending it.
2. To improve quality, learn to objectify words as data. Read your work as an editor.
3. The deadline governs the amount of time for improving the report.
4. Let some time pass before reading drafts afresh.
5. Proof reading becomes progressively more difficult. Trade your work with a friend. Then proof read your corrections.
6. A good thumb rule of editing is, *when in doubt leave out.*

Organisation into sections

The report will include some or all of the following: *(a)* Title; *(b)* Contents; *(c)* Acknowledgments; *(d)* Abstract; *(e)* Introduction; *(f)* Literature Review; *(g)* Methods; *(h)* Results; *(i)* Discussion; *(j)* Recommendations; *(k)* Appendices; and *(l)* References.

Drawing conclusions

Separate the evidence from your interpretation of the evidence. This requires a logical progression during the report from data to interpretation.

Evaluation checklist

A checklist can help you judge the quality of your report.

Perseverance

Don't give up!

The report is the final product of your research project, the standard by which it will be judged. Indeed, the written report is so important in research that some argue that research does not exist until it has been subjected to rigorous independent peer review to verify its quality and published.

For a first study, your examiners fill the review role. They are the only people you have to impress. Publication might be a bit ambitious at this stage, but the ultimate academic standard is clear.

18.7   Annotated references

Desai, V. and R. Potter (eds). (2006). *Doing Development Research*. New Delhi: Vistaar.
    The readings in this book on development research include a section on disseminating results, which is relevant to both this and the next chapter.

Mounsey, C. (2005). *Essays and Dissertations*. New Delhi: Oxford University Press.
    A short guide that contains material on collecting information and structuring reports, including time management, printing and editing.

Walliman, N. (2005). *Your Undergraduate Dissertation: The Essential Guide for Success*. London: Sage.
    Walliman uses a clear structure and language to write about the dissertation as the product of your research.

Many books provide guidance on academic writing, and on planning and writing dissertations and theses.

Using the Results 19

You might have though that doing research is hard—and it is—but now we get to the really hard part. The difficulty is in persuading others to take our advice. Often, we fail in this task. We might think that our research is the pinnacle of intellectual achievement, but others might dismiss our work because they feel that we are obsessive–compulsives and also, arrogant about it.

The solution to obtaining action on research findings, and it is only a partial one, is just the same as in defining the research problem. You are more likely to be successful if you break down a large problem into smaller ones and deal with them one by one. Succeeding in the real world with slow incremental change can often be quietly effective and very satisfying. If it is not, then your field is probably politics, not research.

If you followed the advice given earlier in this book and confined your project to your own institution, the guidance about feedback in Chapter 2 will allow you to meet most ethical and action-related obligations. At the end of your initial research project or course, it is also timely to reflect on the possibilities that research might open for you professionally, if indeed you enjoy research and would like to do more.

Nearly half my career has been spent as an academic, most of the rest as a bureaucrat or consultant. What follows is not based on the literature, but are my own reflections about working on the inside and the outside of bureaucracies. I will discuss:

1. clarity of presentation to decision makers;
2. power versus influence as a researcher;
3. implementation strategies for researchers; and
4. probabilities in decision making.

19.1 Clarity

One of the reasons why research is not implemented is simply that academic reports are often too long and complicated for busy managers to read. Even if they are trained in research methods, managers probably will not have the time to read the details. In this situation, rewrite away from the formal logic of the research report. The research paper was for a particular small academic audience. Now, you have a different one.

A useful technique to hit the reader with your message is to use a journalistic structure. Typically, news articles in newspapers tell the story in the first four paragraphs. Then follows an expansion. If the newspaper is pressed for space, the sub-editor might simply shorten the article by cutting out the last paragraph or paragraphs. In research writing, the last paragraphs are the most important because they express the major findings deduced from the preceding research. Non-academic readers might never get that far, so put the findings and recommendations first, and then justify them briefly.

Use freely:

- Dot points.
1. Numbered items.

An executive summary of 500 words or less should focus on the implications and omit the methodology.

Re-presenting your findings is a necessary but not sufficient condition for action on research. If you do not do it, decision makers probably will not read your research. However, just because they read your recommendations, does not mean that they will act upon them.

19.2   Power and influence

Our ability to create change is an issue of power versus influence. Very rarely do social science researchers have the power to actually make changes in the real world. The best we can usually hope for is influence through persuading decision makers to use our findings.

Exercising influence can be difficult, especially when decision makers do not realise that they have a problem that needs fixing. Even if they do realise it, they will not always look to researchers for advice. For bureaucrats, researchers and universities are not bearers of the golden truth, they are just another group with vested interests. This cynicism is reinforced by every report that recommends funding for ongoing research.

The in-principle value of research in contributing to a climate of accountability is clear, but the growth of public accountability is always slow and is dependent on many things besides research and its presentation. Changes in organisational culture are invariably slow and this is the real impediment to the adoption of research findings, not report presentation. Many bureaucratic cultures are not outcome oriented and might indeed have vested interests in limiting public exposure of organisational performance. The willingness of some enlightened officials to place results in the public domain does not pervade all agencies or the levels within them. Strong decision makers might be willing to admit to problems, but weak ones hide or deny them to make their management look problem free. Outside advice can often conflict with institutional and bureaucratic interests and, thus, be unwelcome.

Additionally, a little modesty helps. Often as researchers, we develop tunnel vision: we only see the problem narrowly from our own perspective. Sometimes, our advice is not very relevant to decision makers because we might overlook factors that are important to them. Indeed, the public servant who appears to ignore our findings and recommendations might privately agree with them, but in governmental systems, officials cannot take actions that contradict government policy. The politicians—properly—carry the day. If we want to change real-world conditions, we have to understand that politics are part of them.

19.3   Implementation strategies

There are several strategies for dealing with this situation. Chances are that you will use different ones as your career progresses. The main strategies revolve around the four types of research defined in Chapter 1.

1. One strategy is to become a specialist researcher in pure and applied research and ignore implementation. You can quite properly define your role as contributing knowledge to be used by yourself and others for further research and for teaching. If you have ability as a researcher and can find the opportunities, this can be a particularly satisfying intellectual life.

2. A second strategy as part of your approach to applied research is to act as a publicist for your own research. Publication of results through newspaper columns, radio and the like can be a bit hit-and-miss. It can sometimes have considerable effect, but often it might not. Columns and publicity are more likely to be effective if they are targeted. Your education research findings might go into professional magazines or sections of the newspaper dealing with schools, for example. You can contribute to in-service sessions in your own organisation or as an outside trainer or adviser.

3. A third strategy is to seek consulting work undertaking policy research. In this situation, the decision makers have realised that they have an issue and contract experienced outside advisers. As a consultant, you are paid by a client (often, but not always, a governmental agency). Your intention might be to influence the client about community needs, for example, but you should not

confuse the potential beneficiaries (the community members to whom you feel a moral obligation) with the client (the organisation that pays you). Contractual obligations to the client come first in the real world, if only because no report equals no income.

Your involvement with the client is essentially an act of faith. You have to trust that your contribution will have an effect on the decision-making processes. You will probably remain unaware of whether this is so because consultants rarely get this type of feedback. A common risk is that consultancy reports can sit on shelves. Even work commissioned and undertaken in good faith might not be acted upon quickly, if at all, or exposed publicly in the interests of freedom of information and public accountability. Commercial contractors may stall reports that threaten their financial interests, which is ultimately what happened to the crime victimisation studies.

Be wary. Clients might not really be interested in dealing with the problem. Some might only be playing political or public relations games. The appearance of acting by engaging consultants might be a smoke screen for their real interests. They might want to delay a final decision, or to pre-empt the outcome, for example, by having the consultants provide 'independent' advice that their programmes have been successful. They might want a consultant who will tell them that an initiative that they support is the best option, or tell them that an initiative they oppose will not work. You can provide contradictory advice to your client but it will certainly be modified, it might well be ignored and probably, you will not be hired again. Your choice here is to not undertake this type of work in the first place.

Consulting is often very interesting because the new situations to which you are exposed create intellectual and professional challenges, and sometimes it can pay well. It is only satisfying in the long term if you are very goal oriented, invest your commitment in the study process and accept that the client is responsible for any long-term outcomes.

4. A fourth strategy is to restrict your research to areas where you actually do have influence. The role is action researcher as a practising professional in your own workplace or community. As a teacher, you might analyse students' performance to see where they need remediation. You might try out a new curriculum and, with your colleagues, attempt to assess its impact in order to improve the quality of your own professional work. As a member of a community group, you might contribute to analysis of issues affecting the community, for example, the possible environmental impacts of a proposed development nearby.

Such a role can be very satisfying, but your involvement in the workplace or community is essentially a political one. Your views will not necessarily be respected just because they are based on research. You will probably be perceived as just another person with a viewpoint. Your belief in the primacy of intellectual analysis might not sit well with, and might even threaten, people with different personalities. Emotions often run rife and can involve you in, even generate, conflict in the workplace and the community.

5. A final strategy is to seek a career that provides opportunity as a decision maker to wield power, for example, as an official who is a consumer of research with a commitment to informed decisions. This role can be very satisfying if you are, say, a research officer in a small, goal-oriented technical organisation where the collective objectives are clear and the team works towards them. However, even these organisations have to deal with the real world of funding and political clients, which impacts the work. Many other types of organisations—both governmental and commercial—focus more on the political processes than the implementation outcomes. These offices attract staff who are fascinated by the political game (whether the parliamentary or the bureaucratic one). They enjoy power and being associated with it. In pursuing political processes that gratify them, they might well ignore research findings that satisfy you.

19.4   Probabilities in decision making

Despite some of that pessimism, you can strike it lucky as a researcher and influence events, often in unexpected ways. If a decision maker does have a problem and your research helps solve it, your findings might be taken up very quickly, and the decision makers are less likely than you to be concerned about the possibility of your findings not working.

As researchers, we become used to thinking of very high levels of probability—95 per cent or 99 per cent in the social sciences—as being required before we accept a conclusion, let alone act upon it in the real world where it might affect people's lives. It can be a shock to discover that bureaucratic systems operate at far lower levels of probability, if they even consider probability at all.

As a bureaucrat, it is possible to reduce all decisions to a binary choice (Act/Do Not Act), toss a coin and make the 'right' decision 50 per cent of the time. A lazy decision maker can create the superficial appearance of success with these odds because bureaucratic systems usually make judgements that might have, perhaps, 70 per cent likelihood of success.

Research can act to increase the likelihood of success: good judgement plus increased knowledge increases the probability of correct decisions. However, few decision makers can hope to achieve anything near the probabilities of success that we regard as acceptable in the sciences.

There are two explanations for this. The first is that there is a distinction between theoretical preference and pragmatic preference (Popper 1979: 13–23):

1. *Theoretical preference* is the scientific quest for truth, especially true explanatory theories, which proceeds through the process of falsifiability.
2. *Pragmatic preference* is the policy concern for practical action, which proceeds through use of the best-tested alternative, that is, the option that has the most information available to support it at the time when action has to be taken.

A decision maker with a deadline for a decision cannot wait for new scientific evidence or be too concerned about scientific scruples over demonstration of cause-and-effect, for example. The decision has to be taken now and can only use the best evidence to date, however inadequate it might be. From a practical point of view, incomplete research results may have to be used because they are the only data available. Urgent decisions are needed, so authorities cannot wait years for more formal research.

The other explanation for low probabilities in decision making is a distinction between the 'statistical significance' of results and their 'social significance'. In the real world, we can only act on things within our control. Statistical findings might rank one variable as the most significant, but if we cannot control this variable in practice, it has no social significance. The following quote demonstrates the issue in relation to official action on student achievement in schools:

> Are these [regression analysis] estimates (which are certainly statistically significant) socially significant? Do they make investment in teacher training programs worthwhile?…The residual [unexplained statistical] effect is stronger than the combined effects of all student, teacher, and school variables measured. Thus, improvement in this residual of factors could lead to far larger improvements in achievement levels than those mentioned above. These residual factors, however, are, by definition, unknown to us. Until they become known to us, they also lie outside our control…The student background variables, on the other hand, are known to us but are outside the control of education authorities. The [statistically less important] school and teacher variables, however, are known to us and are within the range of control of educational authorities. (Husen et al. 1978: 91)

Educational authorities could only act on a statistically less important set of variables involving schools and teachers because they had no power over student backgrounds and home life, or over the unknown residual factors. Researchers might not consider the school and teacher variables to be a priority, but to decision makers, they would be the only usable option. The implication is that some of your results might be acted upon, but not necessarily the ones that you would expect.

19.5   Conclusion

Research is hard, and it is even more difficult to persuade others to take our advice. Often, we fail.

Clarity

Reports for busy managers should be short. Tell the story in the first four paragraphs.

Power and influence

1. Social science researchers can usually only hope for influence through persuading decision makers to use their findings.
2. For bureaucrats, researchers and universities are just another group with vested interests.
3. Outside advice can often conflict with institutional and bureaucratic interests.

Implementation strategies

Strategies for researchers include pure research, acting as a publicist for applied research, policy research consulting work, action research or as a consumer of research.

Probabilities in decision making

1. Bureaucratic systems operate at far lower levels of probability than science.
2. The policy concern for practical action proceeds through use of the best-tested alternative.
3. The statistical significance of results might not translate into actionable social significance.

Whatever your success in implementing research, the study of research methods will not go astray, particularly if you do complete a research project yourself. Regardless of how you use the formal qualifications that might result, you will find that the intellectual benefits remain. Not only will you have a better understanding of how research findings are obtained, you will better understand the lack of method behind much information in the media, such as advertising and publicity.

Additionally, and more important, your own thinking should have improved. You might not apply the full range of techniques in this book, but many aspects will stay with you forever. Personally, measurement scales, cause-and-effect and probabilities clarify all sorts of decisions in my daily life. You might well find other things more beneficial.

In part, the boxed examples in this book were intended to demonstrate just how interesting research can be. My own projects took me into all sorts of countries and places I would not have visited otherwise. The first crime survey in Port Moresby, for example, took me to areas I had never been to despite living in the city for four years previously, and this experience broadened by mind about them. I enjoy teaching and, sometimes, I enjoy administration, but research for me is far more intellectually satisfying. To repeat what I said in the Preface, whatever you take out of this book, I hope research is as satisfying and interesting for you as it has been for me.

Glossary

Abstracting: A higher order intellectual skill that analyses research material for the key principles that might apply to other situations. An abstract presents key concepts, bringing in detail only in outline to show the type of evidence used to support the main ideas. In contrast, a *summary* shows understanding by representing evenly all parts of an article and includes more detail. See Chapter 3: 3.5.

Action research: Research concerned with working on particular activities to make improvements. It is especially used to evaluate the success or failure of new projects or to improve workplace practices. See Chapter 1: 1.1 and 1.3.

Analysis: A higher order intellectual skill that breaks material into parts to explore understandings, doing so through classification, comparison, illustrating and investigating. See Chapter 3: 3.3.

Applied research: Research concerned with topics that have potential for practical application. The research often starts from scientific curiosity, but is not designed keeping in mind a particular way of implementing the results. See Chapter 1: 1.1 and 1.3.

Attribute: An attribute is a characteristic of something. It is a concept or a construct expressing the qualities possessed by a physical or mental object of study. See Chapter 8: 8.1.

Available data: Data from existing sources, usually as documentary evidence in libraries and archives. It can include *primary data*, such as interviews and personal reports from participants in events, and *secondary data*, which is reportage based on others' accounts. *Internal criticism* involves consideration of the meaning of the data, which relates to reliability. *External criticism* involves identifying whether the data is genuine, which is a validity issue. See Chapter 9.

Case study method: A research method undertaking detailed examination of one, possibly two or three particular cases in-depth and holistically. *Ethnography* takes a situation as given and particularly tries to find out what it means to the participants. Commonly, case studies are associated with qualitative research, but often they combine different research techniques. The *comparative case study* method holds variables constant to make comparisons more rigorous. See Chapter 6.

Causation: Identification of the antecedents that caused an effect. To demonstrate cause-and-effect rigorously requires strictly controlled experimental research. Experiments usually look for a single cause (*unicausality*), but researchers need to open to alternate causes, and to *multiple causation* or *equifinality* (equifinality can also mean that more than one cause is necessary for an effect to occur). One cause can also have many effects. See Chapter 8: 8.2.

Control:

1. The management of variables so that their effect can be measured and held constant statistically. See Chapter 8: 8.3.
2. *Control groups* that do not receive an experimental treatment are matched groups used in experiments to compare with experimental groups that do receive the experimental treatment. See Chapter 8.

Correlation:

1. Correlations are measures of a relationship between two variables, usually on a scale from +1.00 to −1.00. This describes an *association* between the variables and does not establish causation unless as part of an experimental design. See Chapter 16: 16.3.
2. *Correlation studies* are usually surveys that measure associations between single and multiple variables. They are not experiments and cannot formally establish cause-and-effect, although they can indicate important avenues for follow-up research. See Chapter 8: 8.5.

Creating: The highest order intellectual skill. It generates new ideas and patterns by constructing, designing, formulating and synthesising. Research requires this level of skill, which is why it is insufficient for literature reviews to just repeat others' ideas. See Chapter 3: 3.3.

Ethics: Standards of professional behaviour. See Chapter 2.

Evaluation:

1. A high order intellectual skill that makes judgements through assessment, critique, judging and rating. See Chapter 3: 3.3.

2. Research concerned with assessing the performance of activities. *Formative evaluation* is action research occurring during implementation and is orientated to improving performance. *Summative evaluations* at the end of activities assess whether they have met their objectives. See Chapter 6: 6.3.

Experimental method: A research method aimed at establishing causation through rigorous quantitative experimental designs. Experiments need to demonstrate that a randomised *experimental group* exposed to a treatment did change, a randomised matched *control group* not exposed to the treatment stayed the same and an *alternative independent variable* did not determine the result. *Quasi-experimental* (as if experimental) designs apply experimental logic to attempt to control factors at play in field research. They follow the principles of experimental design except that randomisation of control and experimental groups is not possible. *Ex post facto* (after the event) designs reverse the experimental method by searching backwards from the post-test, case study or survey to infer prior causes logically. See Chapter 8.

Generalisation: Prediction from a sample to the whole population from which it is drawn. See part of Chapter 1 (1.4) and all of Chapter 5.

Grounded research: Research that is based in participants' experience rather than preceding theories. The role is to review the data and see what patterns might emerge rather than to review theory, deduce hypotheses and use data to test the hypotheses. See Chapter 4: 4.1.

Hypotheses: Informed guesses about the answer to a research problem. A *research hypothesis* predicts a positive relationship between variables so that the hypothesis can be tested and either accepted or rejected, perhaps defining it further through an *operational hypothesis*. *Deductive hypotheses* are derived beforehand from existing theory. *Inductive hypotheses* are derived from grounded data. A hypothesis that is not supported is *rejected, refuted* or *falsified*. A hypothesised relationship cannot be proven absolutely, so the operational test is for its non-existence using the *null hypothesis*, which is a prediction that no difference will be found from expected. *Type I errors* are false positive results (that is, incorrect rejection of the null hypotheses). *Type II errors* are false negative results (that is, incorrect acceptance of the null hypotheses). See Chapters 4 and 14.

Informed consent: Agreement to participate in research based on knowledge of the research and its aims. See Chapter 2.

Interviews: A data collection technique where the researcher asks questions directly of the interviewee. *Unstructured interviews* generate qualitative data by raising issues in conversational form. *Semi-structured interviews* use interview guides so that information from different interviews is directly comparable. *Focus groups* are a form of semi-structured group interview. *Structured interviews* use formal standardised questionnaires. *Interviewer bias* is a risk, especially in ethnographic case studies where the researcher might identify with the participants and not assess data objectively. See part of Chapter 6 (6.6) and all of Chapter 11.

Literature review: A major component of the research proposal. It is an analysis of relevant publications that sets the context for and defines the research topic. The review is always oriented towards narrowing the field to provide a research problem that can guide operational research. See Chapter 3.

Measurement scales: Technically defined methods for classifying or categorising data (whether words or numbers) on the binary, nominal, ordinal, interval and ratio scales. See Chapter 14: 14.1.

Metaphysics: The study of the nature of reality. The *idealist* position is that the world exists only in the mind. The *materialist* position is that it exists outside the mind. The doubting *sceptic* view is that nothing can be proved. A *commonsense* view is *realism*—acceptance that the real world exists, even though this can be neither demonstrated nor refuted. *Philosophical pragmatism* can be used to synthesise these views by treating knowledge as useful in terms of its practical effect. See Chapter 4.

Mixed methods: Combination of qualitative and quantitative research techniques to cancel out their weaknesses. *Triangulation* is a particular application that uses different techniques to study an issue from different angles. A further application is *meta-analysis*, that is, analysis of large numbers of similar studies to see if an overall pattern emerges. See Chapter 4: 4.5 and 4.6

Non-response rate: The percentage of people in a sample who could not be contacted, had moved, refused to answer questions or could not answer for other reasons. See Chapter 5: 5.6.

Objective research (*objectivity*): Research that treats the physical and social worlds as objects that we can sense in some direct form, for example, by seeing them. The objective social world consists of people, for example, as counted in censuses. *Subjective research* (subjectivity) deals with mental constructs that we cannot directly see but which we infer from what people say about them or from various forms of measurement such as attitude scales. Subjective in this sense does not mean personal opinion but research of the subjective. See Chapter 4.

Observation: A research technique where the researcher collects primary data by direct observation. *Structured observation* typically uses observation schedules in formal settings. *Ethnography* takes extended periods in natural settings to learn in detail about particular cultures and the meaning of those cultures to their members. *Participant observation* means that the researcher takes part in the research situation as a member of the group. *Non-participant observation* requires the researcher to be present but not to participate in group actions. Hidden observation occurs when the observer is out of sight. See Chapter 10.

Paradigm: A system of intellectual thought that constitutes a way of viewing reality for the researchers that share them. Paradigms such as positivist and post-positivist research methodologies are *social constructs*, that is, sets of social beliefs. This viewpoint is consistent with a subjectivist school called *phenomenology*, which holds that all researchers are actors whose belief systems are integral to their research. See Chapter 4.

Participatory research: Participatory research considers that research is a political process, that the researchers' own constructs or ways of thinking affect their behaviour, and that this behaviour is not an entitlement from independent scientific rules that override other considerations. In this view, research should be an ethical process of reciprocal social action in which researchers and participants are on an equal footing. See Chapter 2: 2.6.

Pilot study: A form of restricted case study, for example, to trial a draft questionnaire. See Chapter 6: 6.2.

Plagiarism: Cheating through failure to give acknowledgement by copying material from the literature without citation, or by copying the work of other students. See Chapter 3: 3.7.

Policy research: Research based on practical issues of interest to those who make decisions about them. See Chapter 1: 1.1 and 1.3.

Pragmatism: A school of methodology that views knowledge as useful in terms of its practical effect. It puts prime emphasis on research objectives and what is useful in achieving them. *Pragmatic preference* is the policy concern for practical action, which proceeds through use of the best-tested alternative, that is, the option that has the most information available to support it at the time when action has to be taken. *Theoretical preference* is the scientific quest for truth, especially true explanatory theories, which proceeds through the process of falsifiability. See Chapter 4 and Chapter 19: 19.4.

Probabilities: Mathematical predictions about the likelihood of an event occurring. In science, all predictions are based on probabilities. The social sciences usually set 95 per cent as the acceptable likelihood of an outcome occurring. Statistical analysis does not express the outcome of hypothesis testing as *levels of probability* (the chances of being right), but as *levels of confidence* (the chances of not being wrong). See Chapter 4: 4.1 and Chapter 14: 14.3.

Pure research: Research that is concerned solely with scientific outcomes. The purpose is to expand knowledge and to discover new things because they are of interest to the scientist and to science. See Chapter 1: 1.1 and 1.3.

Qualitative research:

1. Research that focuses primarily on the subjective meaning of attributes to individuals or groups of people. In contrast, *quantitative research* primarily focuses on the objective measurement of variables. See Chapter 4 and Section 3.
2. *Qualitative data* is information represented usually as words not numbers, while *quantitative data* is information represented as numbers. See Chapters 15 and 16.

Questionnaires: A research technique where the researcher collects primary data by asking questions and filling out questionnaire forms. Questionnaires are one of many techniques that can be used to collect data using the survey method. See Chapter 12.

Randomisation:

1. Allocation of individuals to control and experimental groups randomly so that their composition is equalised. The assumption in randomisation is that all characteristics, measured or not, will be assigned randomly between the groups and thus, they should not have a significant effect on the results. See Chapter 8.
2. *Random events* are ones where each outcome cannot be predicted individually. See Chapter 14: 14.4.

Rating: Exercise of judgement in numerical coding, requiring inferences to be drawn about the meaning of qualitative data. *Low inference* judgements require little interpretation by the observer or scorer. *High inference* judgements require considerable judgement by the scorer about actions being recorded. *Inter-rater agreement* requires independent and competent judges to agree on scoring and interpretation of the data. See Chapter 10: 10.4.

Relevance: The relevance of research is established by its usefulness to consumers of the results. See Chapter 1: 1.4.

Reliability: The ability to replicate the same research results using the same techniques, that is, to provide results that other researchers could repeat. See Chapter 1: 1.4.

Research methodology: Refers to the broader principles of research underscored by philosophical rationales. *Positivism* is a quantitative methodology that studies the world and people in it as objective things by direct observation according to strict rules. In this paradigm, research is about the scientific rules that researchers follow. In contrast, *post-positivism* views knowledge as subjective, value laden and not based on cause-and-effect. In this paradigm, research is what researchers do. See also, *pragmatism*. See Chapter 4.

Research methods: Key principles of research design, such as the case study method. *Research techniques* are particular approaches for collecting and analysing data, such as observation. *Research tools* are resources used in conducting research, such as computers. See Chapter 1, Section 2.

Research problem: The first stage of research requires a simple, clear and analytical formulation of the topic. Theoretical *questions* are relevant to the development of science, while practical *problems* deal with real-world issues. See Chapter 1 (1.2) and Chapter 3.

Sampling: The total group to be researched is the *population* or *universe*, which is the group to be generalised about. The usual focus of study is a subgroup or sample. Selecting the sample group is *sampling*. The *sample fraction* is the sample as a percentage of the population. A *random sample* gives every member of the population an equal chance of selection from a *sample frame*, which is a list of all the members in the population. A *haphazard sample* is a non-random sample, such as a case study. *Structured samples* include list, proportionate and disproportionate stratified, area, grid and cluster samples. They may be *single-stage*, *two-stage* or *multi-stage*. See Chapter 5.

Semantic differential: Polar opposite adjectives, such as 'high–low', used in defining variables and formulating answer scales in questionnaires and tests. See Chapter 8 (8.1) and Chapter 12 (12.2).

Statistics: Numerical representations of data. *Descriptive statistics* such as percentages and means summarise numbers and can be represented in graphs. *Inferential tests* analyse statistical significance for testing hypotheses and drawing inferences about the strength of findings. *Parametric tests* are based on an assumption of a normal distribution in the data. *Non-parametric* tests do not make an assumption of normalcy. They are especially useful with small samples. See Chapter 16.

Survey method: A research method used for developing generalisations about populations through sampling. Surveys are useful mainly for describing patterns in large groups rather than in-depth analysis of individuals' views. *Censuses* are the most complete type of survey. *Cross-sectional surveys* represent a particular population at a particular time. *Longitudinal surveys* repeat cross-sectional surveys *as trend, cohort* and *panel studies*. See Chapter 7.

Testing: A research technique where the researcher collects primary data through some form of test, usually written. *Criterion-referenced tests* aim to show whether students have achieved a given learning objective, with performance on a test item treated as a behaviour that demonstrates learning. In *mastery tests*, the pass mark is usually set at 80 per cent of the questions. *Norm-referenced tests* aim to find out who scores higher or lower. Performance can be scaled to represent a normal distribution. See Chapter 13.

Validity: The correctness of data (sometimes called *internal validity*). *External validity* is the extent to which research can be generalised to other situations (also called *ecological validity*). *Face validity* is the researcher's judgement. *Construct validity* focuses on the property that a test measures based on theoretical interest in different types of human behaviour. *Criterion-related validity* predicts subsequent performance. *Content validity* focuses on the adequacy with which a test samples particular knowledge. See Chapter 1 (1.4) and Chapter 13 (13.3).

Variables: Variables use numerical values to measure attributes. A variable is a quantity that expresses a quality in numbers so that it can be measured more precisely. An *independent variable* is a presumed cause introduced under controlled conditions during experiments as a treatment to which an experimental group is exposed. A *dependent variable* is the presumed effect measured before (*pre-test*) and after (*post-test*) the treatment to see whether change occurs. A *background variable* is an antecedent that could affect the study. An *intervening variable* is a measurable event between the treatment and the post-test measurement that might affect the outcome. An *extraneous variable* is an uncontrolled event that might affect the outcome during a study. *Alternative independent variables* suggest different causes from the independent variable. A research study can be univariate (studies a single variable), *bivariate* (studies two variables) or *multivariate* (studies three or more). All variables need to be *unidimensional* (that is, capable of being described by a semantic differential to measure one attribute only). *Sample variables* should be tested statistically against the equivalent *population parameters* to see if the sample reliably represents the population. See Chapter 8.

Weighting: Adjustment of disproportionate samples before data analysis to represent the population proportions correctly. See Chapter 5: 5.7.

References

American Psychological Association. (2002). *The Ethical Principles of Psychologists and Code of Conduct*. Washington: APA.

American Sociological Association. (1999). *Code of Ethics*. New York: ASA.

Anderson, L. and D. Krathwohl (eds). (2001). *A Taxonomy for Learning, Teaching, and Assessing: A Revision of Bloom's Taxonomy of Educational Objectives*. New York: Longman.

Arellano, E., T. Barcenal, P. Bilbao, M. Castellano, S. Nichols and D. Tippins. (2001). 'Using Case-based Pedagogy in the Philippines: A Narrative Enquiry', *Research in Science Education*, 31(2): 211–26.

Ary, D., L. Jacobs and A. Razavieh (1996). *Introduction to Research in Education*. Fort Worth: Harcourt Brace.

Babbie, E. (2007). *The Practice of Social Research*, 11th edition. Belmont: Wadsworth.

Badgett, J. and E. Christmann. (2009). *Designing Elementary Instruction and Assessment: Using the Cognitive Domain*. Thousand Oaks: Sage.

Beeby, C.E. (1966). *The Quality of Education in Developing Countries*. Cambridge: Harvard University Press.

Best, J. and J. Kahn. (2005). *Research in Education*, 10th edition. Needham Heights: Allyn & Bacon.

Bhatia, B. (2006). 'Dalit Rebellion against Untouchability in Chakwada, Rajasthan', *Contributions to Indian Sociology*, 40(1): 29–61.

Billingham, J. (2005). *Editing and Revising Text*. New Delhi: Oxford University Press.

Boorer, D. (2004). 'Andragogy: The Lecturers Speak', *Papua New Guinea Journal of Education*, 40(1): 24–30.

Campbell, D. and J. Stanley. (1966). *Experimental and Quasi-Experimental Designs for Research*. Chicago: Rand McNally.

Cozby, P. (2009). *Methods in Behavioral Research*, 10th edition. Boston: McGraw Hill.

Dasgupta, S., M. Huq, M. Khaliquzzaman, K. Pandey and W. Wheeler. (2004). 'Indoor Air Quality for Poor Families: New Evidence from Bangladesh', Policy Research Working Paper 3393, World Bank, Washington.

Department of Education. (1975). 'Duty Statement', Regional Secondary Inspector (Position No. SE 7-15)', Port Moresby.

———. (1980a). 'Agendas and Minutes of Inspectors' Conferences' [various titles], Port Moresby, 24–27 March.

———. (1980b). 'Structure Chart of the National Education Department', *Papua New Guinea Education Gazette*, 14(5): 112.

———. (1980c). 'Minutes of RSI Conference', 24–27 March 1980, Wewak.

Desai, V. and R. Potter (eds). (2006). *Doing Development Research*. New Delhi: Vistaar.

Fien, J., D. Yencken and H. Sykes (eds). (2002). *Young People and the Environment: An Asia-Pacific Perspective*. Dordrecht: Kluwer Academic Publishers.

Frame, Janet. (1961). *Faces in the Water*. New York: Braziller

———. (1989). *An Autobiography* (Collected Edition). Auckland: Century Hutchinson. Reprinted in 2008 as *An Angel at My Table*. London: Virago.

Gall, M., J. Gall and W. Borg. (2006). *Educational Research: An Introduction*, 8th edition. Needham Heights: Allyn & Bacon.

Gaur, A. and S. Gaur. (2009). *Statistical Methods for Practice and Research: A Guide to Data Analysis Using SPSS*, 2nd edition. New Delhi: Response.

Gillham, B. (2005). *Research Interviewing: The Range of Techniques*. Maidenhead: Open University Press.

Guthrie, G. (1977). 'The Tribal System of Appropriation in Aboriginal Australia', *Pacific Viewpoint*, 18(2): 149–66.

———. (1980). 'Stages of Educational Development? Beeby Revisited', *International Review of Education*, 26(4): 411–38.

———. (1982). 'Reviews of Teacher Training and Teacher Performance in Developing Countries: Beeby Revisited (2)', *International Review of Education*, 28(3): 291–306.

———. (1983a). *An Evaluation of the Secondary Teacher Training System*. Report No. 44, Educational Research Unit, University of Papua New Guinea, Port Moresby.

———. (1983b). *The Secondary Inspectorate*. Report No. 45, Educational Research Unit, University of Papua New Guinea, Port Moresby.

———. (1984). 'Secondary Teacher Training Effectiveness in Papua New Guinea', *Studies in Educational Evaluation*, 10(2): 205–8.

———. (ed.). (1985). *Basic Research Techniques*. DER Report No. 55, National Research Institute, Port Moresby.

———. (2007a). *Community Crime Surveys: Interviewer Training Manual*. Port Moresby: Justice Advisory Group.

———. (2007b). *Highlands Highway Crime Study 2005*, Special Publication No. 42, National Research Institute, Port Moresby.

———. (2008). *Urban Crime Victimisation in Papua New Guinea, 2004–2008: A Synthesis*. Port Moresby: Justice Advisory Group.

Guthrie, G. and J. Laki (2007). Yumi Lukautim Mosbi: *Impact Evaluation 2006*, Justice Advisory Group, Port Moresby. Available at http://www.lawandjustice.gov.pg/resources/documents/YLM_IMPACT_EVALUATION_REPORT_FINAL_2201071.pdf / (accessed on 26 February 2010).

Guthrie, G., F. Hukula and J. Laki. (2007). *Bougainville Community Crime Survey, 2006*, Special Publication No. 52, National Research Institute, Port Moresby.

Henn, M., M. Weinstein and M. Foard. (2006). *A Short Introduction to Social Research*. New Delhi: Vistaar.

Hennink, M. and S. Clements. (2004). 'Impact of Franchised Family Planning Clinics in Urban Poor Areas in Pakistan', Applications & Policy Working Paper A04/16, Southhampton Statistical Sciences Research Institute, University of Southampton.

Hewison, K. (2004). 'Thai Migrant Workers in Hong Kong', *Journal of Contemporary Asia*, 34(3): 318–35.

Husen, T., L. Saha and R. Noonan. (1978). 'Teacher Training and Student Achievement in Less Developed Countries', Staff Working Paper No. 310, World Bank, Washington.

International Labour Office (ILO). (2009). 'Evaluation: Sri Lanka: Integrated Rural Accessibility Planning Project (IRAP)—A Component of UNOP's Community Access Programming', ILO Evaluation Summaries, ILO, Geneva.

Iredale, R., F. Guo and S. Rosario (eds). (2003). *Return Migration in the Asia Pacific*. Cheltenham: Edward Elgar.

Israel, D. (2008). *Data Analysis in Business Research: A Step-by-Step Nonparametric Approach.* New Delhi: Response.

Kanji, K. (2006). *100 Statistical Tests,* 3rd edition. New Delhi: Vistaar.

Karuppusami, G. and R. Gandhinathan. (2007). 'Web-based Measurement of the Level of Implementation of TQM in Indian Industries', *Total Quality Management,* 18(4): 379–91.

Kerlinger, F. (1986). *Foundations of Behavioral Research,* 3rd edition. Orlando: Harcourt Brace.

Kline, T. (2005). *Psychological Testing: A Practical Approach to Design and Evaluation.* New Delhi: Vistaar.

Krejcie, R. and D. Morgan. (1970). 'Determining Sample Size for Research Activities', *Educational and Psychological Measurement,* 30(3): 607–10.

Kreuger, R. and M. Casey. (2009). *Focus Groups: A Practical Guide for Applied Research,* 4th edition. Thousand Oaks: Sage.

Kvale, S. (2008). *Doing Interviews.* London: Sage.

Leedy, P. and J. Ormrod. (2010). *Practical Research: Planning and Design,* 9th edition. Needham Heights: Allyn & Bacon.

Maxwell, T. (ed.). (1992). *University of New England Thesis and Dissertation Guide.* Armidale: University of New England.

McKinnon, K.R. (1968). 'Education in Papua and New Guinea: The Twenty Post-War Years', *Australian Journal of Education,* 12(1): 4–5.

McLachlan, B.A. (1965). 'The Role of the District Inspector in Secondary Education 1965–70', paper presented on 10 March 1965 to the Senior Education Officers' Conference, Port Moresby.

McNamee, M. and D. Bridges. (2002). *The Ethics of Educational Research.* Oxford: Blackwell.

Meadmore, P. (1978). 'The Decline of Formalism in Queensland Primary Education, 1950–70', *The Forum of Education,* 37(1): 27–34.

Morrow, M., Q. Nguyen, S. Caruana, B. Biggs, N. Doan and T. Nong. (2009). 'Pathways to Malaria Persistence in Remote Central Vietnam: A Mixed Method Study of Health Care and the Community', *BMC Public Health,* 9(1): 85. Available at http://www.biomedcentral.com/1471-2458/9/85 (accessed on 26 February 2010).

Mounsey, C. (2005). *Essays and Dissertations.* New Delhi: Oxford University Press.

Nepal, N. and A. Calves. (2004). 'Income Generation Programmes in Nepal: Participants' Perspective', paper presented on 14 August 2004 at the Annual Meeting of the American Sociological Association, San Francisco.

Papua Annual Report (1940–41). Melbourne and Canberra: Government Printer.

Papua Annual Report (1947–48). Melbourne and Canberra: Government Printer.

Parten, M. (1950). *Surveys, Polls, and Samples.* New York: Harper.

Perecman, E. and S. Curran. (2006). *A Handbook for Social Science Field Research: Essays and Bibliographic Sources on Research Design and Methods.* Thousand Oaks: Sage.

Persig, R. (1974). *Zen and the Art of Motorcycle Maintenance.* London: Bodley Head.

Popper, K. (1979). *Objective Knowledge: An Evolutionary Approach* (revised edition). Oxford: Oxford University Press.

Punch, K. (2006). *Developing Effective Research Proposals,* 2nd edition. London: Sage.

Ralph, R.C. (1965). 'The Role of the Inspector of Schools in the System of Educational Administration in Papua New Guinea', paper presented on 10 March 1965 to the Senior Education Officers' Conference, Port Moresby.

Scheyvens, R. and D. Storey (eds). (2003). *Development Fieldwork: A Practical Guide*. London: Sage.

Siegel, S. (1956). *Nonparametric Statistics for the Behavioral Sciences*. New York: McGraw Hill.

Strunk, W., Jr and E.B. White. (2000). *The Elements of Style*, 4th edition. Needham Heights: Allyn & Bacon.

Turney, C. (1970). *The Rise and Decline of an Australian Inspectorate. Melbourne Studies in Education*. Melbourne: Melbourne University Press.

Vulliamy, G., K. Lewin and D. Stephens. (1990). *Doing Educational Research in Developing Countries: Qualitative Strategies*. London: Falmer.

Walliman, N. (2005). *Your Undergraduate Dissertation: The Essential Guide for Success*. London: Sage.

Weeks, S. (1985). 'The Case Study Method', in G. Guthrie (ed.), *Basic Research Techniques*, DER Report No. 55. National Research Institute, Port Moresby: 50–59.

Index

About the Author

Gerard Guthrie has been Managing Director of Guthrie Development Consultancy Pty Ltd., Canberra since 2004. He is a Doctor of Philosophy in Education. An educationalist with around 40 years of experience, his career has had two main parts: one as an academic, and the other as a governmental aid official. He has worked in universities, aid management and aid consultancy in Asia, Africa and the South Pacific, particularly China and Papua New Guinea, and also, briefly, in Bangladesh, Bhutan, Botswana, Indonesia, Japan, Kenya, Malaysia, Mauritius, Nepal, Tanzania, Zambia and Zimbabwe.

Dr Guthrie has a background in development theory and practice and in social science research. He has postgraduate degrees in geography, social science and education, with over 180 publications and papers to his name. His own research has included major projects on migration, teacher education and crime victimisation, as well as aid activity design and evaluation. His publications include: *Cherbourg: A Queensland Aboriginal Reserve* (1977); *Mt. Hagen Community Crime Survey, 2006*, co-authored with F. Hukula and J. Laki (2007); *Urban Crime Victimisation in Papua New Guinea, 2004–2008: A Synthesis* (2008); and *The Progressive Education Fallacy in Developing Countries: In Favour of Formalism* (2010).